THE BRAVE BOSTONIANS

ALSO BY PHILIP McFARLAND

FICTION

A House Full of Women
Seasons of Fear

NONFICTION

Sojourners
Sea Dangers

THE BRAVE
BOSTONIANS

Hutchinson, Quincy, Franklin,
and the Coming of
the American Revolution

PHILIP MCFARLAND

WestviewPress
A Division of HarperCollins*Publishers*

Copyright © 1998 by Westview Press, A Division of HarperCollins Publishers, Inc.

Published in 1998 in the United States of America by Westview Press, 5500 Central Avenue, Boulder, Colorado 80301-2877, and in the United Kingdom by Westview Press, 12 Hid's Copse Road, Cumnor Hill, Oxford OX2 9JJ

Library of Congress Cataloging-in-Publication Data
McFarland, Philip James.
     The brave Bostonians : Hutchinson, Quincy, Franklin, and the coming of the American Revolution / Philip McFarland.
          p.   cm.
     Includes bibliographical references and index.
     ISBN 0-8133-3440-3
     1. United States—History—Revolution, 1775–1783—Causes.
2. Hutchinson, Thomas, 1711–1780.   3. Franklin, Benjamin, 1706–1790.   4. Quincy, Josiah, 1744–1775.   5. United States—Politics and government—To 1775.   6. Boston (Mass.)—Politics and government—To 1775.   I. Title.
E210.M15   1998
973.3'11—dc21   97-48399
                                                                                              CIP

The paper used in this publication meets the requirements of the American National Standard for Permanence of Paper for Printed Library Materials Z39.48-1984.

10   9   8   7   6   5   4   3   2   1

FOR
BERNARD BAILYN

Contents

THE BRAVE BOSTONIANS

1

MR. HUTCHINSON

ENDING HIS CURRENT SERVICE as royal governor of Massachusetts Bay, Thomas Hutchinson had much to attend to over the waning days of May 1774. Very soon he and members of his family would be setting sail from Boston Harbor for England; and meanwhile he was busy settling personal affairs, packing, reviewing matters of public concern with his newly arrived successor, and receiving delegations of grateful citizens. On May 30, for example, some one hundred and twenty of the principal merchants, magistrates, clergymen, and lawyers of Hutchinson's native city presented him formally with a declaration of their gratitude: "We, Merchants and Traders of the Town of Boston, and others, do now wait on you, in the most respectful Manner, before your Departure for England, to testify, for ourselves, the entire Satisfaction we feel at your wise, zealous, and faithful Administration." The addressers went on to lament the loss of "so good a Governour"; and on surrounding days, their feelings were echoed in similar testimonials from Boston's Anglican ministers and wardens, from sundry gentlemen of Marblehead, from the principal gentlemen of Salem, from citizens of Milton, from several gentlemen of the law, from the magistrates of Plymouth County, from those of Middlesex County.

At this time in his life, Thomas Hutchinson was sixty-two, a Bostonian who was—at least in one respect, and despite the achievements that such testimonials acknowledged—unlucky. Doomed soon to board ship, he knew himself to be a miserable sailor, prone to all the drawn-out tortures of seasickness, as a single venture to and from England many years earlier had agonizingly demonstrated. On that earlier occasion Hutchinson had been in his late twenties, already admired, a member of the provincial legislature undertaking a mission on behalf of Massachusetts Bay. Then he had remained more than a year overseas in London, attending to his charge concerning a border dispute with New Hampshire. Yet all through his stay in the imperial capital, he had missed home acutely; and when, after another long bout of the requisite suffering at sea, he did finally return to Boston, he had been ecstatic: "does not remember, through his whole life, any joy equal to that of meeting his wife again, after 13 months' absence" in England. The third-person testimony is Hutchinson's own, looking back in an autobiographical memorandum when his life was nearing its end. And now, as May days of 1774 slipped by and the first of June approached, the governor, in what had become his silver-haired and widowed old age, was once more confronting the ordeal of weeks on the high seas, every hour sure to be a trial, every moment taking his racked body farther from the land of his birth that he loved.

Why was he doing it? Here late in life, the gentleman might have retired to his cherished country home on a hilltop in nearby Milton, with his books and garden and glorious views, one view westward across the province as far as Mt. Wachusett fifty miles off, another northward over the beautiful Neponset valley and up the wide, island-dotted sweep of harbor to the spires and steeples of Boston itself, at the foot of hills on the Shawmut peninsula eight miles away. He loved this province, loved Boston, but his Milton home he loved more than anywhere else on earth and would have happily ended his days here, surrounded by memories and familiar scenes.

Yet Governor Hutchinson had requested leave to sail for England. The king having graciously granted his request, the governor would depart the first of June. The reason was partly financial: He had lately been worried about the welfare of his children, two in particular, and hoped to wrangle from the court in Westminster a pension that would recognize past services and provide for his own needs while allowing his estate to remain intact for the benefit of a hapless son and an unmarried daughter. Then too, Hutchinson was feeling exhausted from the demands of his office, having served continuously in positions of trust over long years during these most trying times. He needed a respite, and at a distance. But part of the reason for his venturing to England was, as he saw it, yet again in order to help his strife-torn province, currently agitated because its capital of Boston was to be punished for certain recent unlawful actions that a few citizens had undertaken in defiance of the Crown. It was Governor Hutchinson's hope that his presence at the seat of empire might alleviate the severity and shorten the duration of that punishment.

Merchants and traders approaching the departing governor with testimonials of their esteem shared his hope. The punishment was laid out in an act, passed by Parliament overseas, that only in recent days had reached Boston aboard incoming vessels. Having read the terms of the act, Hutchinson's loyal petitioners were insisting that they did not mean to arraign the justice of what the British Parliament had seen fit to do. Yet the one hundred and twenty-three signatories—Goldthwaits and Inmans and Ervings and Leonards and others equally distinguished—could humbly have wished, as they assured Mr. Hutchinson, "that this Act had been couched with less Rigour, and that the Execution of it had been delayed to a more distant Time." What had provoked Parliament was the spirited destruction last winter, by some sixty disguised townsmen even now not identified, of a precious large quantity of tea belonging to the East India Company, hauled up from ships' holds and hurled onto the tide in Boston Harbor, while the town did nothing to intervene. In angry response, Parliament had passed the Port Act, rigorously couched indeed, which would go calamitously into effect at the first of this coming month, June 1, 1774, on the very day of Governor Hutchinson's departure.

By the terms of the Port Act and under the direction of the well-armed General Thomas Gage, Hutchinson's English successor, the government overseas had resolved to shut down Boston commerce. No less than that. Close the port to all trade coming in or going out, throw all those dockhands and merchants and ship-builders and sailors and artisans out of work, move the provincial government and the customs elsewhere, and keep the town block-aded by water until such indeterminate time as the East India Company felt itself suitably recompensed and King George III had been satisfied that his subjects in Massachusetts were returned to their proper loyalty.

As for that, the petitioners approaching Governor Hutchinson announced themselves ready to reimburse the company at once for its loss. Meanwhile, they would ask of the governor one favor. "We earnestly request that you, Sir, who know our Condition, and have at all Times displayed the most benevolent Disposition towards us, will, on your Arrival in England, interest yourself in our behalf, and make such favourable Representations of our Case, as that we may hope to obtain speedy and effectual Relief."

But that was precisely what Mr. Hutchinson meant to do. He had nothing more at heart, he responded to his well-wishers, than to contribute to the relief of his country in general, and the town of Boston in particular. Moreover, the governor might hope to be listened to when he reached London. Throughout his adult life he had diligently served the province and the Crown, and his reputation stood high in the court at Westminster. In fact, his successor, General Gage, recently arrived in Boston, had brought with him from England a confidential letter, from the minister responsible for the American department, that relayed the king's entire approbation of Mr. Hutchinson's public conduct. That approbation the sovereign intended to make evident to all mankind "by an early mark of his favor." With such satisfactory prospects before him, the governor might provide a final service on this side of the Atlantic by sharing with General Gage his understanding of Massachusetts's troubled affairs. The two did confer through these days of late May, and the grateful general was moved to write his superior in London before the month was out, commending Mr. Hutchinson's knowledge of both province and town. "No Person," the new Governor Gage assured the colonial secretary at Whitehall, "is so capable to give you true Information, or to foresee the Consequences likely to Arise from all that is, or intended to be done."

Information that the American might furnish to Lords Dartmouth and North and other makers of policy in London had been a lifetime amassing. No one knew more than Thomas Hutchinson—no one before or since has ever known as much— about the history of Massachusetts Bay, and no one at the moment had been better placed to inform himself of current conditions there. Hutchinson had been born in 1711, in Boston's North End, in one of the finest houses in town, son of a prominent merchant and great-great-grandson of the Anne Hutchinson whom the earliest colonists had driven into exile for her antinomian beliefs. Thus, Thomas Hutchinson's American roots went deep, to the very start of New England—although if his forebear had dissented notoriously from the prevailing views of her era, her worthy descendant was orthodox throughout a long life, an irreproachable churchgoer and unwaveringly loyal subject of Great Britain.

He had graduated from Harvard College, worked briefly with his father in commerce, married most fortunately, reveled in a growing family, and early entered politics. Hutchinson's career had been a succession of honors and triumphs: town representative to the provincial legislature by his mid-twenties, knowledgeable shaper of provincial financial policy, in time judge of probate for Suffolk County (where Boston is located), judge of the common pleas, chief justice of the superior court, senior member of the provincial council, lieutenant governor, and, since 1771, royal governor of Massachusetts Bay.

Moreover, on more than one occasion his fellow citizens had chosen the gentleman to speak beyond the province's boundaries on their behalf. That early border dispute with New Hampshire had led the legislature to send Hutchinson while still a young man to England to represent the interests of Massachusetts; and later, in 1754, he had been appointed provincial commissioner to a congress at Albany, there to work with the commissioner from Pennsylvania, Benjamin Franklin, in an effort to strengthen a feeble union of colonies as they entered upon a war against the French and Indians.

Thus, the politician had also served as diplomat. And he was a scholar besides. In a busy life Hutchinson had found time to undertake demanding scholarship, and the impressive result was his three-volume *History of Massachusetts Bay*, based on much scouring of records that in many instances are no longer extant. Hence, to this day, Hutchinson's history remains indispensable for anyone considering the subject of early New England. His achievements, in short, public and private, were formidable, so that by the 1760s, according to John Adams, a fellow townsman who knew him well, the then lieutenant governor was already "admired, revered, rewarded, and almost adored; and the idea was common, that he was the greatest and best man in America."

That exalted estimate found confirmation among the humble. Jane Mecom, a Bostonian of the most modest means, Benjamin

Franklin's ill-lettered sister, in fact, who had remained all her life in the town of her brother's and her own birth, felt moved at the end of 1765 to single out Thomas Hutchinson as "the Gratest ornement of our Country, & the most Indefateguable Patrioat . . . may God Protect & Preserve Him still for the Good of mankind & confer on Him the Honour He Deserves."

Many others in the mid-1760s shared the opinion that Mrs. Mecom feelingly expressed. By then, the object of such adulation had reached his fifties, elegant and imposing, six feet tall, "a tall, slender, fair-complexioned, fair-spoken, 'very good Gentleman,'" who, according to the *Boston Gazette* of the time, had captivated "half the pretty Ladies in the colony" and won the loyalty of "more than half the pretty Gentlemen." To be sure, with all his attractions, the widower Hutchinson remained impervious to the charms of those admiring ladies around him. No gossip or breath of scandal ever touched his personal life. After his wife's death in 1754, Hutchinson would never remarry, extending to her memory the loyalty that in a different sphere he accorded his monarch. In truth, the marriage had been an exceptionally happy one ("does not remember, through his whole life, any joy equal to that of meeting his wife again"), a marriage that had lasted nineteen years, ending just after the birth of their twelfth child. "Such was his attachment"—once more it is the elderly Hutchinson himself looking back and recording privately—"that she appeared, in body and mind, something more than human." The admission attests to the remarkable depth of his feeling for her. In his wife's final hour he had been at her side: "With her dying voice, and eyes fixed on him, she uttered these words—'best of husbands.'"

Such a scene was ineradicable. When Margaret Sanford Hutchinson died, the devastated widower had more than a quarter century of life remaining to him. Through all that time he continued faithful to their marriage, as he remained faithful to the other deep attachments and beliefs formed when he was young. His devoted and active family of five surviving children he watched grow into adulthood. He had his numerous friends, his extensive correspondence, his estates and investments, his books and studies, his homes in Boston and Milton, his high public responsibilities to fulfill. A rich and enviable existence, so it would seem. And yet as the contentious years followed one after another into the

1770s, everything around Thomas Hutchinson appeared to be changing. He did not; he stayed the same. But what had once seemed so enviable in his life became bitter. Many in the town had begun looking to others to lead them. The governor's enemies grew vastly in number, and their new distaste for the man turned to loathing.

Now, late in his administration, some Americans were discovering reasons to berate Mr. Hutchinson as a political Pilate, a packhorse of tyranny, a wretch, a slave, a vile serpent, a viper, a villain and a traitor, a "damn'd *arch-traitor*," were calling him even uglier names, although others, to be sure, continued to hold him in esteem. Those worthy merchants of Boston, like the petitioners from Salem and Marblehead and elsewhere, were still wishing him well to the very end, even here on the eve of his departure for England. In doing so, they went out of their way to express the hope that he would have a pleasant passage (unlikely for so poor a sailor), "and under all the Mortifications that you have patiently endured, may you possess the inward and consolatory testimonies, of having discharged your trust with Fidelity and Honour."

Of mortifications there had been many, fierce and unrelenting. But what had brought about so flagrant a change in a reputation formerly so exalted? One cause Hutchinson could readily identify; and that cause derived from one man in particular, once a colleague, a gentleman born like the governor in Boston but who had removed to Philadelphia as a youth and gone on to become internationally renowned. The person who had done more of late than anyone else to damage Thomas Hutchinson's reputation—had by May 1774 managed effectively to destroy it in America—was that same Benjamin Franklin, the humble Jane Mecom's celebrated brother; and Dr. Franklin had gone about the destruction in a singularly underhanded, ungentlemanly way.

2

Dr. Franklin and the Letters

FRANKLIN DID NOT REGARD what he had done as underhanded. On the contrary, he professed to consider it one of the best actions of his life. He, too, was a gentleman, after all, if born into a social rank quite inferior to that of the patrician Hutchinson's. Like Thomas Hutchinson, Benjamin Franklin was a native of Boston, although his birthplace was by no means one of the finest houses in town. The future Governor Hutchinson was born in 1711, in a mansion in Garden Court, off Hanover Street. Franklin had been born some five years earlier, in January 1706, in a very modest two-story peaked-roof cottage near the head of what is now Milk Street, out of which cramped quarters his father had been able to move the large family a few years later. They had moved, in fact, to the North End, only about six short blocks from where Thomas Hutchinson was to grow up in far loftier style.

Franklin's father was a tallow maker. He ended by having eighteen children, of whom Benjamin was the tenth and youngest son. The boy might have been reared as his father's tithe, sent to prepare for the ministry at Harvard, where Hutchinson would later graduate. But he lacked religious inclination. Instead (as is well known, his amazing life having become part of our folklore), Benjamin Franklin signed on when he was twelve as an apprentice in his brother's Boston print shop.

The brothers quarreled, and young Benjamin set out to make his way alone at seventeen where fate and his printing skills might take him, first to New York, soon after to Philadelphia. Before he was twenty, he had visited England for the first time and, in the course of a year and a half in London, mastered the newspaper trade. Returned to Philadelphia, the young man married and acquired what he would turn into the best-written newspaper in the colonies. His annual almanac, printed in his shop, would add to Franklin's wealth and fame. In fact, by the time he was forty, the printer had succeeded so splendidly at his trade that he was able soon to retire from business and devote himself thereafter, with a success ever more impressive, to various scientific pursuits, to his many philanthropies, and to public affairs.

Pursuing one such affair of the public's, Franklin had returned to England in 1757, world famous by that time because of his electrical experiments, honored (this self-educated tallow maker's son) with degrees from Harvard and Yale and the College of William and Mary. His wife remained at home in Philadelphia, then and throughout her life unwilling to risk crossing the ocean; but Franklin set forth on a mission for certain political interests in Pennsylvania—and lingered in London five years.

Those years saw the death of irascible old King George II and the ascent to the throne, in October 1760, of his grandson, a godly young man of twenty-two. The American resident gloried in the change. Like many others, Franklin spoke admiringly of the new and attractive king and exulted with the rest of England in the astonishing triumphs that blessed the earliest years of George III's reign. The elder William Pitt had been leading the country to victory against France and her allies, so that with the Peace of 1763, all the vast forests of Canada and much of India would come under British domination. Never before in history had an empire spread so spaciously over the globe, and never before had so many people been able to anticipate a rule so benign: under law and a pious monarch, by freeborn Englishmen in Parliament assembled, inheritors of all the golden virtues enshrined in the English constitution.

Franklin, who had returned to America briefly in 1762, was two years later back in London, where he would remain this time a decade and longer. He loved England, was well known there, had many interesting, clubbable friends in all walks of life, and was most conveniently established among amiable admirers in Craven Street. Oxford presented the American scientist with an honorary degree, as did the University of St. Andrews. He was a member of the Royal Society, and the first non-Englishman elected to its council. Thus fulfilled and contentedly situated, observing developments from London in the years after Pitt's wondrous triumphs, the Anglophiliac Franklin found understandable an opinion widely held in England: that the American colonies, having shared in the benefits of a victory erasing France as an enemy from their western frontiers, should share in the lingering costs of the war that had brought about such a beneficial outcome.

The Stamp Act of 1765 was the means whereby those colonies would be allowed to assume their portion of the war debt. Franklin did oppose the Stamp Act, favoring devices more voluntary, but presumed when it passed that the colonies would comply. Like others, he failed utterly to anticipate the American response to such a measure. Thus, he was astonished when his compatriots overseas reacted to the new, unprecedented tax with one universal cry of outrage. So fierce and sustained was their protest that Parliament and the ministry were obliged to think again. The Stamp Act was repealed, although in the years that followed, government would continue to seek some means by which Americans might be made to share in the high expense of running the new global empire.

Through those years, in the late 1760s and early into the following decade, Franklin in London watched with dismay as the pursuit of such means poisoned relations between England and America. He loved both lands, felt himself both American and English, took pride in his roles both as a paid servant of the Crown (deputy postmaster general of the colonies since the 1750s) and, simultaneously, as an agent paid to represent the interests of various provinces (Pennsylvania, Georgia, New Jersey) in England. Moreover, from 1770 on, this advocate for the continued happy union of colonies and mother country was being paid to represent yet one more colonial interest. Franklin was serving as agent for the Assembly, or lower house of the legislature, of Massachusetts Bay; and his holding of that office was to prove crucial in what followed.

But why, meanwhile, was the government here in London so bent on pursuing policies inimical to her colonies overseas? It grieved the American, who wondered about it aloud among his friends. One friend—in Franklin's words, "a Gentleman of Character and

Distinction (whom I am not at present permitted to name)"—responded in the fall of 1772 with an astounding explanation. The levying of the Townshend duties, the retaining of bothersome tea taxes, the posting of customs commissioners, the dispatching to Boston of transports full of troops: All those recent governmental maneuvers so vigorously resented overseas had been inspired initially not by the king and his ministers or by Parliament. On the contrary, those hugely unpopular measures arose from proposals that had originated among certain high-placed Americans—New Englanders—who had secretly been forwarding advice here to government in Westminster.

The agent was incredulous. His informant (whose identity remains to this day uncertain) offered proof. He gave the American a packet of letters to study at his leisure.

Nineteen letters were in the bundle, by seven different writers, worthy New Englanders all, to an addressee in London whose name had been in every instance erased. Some letters closed with cautions to keep their contents secret. All had been written four or five years earlier, between 1767 and 1769, and accordingly had much to say about tumultuous conditions prevailing around the time that British troops had first disembarked at Boston wharves. The writers had been deploring anarchic behavior in the town and elsewhere in New England—mobs harrying officials going about their lawful business, threatening them, breaking house windows, setting fires—and some of the earlier letters had even encouraged the dispatching of troops from Britain to control the mobs, while others had gone as far as to propose reforms in the charter that governed Massachusetts, to make the provincial legislature less indulgent of colonial vagaries and more dependent on Parliament and the Crown.

Among the nineteen letters were six in the hand of Franklin's colleague of years past at the Albany congress, the same gentleman who in the late 1760s—by the time the letters were written—had risen to become lieutenant governor of Massachusetts, the same gentleman who now, in 1772, as Franklin sat reading, was no less than governor of that province. Six letters were from Thomas Hutchinson.

To be sure, Hutchinson's letters were—with one conspicuous exception—the most circumspect and the least specific of the lot. His never so much as mentioned troops or emendations to the charter. In fact he wrote nothing that he had not earlier and more than once said publicly. But all the letters taken together did seem to smack of conspiracy. Here were prominent figures in Massachusetts writing covertly to an unnamed correspondent presumably in a position of authority in England, urging the pursuit of policies that would diminish the autonomy of Massachusetts Bay and introduce a standing army among a citizenry at peace with the world. Why would Americans make such recommendations against the interests of their own people? The answer seemed clear. Monies to be raised, through new levies that the troops would help customs officers collect, were to go in part to pay salaries of colonial officials. The matter appeared as mean and sordid as that: Hutchinson and his cronies stood to benefit financially. A handful of high-ranking Americans had secretly set about to feather their own nests at the expense of colonial liberty.

Franklin as agent determined to share his sensational discovery with the Massachusetts Assembly. Paraphrasing or copying would not do; the authenticity of anything less than the letters themselves, in the writers' own hands, would be suspect. Thus, the agent sought and received his informant's permission to send the packet (private letters irregularly come by and assuredly addressed neither to Franklin nor to the gentleman who had turned them over) across the ocean to Mr. Thomas Cushing, Speaker of the Assembly and no friend of Hutchinson's. The letters reached Boston in mid-March 1773, along with a stipulation that they not be published, or even so much as copied. Mr. Cushing was authorized only to show the letters to certain like-minded friends for their information, then return the bundle to the agent in London.

No one but Mr. Cushing need know, by the way, that the letters had come from Dr. Franklin, who was not at liberty to divulge from whom he had received them in any case. Enough that they were in the Assembly's hands. Later, the agent explained what he had hoped to accomplish by involving himself in so questionable a proceeding. Well-placed provincials, made aware of the contents of the letters, might go far toward removing the disaffection that recent governmental policies had engendered in America, for if those hateful policies could be shown to have derived not from the British cabinet but rather from a few contemptible schemers in

New England, then the way would be open for reconciliation between an innocent ministry and the aggrieved colonial population. The ministry could seize the opportunity to disavow what had been based on faulty advice, thereby restoring conditions to their happy state before the Stamp Act and allowing Americans to reaffirm their affectionate loyalty. As for the discredited advisers, true source of such disastrous policies as these latterly followed: In suffering whatever reaction their exposure might provoke, Mr. Hutchinson and his crew could console themselves with the reflection that the awkwardness of their personal fate was a requisite of reestablishing harmony in the empire.

The letters were not to be published or even copied, merely read and returned. But of course they were published in Boston, despite Franklin's explicit instructions. First their contents were broadcast before the rapt Assembly in the Town House, after a period of preparatory rumors as to the shocking revelations they contained. The Assembly was duly outraged. All of the letters were deplored, all seven writers excoriated. But in particular, the fury of the House descended upon Thomas Hutchinson, the American-born, American-bred governor—and author of one passage in the letters that seemed consummately egregious. "There is most certainly a crisis," Hutchinson had written to England on January 20, 1769. "We expect to be in suspense for the three or four next weeks and then to hear our fate"—learn what steps Parliament meant to take to allay the then current tensions. And the lieutenant governor had continued:

"I never think of the measures necessary for the peace and good order of the colonies without pain. There must be an abridgment of what are called English liberties. I relieve myself by considering that in a remove from the state of nature to the most perfect state of government there must be a great restraint of natural liberty. I doubt whether it is possible to project a system of government in which a colony 3000 miles distant from the parent state shall enjoy all the liberty of the parent state. I am certain I have never yet seen the projection." And still the pen that had conceded so much flowed fatefully on: "I wish the good of the colony when I wish to see some further restraint of liberty rather than the connexion with the parent state should be broken; for I am sure such a breach must prove the ruin of the colony. Pardon me this excursion, it really proceeds from the state of mind into which our perplexed affairs often throws me."

But Hutchinson desired to see—was sure there *must* be—a further restraint of liberty! So outrageous a passage, urging English authorities to abridge American freedom, with others in the packet only somewhat less offensive, helped incite the Assembly to petition at once for the governor's removal from office. Remove the lieutenant governor, too, Mr. Andrew Oliver, another injudicious letter writer, the governor's warm friend and his wife's brother-in-law, who at the time that the letters were written (four of Oliver's were among them) had been serving as provincial secretary. The petition imploring that the two officials be removed was accordingly adopted June 23, 1773, and forwarded to Franklin as agent for the Assembly, that he might lay it before the proper authorities in London.

Franklin submitted the petition to Lord Dartmouth, secretary of state for the American Department. The king, of course, would have to approve such an unusual request, and the king's Privy Council would first sit in judgment on it. A date was set for a hearing, to be held in January 1774. But in the interval between the agent's formal presentation of the petition and the Privy Council's convening to consider it, two events occurred that darkened the mood in which the hearing took place.

One event was private, the other public. One occurred in England, the other in America.

The private event assumed the form of a duel. When published in Boston over the preceding summer as a pamphlet, those letters of Hutchinson and his friends had created a sensation both in the colonies and, in due time, back in England. The English functionary to whom the letters had been addressed, hitherto unknown, was identified. He proved to be a Mr. Thomas Whately, correspondent of the Oliver family and secretary to a member of the loyal opposition in Parliament. That is, Mr. Whately as recipient of the letters in the 1760s was now revealed to have been occupying no position of authority after all and thus would hardly have been able to affect governmental policies. Moreover, the letters were all now seen to be personal: None of the writers had written in his official capacity, and none had known (conspiracy theories notwithstanding) what the others were writing.

It happened that by this time, by late 1773, Mr. Whately was deceased. At his death, in June of the preceding year, his private letters had gone to his brother, who only with their appearance in the pamphlet from America was made aware that some (as he assumed) had been stolen from his writing desk. The brother considered and determined that a certain Mr. John Temple could alone have had an opportunity to steal the letters. Accusations were made, denials followed, and a duel between the surviving Mr. Whately and Mr. Temple was fought December 11 in Hyde Park, on the outskirts of London. Whately, wounded, remained unsatisfied—and determined to return as soon as possible to the field of honor.

In light of those widely known facts concerning two gentlemen's near-fatal quarrel still pending, the following remarkable notice appeared in the London *Chronicle*, dated Christmas Day:

Craven-street, Dec. 25, 1773.

Sir,

Finding that two Gentlemen have been unfortunately engaged in a Duel, about a transaction and its circumstances of which both of them are totally ignorant and innocent, I think it incumbent on me to declare (for the prevention of farther mischief, as far as such a declaration may contribute to prevent it) that I alone am the person who obtained and transmitted to Boston the letters in question. Mr. W. could not communicate them, because they were never in his possession [presumably having been removed before his brother's death]; and, for the same reason, they could not be taken from him by Mr. T. They were not of the nature of *"private letters between friends"*: They were written by public officers to persons in public station, on public affairs, and intended to procure public measures . . . Their tendency was to incense the Mother Country against her Colonies, and, by the steps recommended, to widen the breach, which they effected. The chief Caution expressed with regard to Privacy, was, to keep their contents from the *Colony Agents*, who the writers apprehended might return them, or copies of them, to America. That apprehension was, it seems, well founded; for the first Agent who laid his hands on them, thought it his duty to transmit them to his Constituents.

B. FRANKLIN,
*Agent for the House of Representatives
of the Massachusetts-Bay.*

Thus, when his majesty's Privy Council convened a month later to consider the merits of the provincial Assembly's petition to remove the governor and lieutenant governor of Massachusetts, the American agent presenting the petition—Benjamin Franklin—stood revealed as the very person who had clandestinely furnished the letters that had provoked the Assembly to seek the removal in the first place.

The Privy Council was not long in concluding that the Assembly's request was based on "False and Erroneous allegations," and hence was "groundless, Vexatious and Scandalous and calculated only for the Seditious Purpose of keeping up a Spirit of Clamour and Discontent." But much of the hearing was directed (irrelevantly, as he thought) not toward the petition but toward the agent who had submitted it. For the first time in all his years in England, Dr. Franklin was treated with something less than courtesy. He was, in fact, to be humiliated, an old man approaching seventy made to stand a full hour in the crowded Cockpit, the meeting chamber in Whitehall, and hear himself traduced by Solicitor General Wedderburn while thirty-four lords of the Privy Council among crowds of spectators sniggered and applauded in approval. Scorn poured forth, and contempt, and sarcasm; and the noblemen—the duke of Queensberry, the earls of Suffolk and Sandwich and Rochford, the bishop of London, and others—were heard repeatedly to laugh at the cutting wit and urge on the contumely.

All the while, in his suit of Manchester velvet (set aside afterward and not donned again until he was summoned triumphantly to sign the treaty with France that would assure victory in the Revolution), Franklin stood immovably erect, his passive features offering no response as the solicitor general, having charged him with being a thief, advised the prudent to hide their papers and lock up their escritoires when this gentleman came among them. Not only had the American made off with the letters of one brother, but he had kept his handiwork hidden until he had nearly occasioned the murder of the other. Some people coming by goods dishonorably (the solicitor general averred) retain them with the excuse of not knowing whose they are. But Dr. Franklin had known, yet had failed to restore them to their rightful owner. Letters are "as sacred and as precious to Gentlemen of integrity, as their family plate or jewels are. And no man who knows the

Whately's"—as Solicitor General Wedderburn knew them, well—
"will doubt, but that they would much sooner have chosen, that
any person should have taken their plate, and sent it to Holland for
his avarice, than that he should have secreted the letters of their
friends, their brother's friend, and their father's friend, and sent
them away to Boston to gratify an enemy's malice."

Dr. Franklin had insisted that the letters were on public matters.
Then must an official in a public station forgo all private friend-
ships? Not correspond with his friends? Was the American avow-
ing the principle that he had a right to filch private letters of the
lords here in this chamber, in order to apply them to whatever uses
would best answer the purposes of party malevolence? One thing
was certain: The agent could not have obtained the letters by fair
means. The writers had not given them to him. Mr. Whately now
deceased had not. Nothing would acquit Dr. Franklin of the charge
of having obtained the letters corruptly, and for the most malignant of purposes—unless he stole them from the person who had
stolen them in the first place. "This argument is irrefragable."

Franklin stood exposed thus as the prime mover and conduc-
tor—this electrical genius—of the whole elaborate contrivance
launched against an estimable governor's reputation. Having used
confidants and party leaders to manipulate the Massachusetts
Assembly into becoming his tools in carrying out certain sinister
and secret designs, he now dared to appear in turn as their agent
before the lords of the Privy Council, here "to give the finishing
stroke to the work of his own hands."

More, much more poured forth in that vein, through a long hour
as the distinguished American of sixty-eight held himself erect and
expressionless amid snorts of outrage and peals of derisive laugh-
ter. Finally, the ordeal ended. Next day, Franklin was stripped of
his lucrative position as deputy postmaster, a position that he had
honorably discharged for twenty years. In the weeks that followed,
some in England defended the agent's actions, calling in Craven
Street to offer their sympathetic support. But the London press was
filled with the indignation of others who reviled him.

Thus, through this late winter and early spring of 1774, when
Hutchinson in Boston was suffering the slanders of opponents in
the American newspapers, Franklin in London was enduring
English newspaper attacks upon his own character from the oppo-

site political quarter. And even as Hutchinson was making plans to sail for England, Franklin was reflecting that nothing need detain him longer from returning to America.

Soon, then, he would be gone. "My dear Love," the elderly gentleman wrote his wife in Philadelphia at the end of April, "I hoped to have been on the Sea in my Return by this time, but find I must stay a few Weeks longer, perhaps for the Summer Ships. Thanks to God I continue well and hearty, and hope to find you so when I have the Happiness once more of seeing you."

It had been just under ten years since Dr. Franklin had seen his dear Debby last.

3

A Third
Boston Gentleman

A DUEL FOUGHT IN LONDON, rousing Benjamin Franklin as agent for the Massachusetts Assembly to acknowledge his role in the affair of the Hutchinson letters, was the private event that had darkened the mood of the Privy Council when it met soon after to consider the Assembly's petition for removing the royal governor. But a public event on the other side of the ocean in Boston, in the same month of December as the agent's admission, had affected the Privy Council's mood even more adversely. "I suppose," Franklin himself would write Mr. Cushing after the fact, "we never had since we were a People, so few Friends in Britain." December's public event, news of which had reached London precisely one week before the Privy Council convened in January, "seems to have united all Parties here against our Province."

The public event was the Boston Tea Party.

Governor Hutchinson near the scene had had a role to play in the Tea Party. As his majesty's representative in Massachusetts, he had sought to disband the meetings that were gathering in Boston in raucous protest before the arrival of the tea ("He? He?"—cried Samuel Adams in scorn when learning of it—"is he that Shadow of a Man, scarce able to support his withered Carcase or his hoary Head! is he a *Representation* of *Majesty*?"). And when the tea ships were finally tied up at the wharf, Hutchinson had declined to sign a permit that would have allowed them to cast off and sail back home. As he saw it, the governor had no authority to sign such a permit. Popular leaders—Adams and John Hancock and others—

had seen matters differently. In any case, certain townsmen were determined that the cargoes of tea would not be delivered, to tempt thirsty colonists into paying the minuscule threepenny duty each pound of it bore. Instead, disguised and unmolested, on the night of December 16, 1773, they had boarded the ships and scattered the East India Company's treasure, crate by shattered crate, into the harbor, then dropped to the wharf and vanished among the back streets of the town.

When word of the outrage reached London, Franklin, like a great many others (like the Virginian George Washington for one), was appalled. Bostonians should immediately move to make good the destruction of private property, and their agent in London wrote and told them so. But many back in Massachusetts were of the opposite opinion. John Adams exulted over what had been done, as did his cousin Samuel. To be sure, Samuel Adams's lieutenant Josiah Quincy responded to the fateful episode in a manner rather less easy to characterize.

This third Boston gentleman, Mr. Josiah Quincy, like Mr. Hutchinson and Dr. Franklin, played a prominent part in these months that led to war—and a part that intertwined with theirs. Despite his youth, what Mr. Quincy had already accomplished was considerable. He had been born in Boston twenty-nine years earlier, in 1744, but at twelve had moved with his family to Braintree, a village to the south of town, not far from Hutchinson's beloved country retreat at Milton. Quincys had lived in Braintree for generations, a great many of them; before the end of the eighteenth century, their portion of the settlement would in fact be incorporated into another township, renamed (as its name remains) Quincy.

Braintree near the middle of the century was a remarkable community. Small as it was, various notable Quincys were living there, as well as young John Adams (who would become close friends with Josiah Quincy's older brother and would very nearly propose marriage to Quincy's sister), John Hancock (who would marry a first cousin of Josiah Quincy's), and Abigail Smith, John Adams's future wife and the daughter of yet another Quincy, all of them friends of each other.

Josiah's father was one of numerous thriving merchants in this commercial province, and a gentleman highly regarded. Like the father, the son had gone to Harvard, where he had graduated in

1763. The gifted young man had set out at once on a law career in Boston, and soon he had acquired an impressive reputation. It was in court on one early, memorable occasion that the twenty-one-year-old Quincy had found himself moved to compassion for the then lieutenant governor Thomas Hutchinson, victim of a recent offense that all right-thinking Bostonians deplored.

The offense had occurred in the midst of the Stamp Act agitations, on the night of August 26, 1765. A drunken mob had in its mindlessness swarmed over the lieutenant governor's mansion in the North End, that magnificent ancestral home, had driven Mr. Hutchinson and his family fleeing into the night, and had proceeded to dismantle the house brick by antique brick, guzzling cellar wines, taking hatchets to the elegant furnishings—the gilt-framed family pictures, the tea tables and damask curtains and walnut chairs and looking glasses—destroying the gardens, the roof, the cupola, scattering pillow feathers out of windows, throwing plate and crystal and a scholar's irreplaceable documents ("all the manuscripts & other papers I had been collecting for 30 years together") into the surrounding gutters, keeping at their madness until dawn had finally put an end to it soon after four in the morning.

It was hardly surprising that a gentleman so dealt with by the Stamp Act's besotted opponents (Hutchinson had been on record as opposing the Stamp Act in any case) valued order over liberty, dreaded the anarch more than the tyrant. Next morning, the lieutenant governor as justice of the supreme court of the province had arrived dutifully in the courtroom, and young Josiah Quincy had been on hand, deeply affected by the appearance of the victim of such fury. The gentleman had appeared "big with the greatest anxiety, clothed in a manner which would have excited compassion from the hardest heart," even had his thin camlet surtout and plain waistcoat not contrasted so sharply with the imposing scarlet robes of the other bewigged judges. Tears had stood in Hutchinson's eyes, and his face had revealed his anguish.

> What must an audience have felt [Quincy wrote at the time], whose compassion had before been moved by what they knew he had suffered, when they heard him pronounce the following words in a manner which the agitation of his mind dictated?
> "GENTLEMEN,—There not being a quorum of the court without me, I am obliged to appear. Some apology is necessary for my dress: in-

deed, I had no other. Destitute of every thing,—no other shirt; no other garment but what I have on; and not one in my whole family in a better situation than myself."

As it happened, Quincy's compassion for the lieutenant governor would prove short-lived. The young man was soon to become, and to the day of his death would remain, one of Hutchinson's most pitiless foes.

For now, the destruction of Thomas Hutchinson's mansion—an act universally condemned—was seen as an anomaly, the senseless handiwork of the most savage of the Boston mobs. But other mobs would form in months and years that followed, for rather more intelligible reasons, and British troops would debark in the fall of 1768 to deal with them. Thereafter the troops would idle about the town, tauntingly conspicuous in their brick-red uniforms, so that eventually, inevitably, resentment between soldiers and thronging civilians would explode in open conflict.

The explosion came in 1770, on a cold March evening; and Josiah Quincy was to become deeply involved in the aftermath of the violence. March 5, and King Street and the surrounding roadways were again resounding to the everlasting clamor of footfalls hurrying in the darkness, men in pursuit, angry calls and oaths and taunts and challenges hurled, stones, snowballs, oyster shells hurled, cudgels swung. But this time, abruptly, about half past nine before the hated customhouse, had come fierce loud eruptions of gunfire from beleaguered British soldiers, and three of the tormenting mob lay dead, two others wounded mortally, bleeding in the snow.

Lieutenant Governor Hutchinson was sent for. He hurried to the Town House under the alarm of church bells pealing. There, on the balcony overlooking King Street and the very site of the slaughter, Hutchinson faced down the enraged protesters below by promising them justice. And before the year was out, justice was done.

The soldiers who had fired were brought to trial with their captain. To represent them, the English defendants managed to secure two of Boston's most highly regarded attorneys, both supporters of the Popular Party, opposed to British policy in general. That is, both lawyers defending the soldiers had vehemently resented the presence of troops in Boston in the first place. One attorney was John Adams; the other was young Josiah Quincy.

In Braintree, Quincy's patriot father had learned of his son's involvement in the affair with dismay: that he had taken as clients troops who had fired on Americans. Under great affliction, as he put it, the elder Quincy had written Josiah at once, reporting of having heard "the bitterest reproaches uttered against you, for having become an advocate for those criminals who are charged with the murder of their fellow-citizens. Good God! Is it possible? I will not believe it." Such a betrayal had filled the infirm old gentleman's heart with anguish, convinced as he was that the taking of such a part in the trial would discredit the young man's reputation beyond recovery. "I repeat, I will not believe it, unless it be confirmed by your own mouth, or under your hand."

That hand did promptly confirm the truth of the rumor that had shattered an old man's repose. And after acknowledging in writing the accuracy of the report, Quincy had gone on to remind his father pointedly that men are innocent until proven guilty. They are entitled to legal counsel and aid—"and I dare affirm, that you, and this whole people will one day REJOICE, that I became an advocate for the aforesaid 'criminals,' *charged* with the murder of our fellow-citizens."

Events proved the son right. The jury's subsequent verdict of acquittal, after his and John Adams's brilliant defense, was viewed on both sides of the Atlantic as evidence that everyone, friend or foe, could find justice in American courts, even in tempestuous times. Nor did the attorney's deft performance at the trial injure his reputation, as his father had feared. On the contrary, the favorable verdict behind him, Josiah Quincy continued to rise in the inner counsels of the Popular Party that opposed the governing establishment. In late 1772, he was appointed to an important patriot committee, the so-called Committee of Correspondence, charged with keeping other towns in the province informed of administration's various proceedings that might threaten local liberties. And in the late winter of 1773, Quincy set out by ship to visit colonies to the south, partly for his health—he was tubercular—but also in order to meet and talk personally with counterparts in the Carolinas, Virginia, Maryland, Pennsylvania, New York, and elsewhere.

The trip was a great success. Returned to Boston—now a friend of colonial leaders up and down the seaboard—Quincy was on hand at the end of the year to address the frenzied, crowded meet-

ings that preceded the Tea Party, for in addition to being an out-
standing attorney, the young man had early been recognized as
one of the most gifted orators in the province.

In appearance, these three Boston gentlemen—Mr. Quincy, Dr.
Franklin, and Mr. Hutchinson—would have made an arresting contrast. Hutchinson in his early sixties was gaunt and beanpole slender, angular, aged by the cares of office, withered, urbane, aristo-
cratic, stiff, and with only the flimsiest shred of humor, if the
abundant surviving specimens of his writing may be relied upon.
Franklin, approaching seventy, was of substantial bulk ("Mr.
Fatsides," he had dubbed himself privately, and "the Great Person,"
because of his girth rather than his accomplishments), of medium
height, comfortably rumpled, his countenance kindly, humorous,
canny, his manner sage and conciliatory. And Quincy, as he stood
now in late 1773 addressing the excited Boston multitudes: not yet
thirty, pale and slight, nervous, energetic, displaying evidences of
the tuberculosis that would kill him, his eyes crossed (a deformity
far less exceptional then than now), his demeanor impulsive, emotional, vibrant, engaging.

And unpredictable. The young man's views appeared sufficiently radical, and yet in crises, he had a tendency to behave in
unexpected ways. As in defending British troops after the Boston
Massacre. As now, when he spoke in that clear, penetrating tenor
voice (like the music of the spheres, one admiring contemporary
recorded) on the rainy dark afternoon immediately preceding the
Tea Party, stilling the hordes that had crowded into the Old South
Meetinghouse. "Look to the end," he cautioned his fellow
Bostonians. "Whoever supposes that shouts and hosannas will ter-
minate the trials of the day, entertains a childish fancy. We must be
grossly ignorant of the importance and value of the prize for which
we contend . . . to flatter ourselves that popular resolves, popular
harangues, popular acclamations, and popular vapor, will van-
quish our foes. Let us consider the issue. Let us look to the end. Let
us weigh and consider, before we advance to those measures
which must bring on the most trying and terrible struggle, this
country ever saw."

Temperate words—farseeing of course (the measures that night
on Griffin's Wharf did directly bring on the terrible struggle), but
more moderate than might have been expected from one who for

several years had been identified as a fiery leader of radical agitation against every aspect of English colonial policy.

Despite the warning, the tea was destroyed; and no more than four days later, Josiah Quincy had turned about and was unblinkingly writing in the *Boston Gazette* to defend the destruction, blaming the event on local tea agents, Crown appointees, whose stubbornness had forced so drastic a step to be taken.

For Quincy, attorney and orator, was also a fluent journalist; so that during weeks following the Tea Party, while Boston awaited the response from England that must come, he made time for further writing, publishing a series of newspaper articles that recapitulated recent Boston history in order to identify the cause of the town's distress. No doubt lingered in the young man's mind about the source of the present troubles. The lawyer-journalist ended his survey by asserting that one person alone, one single individual, bore responsibility for the current trials of the town, the same who had earlier covertly advocated abridging American liberties. Gone now was any sympathy for what that individual might once have suffered from Boston mobs. Quincy concluded by exposing Governor Thomas Hutchinson as no less than "the first, the most malignant and *insatiable* enemy of my country;— . . . he is the chief author and supporter of the severest calamities under which this people labor . . . he has done more general mischiefs and committed greater public crimes than his *life* can repair or his *death* satisfy;—and . . . *he is the man* against whom the blood of my slaughtered brethren cries from the ground"—that blood of victims of the massacre whose murderers the writer himself had successfully defended.

Such a strident outpouring, characteristic of the age, serves as a specimen of what the governor of Massachusetts Bay was encountering in the papers with dismal regularity during these months preceding his departure for England. It may indicate as well the kind of vituperation that Dr. Franklin on the other side of the water was reading in the London papers directed against his own substantial self, though from the opposite pole of political opinion.

Josiah Quincy's ardor, in print and on the platform, did not go unchallenged. Like Hutchinson and Franklin, he too had enemies. Before long, one such would be evaluating the young man, in what passed for objectivity, as a "pettyfogging Attorney, a firebrand in Politics, tolerable Orator, and an inflammatory Writer," a gentleman "of a sour, gloomy, discontented Temper" who "squints abominably." And even now, during this very spring, this May of 1774, after Parliament had answered the Tea Party with the Port Act, Quincy was to receive an ominous letter from the British Coffeehouse in King Street, haunt of officers and of locals friendly to the Crown. The letter conveyed a warning to a malcontent whose imprudences had put him in hazard of losing his life and having his estate confiscated. Among those imprudences, the eloquent young Quincy at a recent town meeting had expressly charged king, Lords, and Commons with ignorance and effrontery in passing the Port Act, as the anonymous letter writer reminded him; and "not content with these bold speeches, you were the principal mover of sundry votes, passed at this meeting, which can be considered in no other light by Great Britain, than as an hostile attack upon her." Quincy's correspondent urged the young man to reflect on his conduct and renounce it, even though he might already have proceeded too far to be saved. "Let me conjure you," the writer admonished with a certain unction in closing, "to weigh well what I have offered to your consideration, and believe me to be YOUR WELLWISHER."

The attorney chose to answer such unsought advice publicly, and in a manner that displays his doughty spirit. Quincy's reply, in a local paper of loyalist sympathies that his correspondent might be presumed to read, began by noting that threats of danger from an individual unwilling to reveal his name need never deter a citizen from following the path of duty. In the present instance, whether the writer's purpose had been for good or ill was unclear; accordingly, the recipient might suspend his censure but would certainly not extend his thanks. If, instead of hiding behind a pseudonym, the gentleman had sought an interview to express his concern, "his frankness would have been an evidence of his sincerity, and my cordiality on the occasion should have testified my gratitude." In any case, Quincy's residence in town was well known, in Marlborough just south of Milk Street, and he was easily found. Should the anonymous writer choose to call, he might look forward to "the best civilities of my house; and if he will appoint a meeting, I will give him my presence, either alone, or in company."

So much for veiled threats. Perhaps ready himself for a duel if need be, the young attorney remained undeterred. In fact, he was even then, at that same house just around the corner from where Dr. Franklin had been born, preparing a written response—more detailed than his speeches—to the Port Act. When published, the pamphlet, *Observations on the Boston Port-Bill*, would make Josiah Quincy's name widely known, not only in America but overseas, among the highest councils of government in London.

4

Boston in May 1774

Boston papers in late May carried a notice of the new pamphlet for sale. Among pleas for the recovery of runaway slaves and an advertisement for newfangled "Umbrilloes" against the rain (illustrated with an explanatory woodcut) and the announcement that dancing-master William Turner "will attend . . . on grown Gentlemen and Ladies, and assures the utmost Secrecy shall be kept till they are capable of exhibiting in high Taste" was displayed a box informing the public that "To-Morrow will be Published," on Tuesday, May 31, "And Sold by EDES and GILL, in *Queen-Street*, (Price 1 s. 6 d.) Observations on the Act of Parliament For Blocking up the Harbour of *Boston* . . . By JOSIAH QUINCY, JUNR."

As for that, never in peace or war had Boston suffered a blockade. The town to be dealt with thus harshly was at the time, and for years had been, one of the two or three busiest ports in North America—even if strikingly small by our standards. Small in area: The topography of no other American city has changed more than that of Boston, which then occupied a pear-shaped peninsula extending northeastward into Massachusetts Bay. The stem of the pear connected the peninsula to the mainland as the so-called Neck, an isthmus scarcely forty yards wide, bordered by mudflats and sometimes at high tide submerged, so that Boston on occasion became an island. Otherwise, a single road allowed entrance from the mainland between the mudflats onto the peninsula, which in extent was about the size of modern-day Central Park. Bare hills covered much of the space to the west on the peninsula, and three coves—bites out of the pear—further reduced the area available.

But from the start, there had been fresh water on that clump of land that protruded, and no wolves or bears or mosquitoes, facts that help account for its appeal to the original settlers of 1630.

By May 1774, the town that had grown there nestled at the base of the three hills, at the northeast portion of the peninsula around the coves. Small in area, Boston was also still small in numbers, with a population of some eighteen thousand people. Yet what remarkable individuals were among them! Would any modern community of comparable size on which history shone such a brilliant light reveal so many highly gifted? The painter John Singleton Copley walked the streets of Boston that late May, planning his approaching departure for Europe, while the young black poet Phillis Wheatley, grieving the recent death of her beloved mistress, was walking the same streets. The enormously popular, enormously wealthy Mr. Hancock lived in the town, though he was currently indisposed, confined to his Beacon Hill mansion with the gout. And in Queen Street, Mr. John Adams fretted about the gravity of public events, which his cousin Samuel Adams had been moving to exploit in taverns and caucus rooms. Paul Revere was there, and the physician Joseph Warren, whose brilliant promise would be cut down at Bunker Hill, and others only somewhat less well known to history—along with worthies whose names their fellow citizens might reasonably have assumed as likely as any yet mentioned to echo down the ages, except that the gentlemen and ladies alluded to (the Vassalls and Pembertons and Sewalls and such) had chosen wrong and thereby consigned themselves to oblivion.

Those last named were adhering to the party of privilege, variously called the Court Party, the Prerogative Party, loyalists, or Tories. "Tory" is the English spelling of an Irish term meaning "pursuers," applied in the seventeenth century to Irish papists and royalists opposing the republican armies of Cromwell. Later, in the 1680s, the term referred to those in England who supported the claims of the Roman Catholic James, duke of York, to succeed to the throne of his ostensibly Protestant brother Charles II. Throughout the century that followed, Tories accordingly presented themselves as the party of legitimacy and tradition, in England as in America.

Their opponents in Boston were the Country Party, variously called patriots (a term then merely descriptive), Sons of Liberty, rebels, or Whigs. "Whig," like "Tory," dates from the seventeenth century, a Scottish word applied to Presbyterians who supported English Puritan aspirations, and hence were opposed to the royalists, the Cavaliers. Near the end of the century Whigs in England would dispute the Catholic duke of York's right to succeed to the throne, and would rejoice when he was deposed and the Protestants William and Mary replaced him.

In America the term "Whig" came into use only in the late 1760s, to describe those who were protesting then current policies of Great Britain, starting just before the Stamp Act, that were aimed at making the colonies share in the cost of empire. Before 1765, in fact, when the Stamp Act became law, there had been little occasion for Whigs in America. Good feelings had abounded at the start of the decade, in the colonies as in England, as George III was ascending the throne; and affection for the new young king had deepened when his armies triumphed gloriously over France, in Europe and India, in the West Indies and Canada.

The decade advanced. The Stamp Act was passed, then repealed. The Townshend duties were enacted; most of them were repealed. The duty on tea was retained; customs officials were sent to Boston, with troops, to collect the duty. And through it all Hutchinson, his friends the Olivers, and other provincial leaders, once so esteemed and now less so, could only look on in bewilderment and dismay as relations between England and America soured, as patriot voices began to speak out more frequently and forcefully from pulpits and in legislative chambers. Everything was changing. The lower part of the people, as Hutchinson himself put it at the time, had of late acquired such a sense of their importance "that a gentleman does not meet with what used to be common civility, and we are sinking into perfect barbarism."

The Tory cause was doomed, of course. It looked longingly backward to an earlier time, when those lower orders had known and held their place, understanding and respecting the merit of prerogative. The paternalistic Hutchinson and his colleagues among the governing class, bred to rule, knowledgeable about the complexities of government as the humble simply could not be, had from the beginning (as they thought) pursued their duty responsibly. Now as the years advanced into the 1770s, they could do little but persist in their old ways, regarding the present disturbances in the province as an aberration, the mischievous handiwork of a group of incendiaries inflaming the innocent for their own purposes. The ringleaders were known—that palsied, lisping, middle-aged failure Samuel Adams and his pack: Hancock, Warren, young Quincy—all of whose self-serving wickedness must finally be exposed, allowing the multitudes to see their error and return to the ways of their fathers.

Thus, the Tories. Yet oddly, the Whigs, too, represented themselves during these same years not as revolutionaries but rather as the party truly seeking to return to earlier times, before the Stamp Act and like measures had been foisted upon the empire by a small, sinister cabal of politicians in England, bent upon enslaving America. The innocent multitudes in the mother country had been misled, in Whig opinion, and English voters would eventually see *their* error, throw out the villains—the Butes and the Norths and the like—and return the empire to that happy state of mutual respect that had existed so long and fruitfully between the colonies and Great Britain, when both had shared a common love of liberty.

The issues that divided the two parties, in Boston and in London, were expressed less often in terms of taxation than sovereignty. Who was sovereign over the colonies—and hence could tax? Parliament, said the Tories, or (in the ancient phrase) the king in Parliament. The empire simply could not survive otherwise. Any such vast endeavor must have over it one supreme authority under God. Colonials as Englishmen were subject to Parliament. If those living overseas should be foolish enough to set up a rival to that authority, the empire would split apart; no one can serve two masters. Then the various colonies, detached from the mother country, would fall to bickering among themselves and, no longer protected by England's might, would become prey to the grasping ambition of some other mercantile nation far less humane: the French or the Spanish or the Dutch.

True (as many Tories conceded), America in the course of time was destined to grow strong and united and even independent—maybe a century from now—but for now while the colonies grew, and into the foreseeable future, Americans must forswear any ruinous claims of possessing a sovereignty equal to Parliament's. Such autonomy, insisted upon, would mean separation from England; and after separation would come disaster, as predators picked off the enfeebled and inevitably quarreling provinces one by one.

The Whigs for their part argued that the original settlers journeying from England to the New World had specifically freed themselves from the restraints of English society, from all that feudal and episcopal apparatus, when setting out to fashion their new commonwealths at the edge of the American wilderness. Now, after a century and a half, Americans shared with Englishmen back home a loyalty to the Crown and the British constitution, but their own provincial legislatures had been chartered expressly to serve—and had served successfully for decades—as local, responsive parliaments, levying taxes and framing the other laws under which the colonies were beneficently governed.

The argument over sovereignty had been carried on at length, at different levels of society in America and in England, with both Tories and Whigs learnedly citing precedents, arguing with great subtlety and feeling during the years before 1774. Yet all that heartfelt and attenuated clamor had become academic now. The Tea Party had led Parliament to close the discussion by asserting its supremacy at the end of a bayonet. There was to be no more talk. The commander in chief of all British forces in North America, an Englishman, had been appointed governor of Massachusetts Bay, to succeed the civilian native governor Hutchinson. Governor-General Thomas Gage had accordingly arrived in Boston in mid-May 1774, with British troops already in town at his disposal and four more regiments on the high seas not far behind. Parliament had spoken through the Port Act, and there was an end of it; General Gage was here with sufficient force to assure that Parliament's dictates would be obeyed.

What the new governor had seen when he had sailed into Boston Harbor aboard the frigate *Lively* on Friday the 13th of May was, by agreement of the several travelers of the period who recorded their impressions, a singularly beautiful prospect: green islands, the busy harbor full of shipping, the town curving around the coves, wharves jutting forth, homes and churches and public buildings, and the hills rising behind. This was his majesty's premier port in the new world, and the evidence of commerce was everywhere in view: in the ropewalks, the warehouses, the sail lofts, the stores, the ships at the docks, the busy shipyards. Most of the fortunes in town, in fact, had been made from commerce: All that comfortable wealth in Hutchinson's family, the wealth of Quincy's father and of his father-in-law Mr. William Phillips, of Messrs. Hancock and James Bowdoin and the family of Peter Faneuil and numerous others—all of it was merchants' money. And the business of commerce was rarely out of sight. From almost any spot on the peninsula, once Gage had set foot ashore, he would have seen the sea or could have reached it in a moment or two. Streets led down to the bustling waterfront, to the harbor crowded with ships welcomed in Bristol and St. Eustatius and far-off Surinam.

And all that bustle, all that prosperous, clamorous activity was to be abruptly stilled. Parliament had decreed an end to all commerce June 1. The entire town had been condemned unheard, as it were, as Josiah Quincy was noting here at month's end, in his *Observations* on the Port Act, received in the last ships from London. Not only had the town been condemned without a formal hearing, but Boston had not even been asked to respond informally to the charges entered against it. Yet the most ferocious criminals, the lawyer Quincy was reminding readers in his just-issued pamphlet, were not punished until after they had been arraigned before disinterested judges, given the opportunity of defending themselves, and found guilty of whatever they were charged with having done. In the present instance, by contrast, "a whole people are accused, prosecuted by they know not whom; tried they know not when; proved guilty they know not how; and sentenced in a mode which for number of calamities, extent and duration of severity, exceeds the annals of past ages, and, we presume in pity to mankind, will not mark any future era in the story of the world."

That, Quincy argued, was the first injustice of this newly arrived Port Act. The disproportionate severity of the sentence constituted the second of three great wrongs that the act had inflicted on Boston. For what had the town done? What unprecedented crimes had its citizens committed to justify the enactment of such penalties, forfeitures, and pains? Minutes of town meetings from last fall would confirm that the inhabitants had disavowed all riot and disorder. In fact, in the course of the tea crisis, town meetings had been dissolved; the informal gatherings that had followed had included (unlike Boston town meetings) people from surrounding villages and were conducted according to procedures different from those that guided the governing body of the town. How then blame Boston for what was the unofficial work of specific individuals? No, Boston had conducted itself cautiously and prudently throughout the crisis, as the records would show. Moreover, were popular commotions peculiar to this town in any case? "Hath not every maritime town in England been repeatedly affected by them?" And (Quincy might have added) had not other American ports—New York, Philadelphia, Charleston—refused the hated tea as well?

Yet the act, with unprecedented rigor, punished only this one town, the entire town of Boston, guilty and innocent alike. Punished it, moreover—and this was the third great wrong perpetrated—in a manner that precluded redress. For the law had been so framed that the most agonizing pains and penalties would ensue even if the injunctions of the act were scrupulously obeyed. Suppose for a moment (Quincy urged his readers) "that upon the first intimations of the present law, Boston had been as prone to obey the edict of a British court, as the Turk to comply with the mandate of the Divan; let us imagine them as servile, as fawning as a court dependent to a minister of state;—nay, if there be any thing in nature yet more humble and more base, let Boston (in idea for a short moment) be that humble, servile, base, and fawning something: What doth it all avail?"

Nothing whatever. Even if the entire town had will and means, the East India Company over there in London's Leadenhall Street far across the sea could not be satisfied until after the citizens of Boston had called a meeting, come together, consulted, and resolved what to do. "Great bodies are not calculated for speedy decision, any more than velocity of motion. The resolution formed, time must be given for despatches to England, application to the East-India Company, an adjustment with them upon the nice point of 'full satisfaction,'" which the terms of the act were insisting upon. Moreover, the king had to be satisfied as well, while the weeks and months passed, and the universal suffering in the town intensified.

Let the reader consider how much time must elapse before all this could be accomplished. In short, with whatever goodwill well-meaning citizens of Boston might undertake to stay the torrent of evils that had descended upon them and however diligently they might exert themselves to do so, no course of conduct could save them from being overwhelmed in ruin—ruin, moreover, as Quincy observed, that must be visited upon the entire population: upon aged and infirm, rich and poor, women and children, the innocent as well as the guilty.

Observations on the Boston Port-Bill had identified the enormous injustices of Parliament's harsh measure with logic and fervor. His pamphlet once published, the young attorney-author was eager to have it widely read. Accordingly, Quincy transmitted copies to those many new friends—gentlemen of consequence in the other colonies—whose acquaintance he had made on his trip south the year before. And on this final day of May, he took care to see that a copy was delivered as well to his only brother, ten years older, also living here in Boston.

Samuel Quincy was a lawyer, too, earlier involved like his younger brother in the trial of the British soldiers and their captain after the Boston Massacre. Only Samuel had appeared on the side of the prosecution—two brothers in court pleading against each other's brief. A seeming paradox: Samuel's sympathies were loyalist. He was solicitor general of Massachusetts and would live out his life loyal to his king. Yet in the trial, this Crown officer had been obliged to prosecute British soldiers, while his younger brother, the patriot, had defended the same British soldiers successfully against the state's charges.

Such were the contradictions of these contentious times: that the two brothers were professionally opposed, and personally so different in their loyalties, indicates how deeply Massachusetts was divided as this present spring month ended. Very families were divided, to their anguish—so that on June 1, Samuel Quincy, having received a copy of Josiah's latest handiwork, must sit down and share his complex feelings.

"Dear Brother," he wrote, "The pamphlet you presented me yesterday was doubly acceptable, as the billet that accompanied it assures me of your desire to live in amity with an only brother. Such a testimony of your respect I cannot fail of remembering with pleasure. The convulsions of the times are in nothing more to be lamented, than in the interruption of domestic harmony."

The writer went on to express his regret that the meetings of the two had not been so "free, or frequent" of late as they once had

been. Yet because both gentlemen had taken care to avoid conversing on politics, their caution had prevented—and would go on preventing—"a clashing of the fiercer passions." And the loyalist
ended his letter with moving generosity, even eloquence. "God
preserve you," brother wrote brother, Sam wrote Josh, Tory wrote
Whig, on this momentous first of June, "in health and longevity,
the friend and patron, and at length the father of your country, and
the eclat of your own times record you with honour to the memory
of the latest ages, and especially, the prayer nearest my heart, may
you continue, and have reason to continue, the friend and companion of your most cordially affectionate brother. SAMUEL QUINCY."

5

CROSSING THE ATLANTIC

WEDNESDAY, JUNE 1, 1774—the day that Samuel Quincy was writing Josiah—was a day of surpassing beauty in Boston. The sun shone golden on the windows of the little town, and the harbor waters sparkled; and all day long (surviving journals agree), the weather continued balmy and delightful.

At ten that morning, Thomas Hutchinson, his son Elisha, his daughter Peggy, their servants Patrick Riley and the ailing Mark, "a Negro man," with fellow passengers Polly Murray, James Horrop, and a family of four named Gardner, had set sail from Castle Island in the harbor, aboard the *Minerva*, Captain James Callahan. An hour later they had passed troop transports ("one answers 26 days out") arriving in the bay to strengthen Governor Gage's hand through coming weeks, the first of the reinforcements sent from Britain. Alongside the lighthouse at one in the afternoon, the *Minerva* was off Cape Cod bound eastward by eight in the evening.

For the sixty-two-year-old departing governor, the day would have been long and emotional. At the start of it, his excellency had risen for a last time in his Milton home, the country home built thirty-one years earlier, while his adored wife was still alive. A low Georgian structure, the place had been enlarged and much beautified over the decades, sycamores planted, the crest that the home graced cleared to allow for those lovely views—the one to the west and the glorious one northward, out over marshes of the Neponset valley to Boston Harbor that had glittered in sunlight this same splendid day: green islands and the fields with their sheep, the town of Boston itself far off, eight miles to the north, the hills and the tiny spires and roofs near the water's edge.

Early this morning, then, Governor Hutchinson had taken leave of his Milton home and those views, passing on foot among neighbors to bid them farewell, his carriage following behind him down the slope to the Lower Mills. A last time he had climbed into the carriage, seated among its familiar comforts as it bore him to the eastern edge of Dorchester Heights. From there the governor had been rowed the brief distance over to Castle Island, barracks and fortifications somber beneath the flashing banner of St. George out in the harbor. He had stepped ashore on the island shortly before nine o'clock.

If Hutchinson's farewells to his neighbors back in Milton had been cheerful—as an eyewitness later reported—those testimonials that he was taking with him, from local merchants, lawyers, clergymen, and magistrates, would have helped to support his spirits. The private message from Lord Dartmouth, colonial secretary, that General Gage had delivered would have been likewise heartening, conveying as it did, and on the best authority, the sovereign's gracious approval of all that Hutchinson had achieved. And still another consolation would have helped the governor to be of good cheer, even as he faced the miseries of seasickness immediately ahead, even as he was bidding good-bye to everything that he loved: He was to remain in England only a short while.

His son Elisha, arriving at Castle Island with sister Peggy earlier this same morning, had felt confident enough of the travelers' prompt return to leave his pregnant wife awaiting him at her father's home in Plymouth, thirty miles away. Elisha's confidence, like his father's, arose—in Hutchinson's own words later—from a communication conveying General Gage's new appointment, in which the outgoing governor had been assured that the continuance of his replacement in office "would, probably, not be of long duration, and that it was the king's intention that he [Hutchinson] should be reinstated, if agreeable to him, whenever general Gage's services as commander-in-chief should be required in any other situation." In other words, the general and his regiments were to preside only through the early date when the tea damages were paid for, an interval during which Thomas Hutchinson in London would be counseling the ministry wisely about colonial policies most likely to benefit all reasonable parties concerned. That done— and given the notoriously fickle nature of public opinion—the civilian governor might then return to the grateful applause of his fellow Americans in the province, the present crisis behind them all and a fruitful relationship reestablished between colony and mother country. Some such thoughts must have sustained his excellency as the *Minerva*, 180 tons and laden (as his son aboard would observe) like Noah's ark, plunged eastward bearing livestock and landlubbers into the broad Atlantic.

Behind the vessel had been left a town in public mourning, church bells ringing dolefully all the bright day long, as the provincial government set about withdrawing to Salem, and warships held their station in the harbor, henceforth closing the port of Boston to trade.

Ahead lay the ocean, weeks of it. There were light breezes at the start of the voyage, and agreeable weather; yet even so, "the Governor and Peggy were very sick," as Elisha, visited by distressful feelings himself, would note in his diary later. Throughout the lengthy passage, father and daughter would suffer; nor was the son to be entirely free from qualmishness, although in his case, mercifully, nothing so severe as to confine him to his cabin.

Twenty-nine at the time, Elisha Hutchinson had been in business partnership with his older brother Thomas Jr., who was staying behind to look after the house in Milton and tend to the governor's affairs. As for the affairs of the Hutchinson sons, those had been left in shambles. As their father had written this spring to an English correspondent: "Neither of my sons have dared to appear in Boston since the latter part of November"—near the height of the Tea Party agitations—"to the total neglect and ruin of their business." The two younger Hutchinsons, both merchants, had been among the select few named in London the year before as local tea agents for the East India Company. Having refused to renounce so lucrative an appointment, the young men through their stubbornness had made themselves abhorrent to the patriots. Tommy was in Milton now, not venturing out; and Elisha on shipboard, widening the distance between him and the town, might in the boredom of the voyage recollect his own deplorable encounter with patriot passions not so long before.

That encounter had happened in January, in the depths of this past winter, a few weeks after the Tea Party. Elisha Hutchinson and his wife had been so bold as to visit Plymouth to the south of Boston, to see Polly's family. When news of the tea agent's arrival in town had got about, which it promptly did, the church bells had rung as though a plague had descended. Before Colonel Watson's house, a crowd had collected to demand that his son-in-law leave at once. The good people of Plymouth wanted no tea agents among them. But because it was nighttime, the colonel got permission from his indignant fellow citizens to delay the departure till morning. Morning brought a snowstorm, and still the townspeople insisted that Elisha go, get out right now, take the road that led from town and keep on it; and the irate church bells had not stopped ringing until the visitor and his wife were well on their miserable, storm-battered way.

Polly—these few months later, with June arrived—was with her father in Plymouth again, in weather more temperate. Her husband afloat missed her, and would go on missing her, as his letters from aboard the *Minerva* and from England show. His sister Peggy, already seasick in close confines, would miss Polly too. The sisters-in-law were dear friends; it was to Polly that Peggy had written ruefully not long before that she felt sometimes as though she had "been running from a mob ever since the year sixty-five," since nine years earlier, at the time of the Stamp Act crisis, the horrific year when vandals had demolished her family's beautiful home in the North End. For nearly a decade the young woman had felt herself to be in anxious flight, ever since she had been a child of eleven.

Now she and her father and brother were bound for England's more tranquil shores. The voyage on which the Hutchinsons were launched must have seemed interminable, and yet it was speedier than many of the time. The first week passed with light breezes and pleasant weather. Ten days into the passage, the wind increased and blew fresh for two days and longer, "which gave us some idea of the grandeur of the ocean." (The report is Elisha's, the only one of the family well enough to do more than record the barest of facts.) Thereafter the trip passed relatively smoothly, though through weather that was foggy, wet, and cold, "uncommonly cold for the season, so that we have been glad to keep to all our winter cloaths."

Contending against the tediousness of the voyage, the son every two hours recorded courses and wind directions and distances run. His lists stretched on. At sunrise on the 11th, a Saturday, Captain Callahan summoned passengers who were well enough to come on deck to behold "an island of ice, about 3 times as big as the ship, which was slowly approaching us, and I think the weather was as cold as we often have it in January." But little besides the iceberg—and later a death on board—occurred to break the monotony.

Think of the dreariness of it: the wet, the chill, the stench, the crowded quarters and stale food and relentless tossing of the vessel, and the seasickness. Franklin would cross the Atlantic eight times. There was no other way, and no hurrying the necessary passage along. Whatever news traveled between colony and mother country must do so aboard such vessels as this, four to eight weeks in good weather one way. The news of the Tea Party in mid-December had reached London by this slow method only in late January, and Parliament's response had come back to Boston in mid-May, five full months after the event. A woman writes from Boston this same summer to a friend in England. Her letter, dated July 8, acknowledges her friend's letter of March 1, recently received, and thanks her friend for writing without waiting to hear from her, since she had written last on January 31. Consider. Miss Anne Hulton had written nearly six months earlier, January 31, in the midst of winter; by the first of March her letter from Boston had not yet reached Liverpool, where Mrs. Adam Lightbody in turn was writing in the shadow of spring a letter that would be received in Boston not before high summer—a letter, even so, all ignorant of Miss Hulton's wintertime news half a year old by then.

Perhaps no single fact is more important to keep in mind, in understanding an age so different from ours—and how events of that age unfolded—than is this fact of such prodigious delays in news traveling back and forth.

Assuredly, the present voyage allowed ample time for the governor, prone on his berth in the close cabin, to rehearse yet again, in moments when the nausea subsided, the injustice of all those charges that had been leveled against him, effectively driving him on his wave-tossed way. He, a traitor? He, an enemy of his country? "There must be an abridgment of what are called English liberties." On three or four separate occasions ashore, Hutchinson attempted to account for his unfortunate phrasing in what after all had been a private letter illicitly come by, published without his consent and against his wishes. He thought now, had thought then, and to the end of his life would think that the letters had been solicited by his enemies in the colony as part of a plot to destroy him, that the whole episode was monumentally hypocritical, the work of cynics bent upon manipulating public opinion by means of pilfered private documents that they had only after much searching been able finally, triumphantly, to lay their hands upon.

There *must*, he had written, be an abridgment of English liberties; it was obligatorily if regrettably so, in situations where Englishmen had moved so far from the mother country—simply because Americans could not be represented in Parliament, and Parliament was supreme over the empire. The *must* had conveyed not a recommendation, but rather a statement of necessity: *had* to be. He had said as much in public many times, had put it in his history, had written it to other correspondents—although if the governor had known in this particular instance that he was writing for publication, he would have taken care to phrase his meaning more carefully.

The damage was done, however. Lieutenant Governor Andrew Oliver lay in his grave as a consequence, that gentleman's end hastened this spring (as Hutchinson felt sure) by grief over the matter of those letters. The charitable Mr. Oliver, public servant, the governor's brother-in-law and closest of his friends, father of Thomas Jr.'s wife, had been taken ill in the winter and this past March had been laid to rest. Alongside the graveyard, rabble among the so-called Sons of Liberty had gathered disgracefully to hoot in triumph as the body was interred.

Bestirring a mob to that vile behavior would seem to typify the opposition's achievements. Well, the damage was done; yet recalling such memories would have made for bleak interludes aboard the little *Minerva*, doggedly beating eastward toward more hospitable climes.

Twenty-one days into the voyage, Governor Hutchinson's black servant Mark died. The governor had brought the man along precisely in hopes of recovering his health, and for the first week or ten days of the passage, Mark had appeared to be doing well. Then he had taken cold, and grew worse, and on the 21st "died in great distress about six o'clock in the evening, and the next morning was buried in the sea." That, and the cold damp weather, and the high-tossing grandeur of it all were leading Elisha near the end of the voyage to conclude glumly that the ocean was made rather for fish than for humans.

At last, however, and sooner than might have been expected, the helmsman sighted land, and the morning of the 27th, the vessel was alongside the Scilly Isles, and "a fishing boat and half a dozen men came and brought us bream, cabbage, lettice, &c. They belonged to St. Agnes, and told us there are about 20 or 30 houses on that island." Replenished, the *Minerva* sailed on, and next day spoke a brig from Newcastle bound for New York "and desired the Captain to put the ship in the News-papers." And on the following day, June 29, 1774—a Wednesday to match the Wednesday of their departure from Boston four weeks earlier—the Hutchinsons and their shipmates landed at Dover, "between 3 and 4 o'clock in the afternoon, not without some difficulty, there being high wind and large seas."

The governor, who had left Boston on June 1, the day that the Port Act went into effect, had sailed assuming that the suffering of his native town would be brief and that payment for the tea destroyed would be forthcoming. Much news was awaiting him and his party to learn upon landing.

The travelers spent that first day ashore, queasy still, visiting the castle and fort in Dover; officers were billeted there whom they knew, the regiments having earlier been quartered in Boston. Then on the 30th of June between six and seven in the morning, the new arrivals set off in three post chaises for London, breakfasting at Canterbury and lingering long enough to visit the cathedral. The Kent countryside as they proceeded "was really delightful," all the more so in the eyes of people just delivered from four weeks' confinement on shipboard. A midafternoon dinner at Rochester; then at six in the evening, having resumed their journey, they were to enjoy an emotional reunion along the London road.

Billy Hutchinson met the travelers near Dartford, "about 12 miles from Westminster Bridge": Billy, who had first come to England eight long years ago—a lad then, a young man now—Elisha and Peggy's brother, the governor's worrisome youngest son.

Eight years earlier, in April 1766, Billy, then age thirteen, had set sail to make his fortune in England, his family watching with a spyglass from their Milton porch overlooking Boston Harbor until the vessel that bore the boy eastward had finally diminished from sight. Now here he stood, just shy of twenty-two, a young gentleman at home in this island nation, welcoming them, greeting his family on the road from Dover, leading them proprietarily toward the quarters in London that he had leased on their behalf. Hardly two months before, Billy's father had been writing wistfully from Massachusetts to a family friend in England: "I am longing to hear that he has obtained some employment, which may give him a moderate support, and prevent a habit of pleasure and dissipation, or of inactivity and indolence"—traits quite unlike those of Billy's brothers. Both of those older brothers were industrious enough—at least until the Tea Party tumults had demolished their Boston business—Tommy, back in Milton, three thousand miles behind them now, Elisha here with his sister sharing in the pleasures of reunion along the Dover-London road.

Despite everything, this day would have offered much to be grateful for. Elisha and Peggy and Billy and their father were all together, on stable English soil, traveling in their three post chaises toward the metropolis of the empire. And once arrived, his excellency was to be welcomed in as cordial a manner as his warmest friends could have wished. The party reached their new lodgings in Parliament Street, Westminster, this same evening of June 30, between eight and nine. Tired though he was, "the Governor immediately acquainted Lord Dartmouth of his arrival," Elisha noted, "and received an answer, desiring to see him at his Lordship's house the next day at noon."

Thus, the two Crown officials, frequent correspondents in recent years, would meet at last face to face, July 1. But Thomas Hutchinson's first full day in London was to include an encounter even more memorable. After all the vilification back home, after the long weariness and discomfort of the voyage, the American governor not yet in London even a full day would find himself on the morrow ushered promptly into the very seat of power, accorded a superlative early honor, one as unexpected as it was exalted.

6

A FLATTERING RECEPTION

THAT NEXT DAY, the first of July, Governor Hutchinson called as requested at Lord Dartmouth's town house in St. James's Square, only a short distance from his own new quarters in Parliament Street. For an hour around noon, the two officials visited together cordially, whereupon the secretary of state surprised his guest by making a most gratifying proposal.

Now in his forties, the earl of Dartmouth had for a long time been regarded as a friend of the colonies; and even this late, into the summer of 1774, this particular official retained much of his popularity overseas. His reputation among Americans had been established eight years earlier, when, as president of the Board of Trade, his lordship had supported repealing the Stamp Act. Provincial legislatures had voted him their thanks at the time; and later, in 1772, when he had been appointed secretary of state for the American Department, the provinces had rejoiced over what had appeared to be a conciliatory gesture on the part of government. Franklin, along with many others, had entertained high hopes that under the generous-spirited Dartmouth's guidance, relations between England and America would shortly improve.

The youthful-looking nobleman was immensely wealthy, father of seven sons, godly ("the Psalm-Singer," his few enemies mockingly called him), and well connected. Lord North, prime minister, was Dartmouth's half-stepbrother; and in their young manhood the pair had managed the delicate task of touring Europe together over two years and returning home close friends still. An avid agriculturalist, truly noble, "the Daniel of the age," the earl of Dartmouth was that rarity, a pious English politician, to be found at his prayers while his colleagues were more likely at the ring or the turf, the brothel or the gaming table.

One of his lordship's numerous philanthropies might be particularized. He had served in the 1760s as trustee of certain funds collected in England to benefit Moor's Indian Charity School in America, recently established to train Indians for the ministry. Upon moving in 1769 from Lebanon, Connecticut, to Hanover, New Hampshire, the thriving little academy had changed its name in the trustee's honor (without his permission, against his wishes) to Dartmouth College.

The nobleman pursued various other interests to benefit worthy causes at home as well as overseas. He was a patron of poets and clergymen, and he furthered the building of chapels throughout Britain to serve the spiritual needs of working people. His acquaintances, moreover, reached well beyond the narrow range of the privileged class in which he had been reared. A year earlier than the present 1774, Dartmouth had received the remarkable slave poet Phillis Wheatley, on a visit to London from her pious Boston home, and had presented that devout young woman (who had earlier written one of her fluent poems extolling the minister's abundant virtues) with an inscribed copy of *Don Quixote.* Now, in his official capacity, he was welcoming yet another Boston visitor, altogether different, with whom he had been in frequent professional correspondence recently, even as the colonial secretary had corresponded regularly with all the royal governors up and down the Atlantic seaboard.

The governor of Massachusetts Bay was making a first call upon the secretary of state for the American Department; and "after near an hour's conversation," as Hutchinson would soon set down, "his Lordship proposed introducing me immediately to the King."

To his majesty George III in person! Of course, such condescension was flattering to a subject who had brought to England an allegiance undiminished. But Mr. Hutchinson was hardly dressed for court. Even so, the sovereign (Dartmouth explained) would be leaving later today for his country palace in Kew, not to return to nearby St. James's Palace before next Wednesday, five days hence. For that reason the opportunity to attend the current levee had been urged, and for that reason, though with appropriate misgivings, accepted.

Dartmouth thereupon retired to have servants dress his own self properly—and proved so long about it that the gentlemen reached the palace only after the levee had ended. Disappointment was forestalled when "his Lordship going in to the King, I was admitted," Governor Hutchinson noted with pride, "contrary, as Ld Pomfret observed to me, to custom, to kiss His Majesty's hand in his closet," in private.

The ensuing conference between King George III and his loyal subject lasted, as Hutchinson took care to inform his numerous correspondents, nearly two hours. When returned to his new quarters in Parliament Street ("a handsome drawing-room, a dining room, four chambers, and a kitchen, well furnished, besides rooms for servants"), the governor set about recording his sovereign's inquiries and his own responses as accurately as he could recall them: what remained clearest in his mind, and as nearly as possible in the order in which the questions had been put.

The royal impression emerging from that thorough and valuable record is consistent with the George III whom history has come to know: painstakingly conscientious, proper, methodical—not to say plodding—and obsessed with detail. His biographers have assured us that this monarch could recite the names of every one of his bishops as well as the successive parishes in which each bishop had served, the names of members of all the faculties at Oxford and Cambridge, the names of the officers in each of his regiments, of all the officers in the navy, of the ships to which those officers were assigned, that he had even memorized the soundings of all the principal harbors in Europe. Thus, having graciously inquired after Mr. Hutchinson's family and about the American's health ("Much reduced Sir by seasickness," was the answer to the latter inquiry, "and unfit upon that account, as well as my New England dress, to appear before your Majesty"), the sovereign proceeded to query his provincial subject in meticulous detail on conditions and persons left behind in Massachusetts Bay.

George III, by the grace of God king of Great Britain, France, and Ireland, duke of Brunswick-Luneberg, archtreasurer and elector of Hanover, and Defender of the Faith, was, upon the arrival of this first day of July 1774, just short of one month into his thirty-seventh year on earth. At the time, he had already passed fourteen years of a reign that would extend through six eventful decades in all, from 1760 to 1820. And it was only now, during these same summer months, that the ruler whose youthful accession to the throne had inspired such acclamations of hope and joy was forfeiting the affection of his colonies in America. Only now, fourteen years into his reign, had disgruntled subjects overseas finally begun to identify his majesty personally with the grievances heretofore blamed on Parliament and the king's various ministers. The harshness of the recent Port Act had urged them forward in assigning such blame. Accordingly, the anniversary of King George's birth, June 4—shortly after the act had gone into effect—had been acknowledged in much of America with only the most perfunctory toasts and parades and illuminations: in Boston certainly, and as far afield from that center of troubles as Philadelphia, where "scarcely, if any, notice was taken of it in this city, by way of rejoicing: not one of our bells suffered to ring, and but very few colors were shown by the shipping in the harbor; no, nor not one bonfire kindled."

The king and the loyal subject before him would as yet have known nothing of such glum shifts of opinion; nor would Hutchinson have found blame to assign to his royal highness in any case. George III seemed on all counts a sovereign of merit: honorable, diligent, appropriately regal in bearing, a loving husband and father, and well informed. Tirelessly, conscientiously, his majesty sought out information concerning the world he lived in and ruled over, as he was doing now, in querying Mr. Hutchinson about the famous letters that had earlier so outraged Americans when published. Who had sent them over from England?

"Doctor F., may it please your Majesty, has made a publick declaration that he sent them, and the Speaker [Mr. Cushing] has acknowledged to me that he recd them: I do not remember that he said directly from Doctor F., but it was understood between us that they came from him." Franklin, the governor went on to explain, had specified that the letters were to be communicated to six persons only, then sent back without copies taken.

The king asked who were the six? When Hutchinson named them: "Mr. B[owdoin] I have heard of," his majesty said. "Who is Mr. Pitts?" And "I have heard of Dr Ch[auncy] and Dr Cooper, but who is Doctor Winthrop?" And "I have heard of one Mr Adams, but who is the other?"

A lawyer, sir.

"Brother to the other?"

"No, Sir, a relation," Hutchinson replied. "He has been of the House, but is not now. He was elected by the two Houses to be of the Council, but negatived."

And where, the king wondered, is Dr. Franklin at present? To which Lord Dartmouth, in attendance, volunteered:

"I believe, Sir, he is in Town. He was going to America, but I fancy he is not gone."

Dartmouth seized an opportunity to show his sovereign the complimentary addresses that citizens of character in Massachusetts had tendered their governor on the occasion of Hutchinson's recent parting from them. "I do not see how it could be otherwise," the king was pleased to respond. He was sure that Governor Hutchinson's conduct had been "universally approved of here by people of all parties." The governor in turn felt happy that his official behavior had merited his majesty's favor. "I am intirely satisfied with it," the king affirmed. "I am well acquainted with the difficulties you have encountered, and with the abuse & injury offered you." Was it not true that Bostonians had gone so far as to threaten to pitch and feather their governor?

"Tarr and feather, may it please your Majesty; but I don't remember that ever I was threatened with it."

"What guard had you, Mr. H.?" the king inquired.

"I depended, Sir, on the protection of Heaven," Governor Hutchinson answered rather loftily. "It has been my good fortune, Sir, to escape any charge against me in my private character. The attacks have been upon my publick conduct, and for such things as my duty to your Majesty required me to do, and which you have been pleased to approve of. I don't know that any of my enemies have complained of a personal injury."

The king expressed curiosity about Hutchinson's private life. "I think you generally live in the country, Mr. H.; what distance are you from town?"

Thus, for a moment the American was encouraged to dilate on his beloved and much-missed home in far-off Milton. "I have lived in the country, Sir," he answered, "in the summer for 20 years; but, except the winter after my house was pulled down, I have never lived in the country in winter until the last. My house is 7 or 8 miles from the Town, a pleasant situation, and most gentlemen from abroad say it has the finest prospect from it they ever saw."

Retreat with its windows so clear in his mind's eye—view seaward from the portico, the parlor view looking west—destined to stand on the hilltop into another era, for nearly a century longer—

His majesty was reverting to public affairs. Pray, what does Mr. Hancock do now? And Mr. Cushing? And what gave Mr. Samuel Adams his importance? ("A great pretended zeal for liberty, and a most inflexible natural temper," was the answer. "He was the first that publickly asserted the Independency of the colonies upon the Kingdom, or the supreme Authority of it.")

And why, the king wondered, do your ministers of the gospel generally join with the people in their opposition to government?

For that, too, Mr. Hutchinson had an answer. "They are, Sir, dependent upon the people. They are elected by the people, and when they are dissatisfied with them, they seldom leave [off] till they get rid of them."

Such a practice seemed to the king very strange, even dangerous. But the majority of New Englanders were, as the governor explained, "what are called Congregationalists," dissenters from the Church of England.

"Pray, what were your Ancestors, Mr. H.?"

"In general, Sir, Dissenters."

"Where do you attend?"

"With both, Sir. Sometimes at your Majesty's chapel"—that is, at King's Chapel in Boston, among the Anglicans—"but more generally at a Congregational church, which has a very worthy minister, a friend to Government, who constantly prays for your Majesty, and all in authority under you." The worthy's name was Dr. Pemberton.

"I have heard," said the king, "of Doctor Pemberton that he is a very good man."

In that style the royal questions continued, many about Massachusetts Bay. "Pray, Mr. H., does population greatly increase in your Province?" "Why do not foreigners come to yr Province as well as to the Southern Governments?" "What is the reason"—Farmer George here speaking—"you raise no wheat in your

Province?" "To what produce is your climate best adapted?" "New York, I think"—George as king once more—"comes the next to Boston in their opposition to Government?"

But, respectfully, Mr. Hutchinson would have awarded so doubtful a distinction to Pennsylvania—and might have made a case for Virginia. The king commented that Rhode Island was "a strange form of Government." Who was the governor there now? A gentleman named Wanton, a sound loyalist. And, "How is it with Connecticut?" And, "What number of Indians had you in your Government?" Thus, through a most flattering interlude in the royal closet, wide-ranging monarchal inquiries followed upon each other. "Lord D. feared I was tired so long standing," Hutchinson noted later. "I observed that so gracious a reception made me insensible of it."

But after all that while together, King George and his provincial governor emerged from their conference with distinctly different impressions about what had been said regarding perhaps the most important of the many subjects considered. The subject had been among the first inquired about: "How," the king had wondered, "did the people receive the news of the late measures in Parliament?"

Those measures included a stern series of bills that his majesty had approved in May and early June. Unlike the temporary Port Act, the additional acts would permanently and drastically reform the government of Massachusetts Bay in order to make it more amenable to royal control.

"When I left Boston," Hutchinson answered, "we had no news of any Act of Parliament, except the one for shutting up the port, which was extremely alarming to the people."

But if he voiced such concern—or said what he soon was writing General Gage in more detail that he had said—King George did not hear it. What Governor Hutchinson would explain to Gage by letter three days later, on July 4, as having been remarked regarding the Port Act at the recent conference with his sovereign was this:

> In the course of conversation the King asked me how the late Acts of Parliament were received at Boston? I answered, that when I left Boston, I had heard only of one, that for shutting up the Port, which was to take place the day I came away: that I had heard, since my ar-

rival, that another Act had passed, which I had not seen, nor had I been able to obtain a particular account of it. That the first Act was exceedingly severe, I did not presume to say, or think it was more so than was necessary, but it must bring the greatest distress upon the town, and many of the tradesmen who depended upon the ships had left the town, and others were leaving it when I came away, and that it would make me happy, if [in] any way, consistent with His Majesty's honour, I might be instrumental, whilst I remained in England, in obtaining their relief. The King thereupon expressed his inclination and desire to grant it when they could put it in his power.

The governor thus portrayed himself as having forthrightly expressed his concerns to his sovereign about the costs of the Port Act—and reiterated his doubts regarding the act three days later, in writing another associate, the provincial secretary, in Boston: "In the long conference I had with the K. I made it my chief object to represent matters so as to obtain relief for the T. of B[oston] on the easiest terms."

But if Hutchinson had ventured such sympathetic representations, King George at the interview had heard something quite different. His majesty (being human) had heard, in fact, precisely what he had wanted to hear.

7

EARLY WEEKS IN ENGLAND

THE KING WAS NOT LONG IN SHARING what he had heard. Removed to Kew, George III informed his prime minister privately by note (marked with Georgian fastidiousness, half past 9 P.M., July 1, 1774) that he had that day met with Mr. Hutchinson, late governor of Massachusetts Bay, and was now well convinced that the Bostonians would soon submit. "He ownes," his majesty wrote Lord North definitively of the governor, "the Boston Port Bill was the only wise effectual method that could have been suggested for bringing them to a speedy submission."

The only effectual means—the only wise method—for dealing with Boston was a blockade. So much for the American's initial success in persuading his sovereign of the hard case of merchants and other innocent sufferers back home, in order to obtain the relief for which they had pleaded before his departure.

Yet as these early days in England unfolded, Mr. Hutchinson did feel exhilarated by what appeared to be opportunities abounding for his doing good. On his very first full day in London, he had been able to confer privately and at length with George III in person; and in days that immediately followed, the governor found means to cultivate his acquaintance with the influential Lord Dartmouth, who proved to be "friendly to the Province and to me personally beyond conception." Moreover, by mid-July the American had had a long private interview with the amiable prime minister, Lord North, at his residence in No. 10 Downing Street. And from all this conferring Hutchinson had succeeded in establishing unambiguously—and was authorized to write as much to General Gage—that Bostonians were not obliged to draft any formal statement of submission about the matter of the tea. The point had earlier been left in doubt; but no official submission to Parliament's authority was expected (which was a good thing: The governor knew his obstinate fellow townspeople well enough to be certain that no such show of deference would have been forthcoming). Simply pay for the tea, then, and refrain from disorderly behavior henceforth, and government here in London would be satisfied. Actions speak louder than words, the king had observed sagely, and Lords North and Dartmouth had of course concurred.

Able so early to clear up a vital confusion—and to Boston's advantage—the governor had hopes of even greater success on behalf of the province in the near future. What he could learn of matters back in America sounded auspicious. "My advices to the 9th of June," he noted in mid-July about Whig efforts back home, "are that the opposition to Government lost ground, and that there was no encouragement from their correspondence in the other Colonies." That is, word now arriving from overseas indicated that Boston, as of nine days after the Port Act had gone into effect, was being left to its fate; Pennsylvania, New York, and the other provinces had declined to involve themselves in troubles between the quarrelsome Yankee town and the mother country.

That, of course, was the news that one wishing the empire perpetuated would want to hear. Waiting and fretting and hoping, the governor—between making numerous social calls—set about establishing his household in unseasonably chilly London. He purchased a coach, engaged a coachman, footman, and cook, and began looking out for a place in the country to lease. But really, his reception here was exceeding anything that he could have imagined. Everyone was kind. Lord Loudoun, one July day observing Hutchinson at his window in Parliament Street, "came immediately over, and treats me with great goodness and condescension." Lord Hillsborough found him out and made the strongest professions of affection and esteem. Lord Hardwicke, expressing his own esteem, desired that the governor would come to Richmond and dine with him tomorrow. Lord Mansfield and the lord chancellor both treated Mr. Hutchinson with singular marks of favor. And in the company of Lord Suffolk he "never met with greater civility."

With all these and the many others whose cordial attentions were soon filling his busy days, the newcomer found conversation turning again and again to Boston. Two assumptions informed the talk, both assumptions profoundly, fatally in error; and yet the English were so sure, and here at their tables sat this knowledgeable American, just arrived from the scene, to confirm, first, that his countrymen would never fire on English soldiers (Lord Hardwicke on the 9th, for instance, "often repeated, that he had no apprehensions of rebellion, or forcible opposition to the King's Troops") and, second, that the various colonies, with all their different cultures and interests, would never be able to act in concert. Hutchinson clung to both those misapprehensions as firmly as did his affable hosts, and in their company—even as he sought to serve his unhappy homeland—he became all the more convinced that one course of conduct alone was admissible. It was so simple: Pay for the tea, and make no further disturbance. All else would follow. The Port Act would be repealed, and speedily, and the tea tax speedily rescinded.

The governor's conversations with high-ranking Englishmen persuaded him, in addition, that Parliament, having passed its coercive measures, felt itself in too far to back down. "I know it is expected that the more determined the Colonials appear"—as they had been resolute at the time of the Stamp Act—"the more likely it will be to bring the Govt here to their terms. I do not believe it. The present Ministry seem determined not to yield." Times had changed. The governor had talked, as he put it, with flaming patriots and fawning courtiers alike, and all agreed. The colonies must acknowledge Parliament as the supreme authority in the empire. That was the crux of it: If not in so many words, then by their attitude, the colonies must yield to that supremacy. Parliament would not tax—was well aware that revenues from taxes were hardly worth the expense of collecting them and that the real rewards for England lay in trade with America—yet Parliament as supreme authority must be acknowledged to have the *right* to tax.

Mr. Hutchinson's countrymen would come to see the reasonableness of England's position on these matters of the tea, taxes, and sovereignty. And when they did, differences between colonies and mother country would be bridged. All the while the governor felt encouraged to think that his being in London was leading to the speedier relief of Boston than would have been possible otherwise. He went on visiting and explaining, then back in Parliament

Street sat at his desk and wrote his many letters to New England, transmitting what he was learning: that the English were in too far now, and united, that the Americans must not deny Parliament's right to tax—even though all sides here affirmed that there was no intention of taxing the colonies henceforth and that the present tax would be removed as soon as the tea was paid for. All of it so easy: "I cannot but therefore hope," Hutchinson was actually writing to New England July 20, "that the measures which you shall have taken for satisfying the East India Company for the loss of their Tea, and the evidence which you shall have given of a disposition to promote order, and a due submission to government, will enable me to obtain for you the desired relief before I can have an answer to this letter."

Here in midsummer, to be sure, most of the nobility and gentry were out of town at their country seats, where Hutchinson was urged to visit them. Many such invitations he accepted, in order (as he wrote home) to be of more service to Americans. He called on Lord Hardwicke at Richmond, on Lord Mansfield at Kenwood, on Lord Suffolk at Bushy Park, on Mr. Welbore Ellis at Twickenham, on Sir Francis Bernard at Aylesbury. And near the end of the month, the governor was traveling toward Oxford with his elder son and his daughter on yet more visits—but had to break off and return to London because Peggy was unwell.

Both she and her father had continued enfeebled from their seasickness, and Peggy had been struggling with an ugly cough besides. Now, as August began, the young woman was back in Parliament Street and writing Elisha's wife at last, her dear sister-in-law at home in Plymouth, dismayed to be only now getting around to doing so. "Is it possible I should be in London a month and not have wrote to you?" Peggy's mind was transported to the departure from New England two months earlier, aboard the wretched *Minerva*. "It seems a little age since the chariot drove from the door and conveyed me from so many dear friends, to suffer more than I should have thought possible for me to have borne. I had not left you many hours," she wrote Polly, "before I was the most miserable creature on earth: it is impossible for me to describe or give you any idea of what I endured the first fortnight: the second was bad enough, and I am not yet what I used to be." Nothing material of so unreal a voyage could the correspondent now recall but one grim interlude: the death on board of poor Mark, their Negro servant, who had been buried at sea in midpassage.

Doleful remembrance. As for London, "London my dear is a world in itself"—something to behold once in one's life and to talk of ever after. But Peggy preferred the country round about, a perfect garden for seventy miles in whatever direction. Still, she could not find much to say for the local climate: "The weather has been as cold as our Novembers, and excessively damp, except two or three days, and I have not been free from a cold since I came."

With all that, there had been compensations. This royal governor's daughter had been presented to their majesties and had met with a most gracious reception. And London offered other pleasures that she might tell of: museums, dinners, monuments, parks, assemblies. The watchmen out the window were sounding past ten o'clock, however, which (to be sure) "is but the beginning of our evenings; but as I have another letter to write to go to-morrow, I must bid you good night." And Peggy finished her overdue letter to her sister-in-law as August 2, 1774, was approaching its end.

That same day, communications within a sack of mail delivered from Boston had brought the young woman's father fresh and disagreeable news. He had dutifully forwarded this latest information to Lord Dartmouth, who called at the governor's lodgings the following morning.

The usually equable Dartmouth was upset. Returning Hutchinson's letters, his lordship "expressed his concern at the contents: spake with great emotion, that he was not one who thirsted for blood; but he could not help saying that he wished to see H[an-coc]k and A[da]ms brought to the punishment they deserved: and he feared peace would not be restored until some examples were made, which would deter others."

What the news just arrived related was the misbehavior of the Massachusetts Assembly in mid-June. In accordance with his orders, Governor Gage had on June 1 (as the *Minerva* was setting sail) moved the provincial capital from Boston fifteen miles north to Salem; it had not been fitting that a disobedient town should serve as the capital, transacting the king's business. In Salem, then, the Assembly and the Council, lower and upper houses of the legislature, had duly convened. Deliberations had followed, committees had been formed; and Governor Gage had been led to believe that one such committee was considering the most appropriate means for reimbursing the East India Company for its loss of the tea.

On June 17, the committee was to report to the Assembly. The indefatigable Samuel Adams had guided what followed. The Assembly had met that day, and the doors of the Salem courthouse were abruptly locked. In due time an assemblyman of loyalist leanings had emerged, ostensibly to answer a call of nature. Instead, he had hurried to the governor, all unsuspecting, to warn his excellency of what was happening behind those locked doors. Nothing at all had been said among the legislators about reimbursing the East India Company. On the contrary, the Assembly was bent on business altogether different—and disloyal.

Gage had immediately sent the provincial secretary with an order dissolving the legislative body. Secretary Flucker had arrived posthaste at the courthouse, but the doors had remained locked, even to him, so that he was reduced to reading his proclamation from the steps outside. Meanwhile, within, the assemblymen had proceeded to agree on sending delegates to a congress of all the colonies, which the various provinces and their committees of correspondence had begun talking about convening as early as possible. The Assembly had selected five delegates, including Samuel Adams, to attend the congress. It had appropriated money to pay the delegates' expenses. And it had urged that all the surrounding towns and villages, and all the other provinces of America, be encouraged meanwhile to give what aid they could to the people of Boston, fettered and suffering behind their blockade.

The legislators' actions were thus in no way conciliatory, were on the contrary defiant and provocative. Of course, the doors had to be unlocked at last. When they were and the members dispersed, Gage would manage without the Assembly henceforth. But no effort at all made to pay for the tea! This news reaching London in early August was, as Hutchinson noted, at the very least disagreeable, yet he would not let himself be discouraged. Under Governor Gage's firmness and with the arrival of troop reinforcements, so many Bostonians of consequence would by now be openly supporting government, "and so many more who secretly think with them" but had earlier been intimidated by those rowdy Sons of Liberty would be openly declaring their loyalty, "that I cannot but hope they will in a short time prevail."

Thus, he wrote Tommy Hutchinson, back home in Milton, on this 3rd of August and added that Lord North remained unconcerned, or certainly appeared unconcerned, "and says that order and government must take place in the Colonies, whether it be sooner or later depends upon themselves: in the mean time they can hurt nobody but themselves." On another subject, "Don't forget the Cranberries," the governor went on to remind his son, six or eight bushels of them to be sent across, the largest and fairest, but not too ripe. And when Tommy had leisure, be so good as to make a list of books missing from the principal sets in the bookcase; perhaps the governor would be able to complete some of the sets in his strolls around the city. And send along the dimensions of the parlor floor in the Boston house, and that big Stonington cheese, which Mr. Hutchinson wanted to give as a gift here, and send the Boston papers, unavailable in London.

Well, on this August day, anxious as he was, and obviously homesick, the governor could take comfort from one remark of Lord Dartmouth's during his call this morning. "Nothing gives me so much relief," his lordship had been pleased to observe just hours ago, "as the consideration that you are sitting at this time in that chair." That was handsome; and later this same afternoon Hutchinson would go to court to attend the investiture of two knights of the Bath, and there be graciously inquired of by his king "concerning the climate in America, &c." Assuredly, George III, like his prime minister, appeared serene. This day "the King, notwithstanding General Gage's letter, &c., had been sent him, said ... — 'Well: matters go on well in America: they are coming right.'"

Coming right? Go on well? The same imperturbable complacency persisted with Lord North, on whom the governor called by appointment for an hour on August 11. Eleven in the morning, and the king's first minister was calmly discounting the news of any resentment or defiance from overseas. "He said he did not expect less from the late Acts than what has happened: he did not, however, conceive them less necessary than he did before: he was not apprehensive of any great matters from the proposed Congress."

Indeed, as August wore on, the mood in England seemed increasingly one of indifference toward the American possessions. "I am told," the governor wrote General Gage on the 12th, "that there appears more indifference about the disturbances in America than there ever did before. 'Let them suffer by their confusions,' it is said, 'if they are so obstinate as not to be content with the easiest government in the world. Nobody suffers here except a few merchants who possibly may make more bad debts than otherwise they would have done.'"

For his part, Mr. Hutchinson did not share the complacency of his English friends. Rather, his spirits had begun to droop. Word reaching London in late summer from overseas, whether from southern or northern or central colonies, concerned nothing but the proposed general congress that was to meet in Philadelphia. To the governor, such an assembly seemed not only illegal but absurd. His syntax grew murky as he contemplated the change of policy that his countrymen appeared bent on pursuing. "I cannot but hope," he wrote glumly to New England, "that the result of such a Congress, under the best form which could be devised, absolutely illegal, and as some of the members are said to be constituted in the present instance contemptible, will be treated accordingly, and have very little weight. Until we hear further from you no step can be taken: not a word can be said which will have any tendency to serve you."

The proper course had been so obvious: Pay for the tea and avoid further turmoil. As it was turning out, the governor could do nothing but bide his time. He felt disconsolate. Short weeks ago, on his arrival in London, all had looked hopeful, whereas now "the prospect is so gloomy that I am sometimes tempted to endeavour to forget that I am an American, and to turn my views to a provision for what remains of life in England; but the passion for my native country returns, and I will determine nothing until your case is absolutely desperate."

In mid-August, calling on Dartmouth yet again, Mr. Hutchinson was gratified to learn that the king was desirous of knowing what mark of favor the American might accept for his previous services. If being created a baronet was agreeable, it should be done immediately. But the governor hardly had the means to support so high a rank and offered the insufficiency of his fortune as an objection. His lordship "would not wish me to take anything less." Thus for now, that matter was set aside.

The next day, the 16th, Hutchinson and his family took tea with Captain Callahan aboard the *Minerva*, as the vessel prepared to depart on its return voyage to Boston. The governor's notation is brief,

not a hint of his feelings among the familiar sights of earlier suffer-
ings aboard, the familiar creosote smells: "P.M. Went on board
Callahan, and drank tea." Elisha, writing home to his Polly, was
more communicative: "To-day we have all been on board Callahan's
ship, and if I consulted my inclination only, I should certainly take
my old bed again: but the last accounts from New England are so
discouraging, that I don't know what you would do with me if I was
there at this time." The young husband separated from his wife
could only hope that over the winter, affairs would take on a more
agreeable aspect. For now, however, there seemed very little likelihood of the Hutchinson family's return to America anytime soon.

Nothing remained to do, then, but idle and visit and wait.

One other matter, to be sure, had preoccupied Governor
Hutchinson during these early weeks in and around London. It
concerned Dr. Franklin and the letters. The king had brought the
subject up during his interview that first day at court; on that occasion Lord Dartmouth had assured his majesty that Franklin,
though having talked of returning to America, was still in town.
Before long, Hutchinson was being pestered by Mr. Temple, the
gentleman who had been accused of stealing the American officials' letters and turning them over to Franklin (and had fought a
duel with Mr. Whately because of the accusation). Temple was
everywhere, wheedling and explaining that he was in reality Mr.
Hutchinson's friend and had been innocent of any involvement in
an episode that had caused the governor so much distress.

As for Franklin himself, Hutchinson was noting at the end of
August: "I have never seen Doct. F. . . . since I have been in Eng."
But he had heard much of the man. Early on, scarcely a week after
the governor's arrival, Mr. Charles Jenkinson, privy councillor and
vice treasurer of Ireland, had assured him, as he noted in his diary,
that the ministry and Parliament had tardily determined to pursue
their present vigorous measures against the colonies—the Port Act
and the other severe acts recently imposed—only because of
"Doctor F.'s extraordinary letter, which he published relative to
your Letters. This alarmed Administration, and convinced them it
was high time to exert themselves when so dangerous a conspiracy
was carrying on against Government."

Again, Lord Dartmouth at his house in St. James's Square was
informing his new American friend on August 31 that a gentleman

had told him of hearing Dr. Franklin discoursing about the steps that the congress overseas would likely take, "and Lord D. added that he did not doubt it was his (Franklin's) own plan"—that is, that the whole idea of having a congress of the colonies was yet another contrivance of the subtle and meddlesome agent of the Massachusetts Assembly.

If so, all that could be achieved by such a course as the doctor had recommended—granting that he did recommend it—was to raise resentment in England. Nothing such a congress might do would bring Boston relief, now or in the future. Such a meeting was foolishness on the part of participants in any case—a recourse, the governor confided to an English correspondent, "which I think will make them very ridiculous, but I flatter myself can have no serious consequences."

Mr. Hutchinson might accordingly dismiss the congress from his thoughts. Of Boston, however, he could only write plaintively at the end of August: "Providence, I hope, will avert its total ruin." This reluctant resident in England would have thought it the happiest event of his life could he have been the instrument for sparing his native city: "The prospect of it was very favorable when I first arrived."

8

DR. FRANKLIN LINGERS

PEOPLE (THEN, AS IN TIMES BEFORE AND SINCE) saw conspiracies everywhere. The good people of Boston were persuaded that a
cabal of ministers in England had conspired to manipulate
Parliament, contrary to the will of a deluded English nation, to enact a series of measures aimed at enslaving America, as they had
earlier enslaved Ireland. Recently, those measures had been seen to
emanate shamefully from a conspiracy of high-placed, duplicitous
Americans, traitors all. Likewise, people in England thought that
merely a handful of self-serving, malevolent Bostonians were conspiring to mislead an honest Massachusetts citizenry, inflaming
their minds against the easiest government in the world. Mr.
Hutchinson was convinced that those same Boston agitators had
conspired with their agent in London, Dr. Franklin, to root out
whatever feeble means might be unearthed, even private letters
several years old, to defile the king's loyal servants. Solicitor
General Wedderburn, pounding the table as he castigated Franklin
before the Privy Council, had conjured up an assembly of well-
meaning farmers overseas duped by the artful agent's tools, such
fellow conspirators as Cushing and the egregious Samuel Adams.
Not many weeks ago, Mr. Jenkinson had been describing to his new
friend Hutchinson the alarm that Parliament had taken over Dr.
Franklin's admission in the newspapers of having surreptitiously
transmitted private letters of others to the Massachusetts Assembly,
an acknowledgment that had "convinced them it was high time to
exert themselves when so dangerous a conspiracy was carrying on
against Government." And Lord Dartmouth just now, this last day

of August, was suggesting to Mr. Hutchinson that that same guile-
ful Franklin appeared to be the prime mover behind the congress
currently assembling in the colonies, the doctor conspiring yet
again against the interests of the empire.

None of all this about conspiracies was true. As for Franklin's involvement with the congress, not a page among his voluminous
papers suggests that he was advising any of the delegates now
making their way from the various colonies toward Philadelphia.
A year earlier, to be sure, in a letter of July 1773, the agent had privately approved of a proposal originating among the Virginia
House of Burgesses, whereby committees of correspondence were
to be established up and down the seaboard to share information
from province to province in those unsettled times. Brave spirits
are among the Virginians, Franklin had written then. "I hope their
Proposals will be readily comply'd with by all the Colonies. It is
natural to suppose . . . that if the Oppressions continue, a Congress
may grow out of that Correspondence. Nothing would more alarm
our Ministers; but if the Colonies agree to hold a Congress, I do not
see how it can be prevented."

Yet in Franklin's view, such a gathering would assemble only for
the purpose of restoring the empire to its former harmony. A congress might, for example, draw up a constitution, mutually agreed
upon with England, that would identify America's rights and duties, thereby removing grounds for future misunderstandings between colonies and the mother country.

The truth is this: Far from conspiring to shape events in the New
World, Dr. Franklin—too American for the English, too English for
the Americans—had for some time been regarded with suspicion
not only in Westminster by members of government but also in
Pennsylvania and Massachusetts by a number of patriot leaders.
Samuel Adams did not trust him, for one. Nor did Josiah Quincy. A
confusion lingered in the colonies about the agent's attitude toward the Stamp Act eight or nine years earlier—whether he had
approved of its passage. Some said he had planned to profit from
the act himself. Quincy earlier, on May 3, 1773, while traveling in
Pennsylvania on his tour through the provinces, had heard confirmed "what I ever believed—that a certain North American Dr. is
a very trimmer—a very courtier," having been "the first proposer
of the STAMP ACT." In other words, unspecified sources in Phila-

delphia were going so far as to charge, eight or nine years after the fact, that Franklin had suggested the odious measure to the ministry in the first place.

Assuredly, the doctor-courtier, comfortably ensconced for a decade in England, had profited for years from a position in government as deputy postmaster for America, and Franklin's son was continuing to serve as royal governor of New Jersey. In addition, and during this very spring of 1774, the agent's unpopular response to the Tea Party had reached Boston, that ill-received reaction to what Franklin chose to term a violent injustice. The agent for the Assembly could only hope (he had written Mr. Cushing on February 2, soon after news of the Tea Party had arrived in London) that the Massachusetts legislature would move promptly to reimburse the East India Company for its loss. "This all our Friends here wish with me." Maybe war will come, as some are now threatening; but, Franklin had cautioned his constituents, let not "an Act of violent Injustice on our part, unrectified," provide England with the plausible pretense for starting such a war. That attitude toward the Tea Party would hardly have recommended the writer to Samuel Adams, even then exulting over Boston's brave defiance.

When Franklin wrote, in February, much more than the Tea Party had been on his mind. Precisely four days earlier, the colonial agent had been publicly branded a thief before the Privy Council and a packed hall of hostile, noisy spectators. Within a day or two of that humiliation, he had been curtly dismissed from his position as deputy postmaster for America: "You will therefore cause your accounts to be made up as soon as you can conveniently." Put your books in order and get out. Meanwhile, Mr. Whately, the brother of the deceased gentleman whose letters had found their way into Franklin's hands, had initiated action to bring the American to court and compel him to tell how he had come by someone else's private property in possessing himself of those letters. Jail, conceivably, lay at the end of that legal process. In truth, there seemed little reason for the doctor to linger in England any longer. Under the circumstances, he could be of no further service as agent for the colonies. He therefore wrote Cushing that he was resigning from the agency, then in mid-February wrote his wife in Philadelphia that he would be sailing home within three months, was waiting only for the arrival of the April packet with the post office accounts from America to settle before departing.

While he waited, the doctor must seek to vindicate himself amid the slanders that the solicitor general had heaped upon him. "It may be supposed that I am very angry," Franklin wrote the speaker of the Assembly in Boston in mid-February. Yet what the agent felt on his own account was, he said, half lost in what he felt for America. The matter seemed remarkably simple. Governor Hutchinson and Lieutenant Governor Oliver had simply forfeited the confidence of those—the people of Massachusetts—over whom they had been appointed to preside. The Assembly had petitioned for the removal of the two officers. The agent of the Assembly had laid the petition before the Privy Council. For his pains he had been slanderously abused and the petition rejected as scandalous, groundless, and vexatious.

"When Petitions and Complaints of Grievances are so odious to Government, that even the mere hand that conveys them becomes obnoxious, how is peace and union to be maintain'd or restored? Grievances cannot be redress'd unless they are known," Franklin (anonymously, as "A Gentleman from London") wrote in self-justification for the Boston newspapers; "and they cannot be known but thro' complaint and petitions; if these are deem'd *affronts,* and the messengers punish'd as *offending,* who will henceforth send petitions? Who will deliver them? The consequences are plain!"

And plainly government's present course was fraught with the gravest danger. A people denied the right to petition their king must swallow their grievances and grow ever more sour with discontent. Franklin, as he insisted again and again, had come by the Hutchinson letters honorably. But what did that matter? However come by, the nature of the letters remained unaltered, and they had furnished the ministry in London with a golden opportunity. "If they had been wise," the doctor, still and forever during these weeks worrying the issue, wrote to Boston near the end of February: if the ministers had been wise, "they might have made a good Use of the Discovery, by agreeing to lay the Blame of our Differences on those from whom by those Letters it appear'd to have arisen"—by blaming the traitor Hutchinson and his henchmen—"and by a Change of Measures, which would then have appear'd natural, restor'd the Harmony between the two Countries. But—"

He broke off in exasperation before the incomprehensibility of governmental pigheadedness. Yet even now, resentment persisted against the agent who had acted, as he thought, only for the common good. "You can have no Conception of the Rage the ministerial People have been in with me, on Account of my Transmitting those Letters." One consequence was that Franklin would be allowed no further dealings with government, so that months later, in the fall (even then still in Craven Street), he would record that he had not been in the company of a minister since the Privy Council ordeal.

Not that he was idle. During his remarkable long life, the doctor was never idle. He had a good conscience still, "which wonderfully supports a Man on such Occasions," as well as the satisfaction of having discovered that he had lost not a single true friend by government's attempt to disgrace him. Writing in the third person, he had noted in mid-February that, in the aftermath of what was intended as a public disgrace, Dr. Franklin's "House has ever since been filled with Visitants, who come purposely to shew their Regard for him, and express their Indignation at the unworthy Treatment he received. Some, who could not come, have written him Letters to the same Purpose."

The agent answered those, and—following an unvarying practice—the many other letters, from France, from Holland, from Philadelphia and Boston and elsewhere, that were delivered to him over these months on an astonishing range of subjects: political, scientific, domestic. Certain people—Dickens, Goethe, Jefferson, Franklin himself—take one's breath away by the totality of their involvement with life, by the apparent fullness of each day they lived. Now, through the spring of 1774 the American (sixty-eight, he was) was writing widely, to private correspondents and for the colonial and English newspapers, on the current imperial crisis; but he was writing as well on such matters of interest to various friends as the behavior of electricity passing through a vacuum in a bent tube, the ends of which have been immersed in mercury, on the results of certain experiments on torpedoes that a colleague had undertaken, on the geological characteristics of Pennsylvania ("abundance of Lime-Stone and Marble, no Flint . . . yet it is supposed that Flint is to be met with in some Part of the Country, since Heads of Arrows made of it by the ancient Inhabitants, are some-

times found in Ploughing the Fields"), on the condition—answering a query—of free blacks in America ("The Negroes who are free
live among the White People, but are generally improvident and
poor. I think they are not deficient in natural Understanding, but
they have not the advantage of Education"), on certain odd experiments involving setting pond waters in New Jersey afire—how the
flames were ignited and what might have caused them—on
sunspots, on the method of making Pyrmont water from fixed air
("Your Brother Chymists are now every where in Europe, busy in
working upon Fix'd Air"), on various gifts of books to Harvard
College and to the Library Company of Philadelphia, on ways of
preserving animals and other "Subjects of Natural History."

In addition to such wide-ranging concerns, and added to his frequent correspondence with the Massachusetts Assembly, Franklin
this spring and summer wrote at length to and heard at length
from the Assembly of New Jersey, the Assembly of Georgia, and
the Assembly of Pennsylvania, all of whose different interests he
was representing. He wrote anonymously (as was the custom then)
for the newspapers. To sympathetic friends, this inveterate social-
izer suggested contents of protests against recent governmental
measures and joined in signing those protests when they were
ready. There were, as ever, personal letters of introduction for so
celebrated a public figure to write and helpfully receive. And as he
set about arranging his affairs to leave England, his domestic correspondence was of course active: letters to his son in New Jersey, to
his son-in-law in Philadelphia, to his sister in Boston, to his wife in
Philadelphia.

"My dear Love," we have seen him writing Deborah, his wife,
April 28, "I hoped to have been on the Sea in my Return by this
time, but find I must stay a few Weeks longer, perhaps for the
Summer Ships." And a week later, May 5, to the same correspondent: "My dear Child, Our Family here"—the Stevensons in
Craven Street, where Franklin had, with interruptions, been lodg-
ing in his four rooms and a sitting room some fifteen years in all—
our family "is in great Distress. Poor Mrs. Hewson [his landlady's
daughter, one of Franklin's multitudinous admirers, who would be
beside him at his own deathbed] has lost her Husband, and Mrs.
Stevenson her Son-in-law. He died last Sunday Morning of a Fever
which baffled the Skill of our best Physicians. He was an excellent

young Man, ingenious, industrious, useful, and belov'd by all that knew him. She is left with two young Children, and a third soon expected."

Dr. Hewson, thirty-four, had contracted an infection dissecting a corpse and had succumbed in a matter of days. It would have been hard for the grieving young widow's avuncular friend to set out for America at such a time. But other reasons were emerging for Franklin to postpone his departure. He had relinquished his duties as agent for the Massachusetts Assembly to Mr. Arthur Lee, his designated successor. Mr. Lee, however, had chosen this season inopportunely to depart on a tour of Europe. Thus, June 1, to Cushing: "Mr. Lee is gone to make the Tour of France and Italy," Franklin was obliged to write, "and probably will be absent near a Year. . . . I had resign'd your Agency to him, expecting to leave England about the End of this Month; but on his Departure he has return'd me all the Papers, and I feel myself now under a kind of Necessity of continuing till you can be acquainted with this Circumstance, and have Time to give farther Orders."

Then by early June, Parliament had passed and the king had approved additional punitive measures that would alter the government of Massachusetts permanently. The Port Act was to be followed by those further severities, through the collective terms of which councillors (members of the upper house of the Massachusetts legislature) would no longer be elected but rather would be appointed—and thus be beholden not to the people but to the king who, through his Privy Council and governor, had appointed them. The royal governor's wishes would that much more easily be enacted into law. Moreover, royal officials in Massachusetts whose pursuit of their duty (in quelling a mob, say) might lead to a provincial's death were from now on to be tried not in local courts but in the courts of other colonies, or even in England— to the encouragement of harsh and arbitrary enforcement of the law, to the disparagement of Massachusetts justice, and to the great disadvantage of plaintiffs, required to gather local witnesses and (if they could be persuaded to leave home) bring them vast distances at high cost and inconvenience to a venue far less sympathetic to the plaintiff's case. Troops, moreover, might hereafter be quartered in whatever vacant buildings were available, regardless of the feelings of local owners. Juries, whom freeholders had for-

merly elected, were now to be chosen from lists provided to the
sheriff, the governor's appointee and creature. Finally, town meetings would in the future convene only once a year, and not to talk
politics either—merely to select town officers and then disband.

Other permanent disruptions and outrages of local custom attended this latest battery of legislation, which Franklin took pains
to protest vigorously in open letters to Lord North in the newspapers and in petitions that he and Mr. Lee had worked out together
and got numbers of Americans living in London to sign, as well as
in satires and letters to be published in newspapers overseas.

But the punishment of Boston and Massachusetts Bay by these
recent additional acts seemed so extreme that the doctor was
moved in time to take heart. Such measures, visiting wrath upon
the innocent, were bound to awaken a protest even among decent
Englishmen, and the ranks of the protesters would grow if only
Americans held firm. What his countrymen must do, Franklin was
led to advise them during the summer, was this: Hold firm, and eschew purchasing English goods. Eschew all luxuries from England, while learning to manufacture necessities yourselves. Soon
enough English merchants would feel the pinch and (as they had
in the midst of the Stamp Act protests nine years earlier) join right-
thinking others here in the mother country to bring down the present ministry and replace it with a government more reasonable,
moderate, and humane. It would take a little while, but the
colonists should stand firm; for government's "Tyrannic Measures" were certain at last to cost it the confidence of the English
people.

In the interim, Dr. Franklin, troubled and restive, was to learn
what some were saying about him in his native Boston. His
youngest sister, seven years his junior and his only surviving sib-
ling of all those seventeen who had grown up in their father's
household, still lived there, indeed had lived in Boston all her
straitened life. The doctor was devoted to this spirited Jane
Mecom, a widow struggling with penury and a number of worrisome grown children. Regularly, she wrote her illustrious brother
ill-spelled, vigorous letters, detailing her burdens and faith, and
her pride in him; and Franklin faithfully responded, not only with
words but with concrete help—clothing, money—that evoked
deep gratitude and led the humble matron finally, in timid fear of

blasphemy, on one occasion to compare her great, dear benefactor, remarkably enough, to Jesus.

Now, however, Mrs. Mecom had been pained by a report about one so worthy that was currently going the rounds. They were saying in Boston that Franklin was begging to have his post office job back, would agree to give up his various positions as colonial agent and settle in England permanently if government would only reconsider and oblige him. This Mrs. Mecom assumed was untrue, but in May she passed the gossip along anyway; and late in July, Franklin answered the charge.

It was a falsehood, he assured his sister, "an infamous Falshood, as you supposed." The same report had been heard every now and then in London: "that I am using Means to get again into Office. Perhaps they wish I would.—But they may expect it 'till Doomsday. For God knows my Heart, I would not accept the best Office the King has to bestow, while such Tyrannic Measures are taking against my Country."

One detects in the words the deepening of the doctor's resentment, the stiffening of his resolve. Many of his compatriots, all up and down the Atlantic seaboard, were simultaneously—as this summer of 1774 advanced—sharing Franklin's growing outrage at ministerial behavior. Before the various coercive acts of late spring, Americans in large numbers agreed with the agent overseas in deploring New England rowdiness: the Tea Party, tar-and-featherings, mobs bellowing through Massachusetts streets. But colonial attitudes were changing. By summer, many in America were having fresh thoughts about the Yankee port behind its blockade, at the same time that Franklin in England was distancing himself from the ministry that had earlier dissociated itself from him. "They have done me honour by turning me out," he was assuring Mrs. Mecom now, "and I will take care they shall not disgrace me by putting me in again." Then added: "All this to yourself.—To the World such Declarations might seem incredible, & a meer puffing of ones own Character: therefore, my dear Sister, show this to no body: I write it meerly for your Satisfaction; and that you may not be disturb'd by such Idle Reports."

But if the devoted Jane Mecom in Massachusetts had been thus troubled by adverse rumors about her brother, Franklin's son in New Jersey wrote his honored father with a different story to tell.

The royal governor of the province, as William Franklin was, had written during a visit to Philadelphia on May 3: "It seems your Popularity in this Country, whatever it may be on the other Side, is greatly beyond whatever it was." That very day the people of Philadelphia were planning to burn—in fact did burn in effigy—Solicitor General Wedderburn, Dr. Franklin's tormentor at the Privy Council and, still highly irritated, set fire as well to an effigy of Thomas Hutchinson. So much for Franklin's enemies; and "you may depend, when you return here," William assured his father, "on being received with every Mark of Regard and Affection."

The doctor's winter humiliation before the Privy Council, widely reported to an indignant America by the spring, had brought about this revision of opinion toward their fellow countryman. Through his summer of lingering in and around London, Franklin was made ever more aware that he would be warmly embraced on his return home. Perhaps he could leave England aboard the September packet. But even as he planned this later departure, with the congress set to assemble in Philadelphia in early fall, friends had begun urging him to remain where he was until the results of its deliberations might be known. Who better to present those results to the ministry in Whitehall?

All the while that he delayed, and out of the depths of his public chastisement in February, the agent's standing with Americans was continuing to rise. In England, in the meantime, as summer days advanced into August and he awaited with others on both sides of the Atlantic news of what the congress might decide upon, this recent object of the solicitor general's scorn was to be honored with a particularly high distinction. Franklin was invited, all unexpectedly, to visit and confer with no less than Britain's greatest living statesman. Earlier, the American had sought and hoped for just such an audience, in vain. Now finally, the most admired of all living Englishmen had himself voiced a desire to meet with Dr. Franklin. In its way, the honor was hardly inferior to Hutchinson's a month earlier, when the governor newly arrived from Massachusetts had been admitted into the very closet of the king.

9

CHATHAM

WILLIAM PITT, FIRST EARL OF CHATHAM, some would call the greatest English statesman who ever lived. Others more cautiously would identify him as the greatest statesman between Elizabeth I and Winston Churchill, with the latter of whom he has often been compared. Like Churchill, Pitt spent much of his life in opposition, regarded suspiciously by the various ministries in power. Like Churchill, he was a traditionalist, an arch-Englishman, an imperialist, a deep student of history, who in times of peace warned repeatedly of the need to maintain Britain's military strength. In one bleak time of war, Pitt, like Churchill, assumed the role of prime minister and led his nation to an astonishing triumph over a host of enemies. Both were great friends of America. The two men were, incidentally, singularly loyal and devoted husbands. Publicly, both were often imperious, haughty, and wrong, though in the greatest matters history has proven both to have been superlatively right. And like Churchill, Pitt was, in wartime and before and after, a thunderous, inspiring speaker, dominating Parliament with the power of his voice, the apt vigor of his language, and the distinctiveness of his oratorical style, that last of course lost to succeeding ages yet invariably remarked upon with stunned admiration by his contemporaries.

"Heavens, what a fellow is this Pitt!" Ministers noted the "amazing powers and influence Mr. Pitt has, whenever he takes part in debate." When he was to speak, members filled the chamber in eager anticipation; and in speaking, he alone was able to hold that often raucous bunch of parliamentarians so rapt that (as was reported by more than one of them, using the same homely cliché) you could hear a pin drop.

To speak so well, to articulate thought in ways that inspire, is no small thing. Yet Pitt's achievements went far beyond speech making. In the 1750s, with England vastly outnumbered and beset by formidable enemies—France and her several allies—the Great Commoner, as he would come to be known, had assumed direction of the massive war effort that was being made around the world, in Europe, in Canada, in the West Indies, in India; and, as tirelessly and intensely involved as Lincoln during another crisis-laden interval, as involved as Churchill during yet another, Pitt had brought the war to within clear sight of a triumphant conclusion, laying the basis for an enormous new empire that would embrace Canada on one side of the globe and India on the other. In particular, the glorious year 1759, his annus mirabilis, had seen victory after victory reward the statesman's efforts: Admiral Hawke at Quiberon Bay, Clive in India, General Wolfe at Quebec. "Can one easily leave the remains of such a year as this?" Horace Walpole wrote ecstatically in the course of it, in October, with triumphs yet to come. "It is still all gold. . . . Our bells are worn threadbare with ringing for victories."

But soon after the start of a new decade in 1760 and the beginning of a new reign under George III, with the war all but won and a new empire gained, Pitt's setting of his country's course would end; like Churchill, he was relieved of the helm with his dazzling successes still bright in memory. The fresh young king had his own plans, and his own ministers to see them through.

Time passed; issues changed. Then, in mid-decade, during the Stamp Act crisis, Pitt rose again in the House of Commons to speak out forcefully and effectively, now against government's new policy of levying taxes on the American colonies. "They are the subjects of this kingdom," he scolded his listeners, "equally entitled with yourselves to all the natural rights of mankind, and the peculiar privileges of Englishmen: equally bound by its laws and equally participating of the constitution of this free country. The Americans are the sons, not the bastards of England. As subjects they are entitled to the common right of representation and cannot be bound to pay taxes without their consent."

That point the orator would express over and over again, in vivid, persuasive language; and his words were transcribed and carried overseas, to be published in American newspapers. Colonials adored him, not only for his earlier success in driving the French out of Canada but now for his support in the cause of their liberty. "The gentleman asks," he thundered at the opposition in the House of Commons, "when were the colonies emancipated? I desire to know when they were made slaves." And Pitt's support was finally, perhaps as much as any other single factor, responsible for the change of feeling in England that had led in 1766 to the repeal of the hated Stamp Act. At any rate, the Americans thought so: that they owed the triumph of their cause principally to one man in Parliament, to the Great Commoner William Pitt. Statues went up to him, in Dedham and in Charleston and in New York City. Colonial leaders extolled him, and colonial legislatures voted him their heartfelt thanks.

It was not as simple as that, of course; more than Pitt's eloquence had been needed to effect the repeal. Among other factors, the fears of English merchants, faced with American boycotting of their goods, were needed. Things are seldom simple. Pitt himself assuredly was not simple—was rather a figure of baffling contradictions. In this very summer of 1766, for instance, the Great Commoner, having won the battle to repeal the Stamp Act, proceeded to accept a peerage from that Stamp Act advocate King George III, to the dismay of his followers becoming Viscount Pitt of Burton Pynsent and earl of Chatham in the county of Kent. At the same time, the new nobleman agreed to form a cabinet and assume the position of first minister again, but now not from the Commons; rather, from among his peers in the House of Lords.

In his correspondence with the king, this champion of liberty resorted to a prose style exorbitantly obsequious, even for an age of elevated language and formulaic phrasing. Chatham's letters, in which he begs to lay himself with all duty and submission at the feet of the most gracious of all sovereigns, "to pour out a heart overflowing with the most reverential and warm sense of his Majesty's infinite condescension," and so on, strike the modern ear unpleasantly. But that was merely another of the man's contradictions. He whose speeches, as his listeners transcribed them, are forceful and vivid and fresh used a style exasperatingly pompous and periphrastic in his writing, on whatever subject. "Pitt's love letters, alas! survive," one of his biographers laments; for though the feelings that those private documents express are admirably amorous, the manner of expressing such feelings, even of expressing profound domestic love, is as often as not heavy-handed, awkward, tortured, and—the word returns insistently—pompous.

Chatham's excessive love of pomp was but another contradiction in the character of this abstemious gentleman, who professed to long for nothing so much as the simplicities of agrarian life. He was a simple man, he asserted more than once, uncorrupted by public office (which was true), innocent of political skills, happy only among his cattle and sows, managing his estates, planting and harvesting his acres. And to be sure, what proved to be a long public career was led by one very private in nature, one whom only his family finally knew well. But those acres in Kent and Somerset to which Pitt retired on occasion were hardly simple or humble. In their grand elaboration—wings added to his manors, trees planted, neighboring lands purchased and houses leveled to improve his views—the squire consumed a large fortune, indifferent to expense. And his multitudes of servants in the familiar blue-and-silver livery, his parade of coaches whenever he traveled, the ostentatious domestic establishment of this "simple" farmer were hardly inferior to those of the wealthiest duke in the land.

Pitt's, the new Earl Chatham's, assumption of leadership in the summer of 1766, after the repeal of the Stamp Act, was short-lived. One of the more teasing "what-ifs" of history lies in that fact. Could his wise direction of government, vigorously exercised at so crucial a time, have saved the empire? But the king's first minister fell ill soon after assuming power, and for long months was indisposed, withdrawing to drink the salubrious waters of Bath and nurse his ailments in his West-country estate in Somersetshire.

The nature of his illness is another of the bafflements surrounding this puzzling man. Throughout his adult life, Pitt was visited by mysterious and utterly crippling and inopportune indispositions. His countrymen did not understand, nor is what ailed him altogether clear even now. Manic depression? Bright's disease? Gout was what they called it then—a traveling gout of the extremities, the bowels, the head. But its symptoms were severe: loss of appetite, sore jaws, prolonged insomnia, eruptions on the skin, lameness, depression. When whatever the illness was visited him most acutely, the man could do nothing, nothing at all—would sit alone in darkness for hours that stretched into days, unable to endure company, unable to abide even the sound of his beloved children, his food left quietly at a hatch in the hallway. Ministers, dukes, the king himself would plead for only five minutes of his time—and be answered, through his faithful wife as amanuensis, by an assurance of the utter impossibility of even that much intrusion on his suffering. Then magically, the convalescent would be better—would abruptly reappear in Westminster wrapped in flannels, trussed, his foot in his special "great shoe," and, even unwell, supporting himself on black crutches, would proceed to speak to issues as none other in Parliament could, rallying his forces once more to protest the courses that government was pursuing.

During this present illness of 1767 that stretched on beyond a year, beyond two years, Chatham's lieutenants filled in for him as best they could, awkwardly biding their time. But it would not do. Another government must be formed, and his lordship in the late 1760s and into the new decade was once more in opposition, when able to function at all.

He seldom attended sessions of the Lords now, rarely spoke in public. By 1774, Chatham had reached his midsixties. Yet although for the most part inactive in affairs of government, he remained a force to reckon with, partly because of his strong, clear views on issues, partly because of the vast love and gratitude that Englishmen continued to feel for a figure who had become virtually a national institution, partly because of the feebleness of any concerted opposition by those in Parliament who were unhappy with the present government. Sick or well, the great Lord Chatham was the logical choice to rally around. If only he might be persuaded to return once more to power, to deal with the growing colonial crisis that the folly of the present ministry had foisted upon the nation.

And indeed, in this very summer of 1774, the statesman—his illnesses abated for the time—was bestirring himself to learn all that he could of American sentiments: their grievances, their hopes. He felt that ministers often make mistakes because they do not trouble to inform themselves thoroughly about matters on which they are acting. Chatham in the present instance did not mean to commit that error.

Of recent American actions, he was persuaded, and had asserted publicly (in his first speech in two years, on May 26), that Bostonians had behaved criminally in destroying the tea last December. Too ill to cast a vote on the Port Bill, he did support the measure, although urging that its harsh terms be revoked as soon as the tea was paid for. As for the other bills that Parliament had gone on to enact in late spring—those additional coercive acts permanently emending the government of Massachusetts Bay—those were more troublesome. With a voice that his illness weakened, Chatham had risen in the Lords and expressed his doubts about the Quartering Act and those other formidable measures. Their easy passage soon after, despite his protests, had urged the statesman to apply himself to learning this summer all that he could about the current difficulties between colonies and mother country that were grown suddenly so alarming.

Toward that end, his lordship was in touch with a number of Americans, with Mr. Samuel Wharton from Philadelphia, Mr. Temple from Massachusetts, Mr. Stephen Sayre from New York. All the while he was feeling better, more like his old self than in years. And reinvigorated, he reflected that no such survey as the one now engaged in would be complete without consulting the most famous—and arguably the most informed—of all Americans. Before summer's end, Chatham had initiated just such a consultation, with Benjamin Franklin.

That August, Franklin had chosen to pass the dog days agreeably away from hot, crowded London in the country, staying with English friends, as he had done on many earlier occasions. The American had been in Brighton, then late in the month made a visit to a friend's seat, Halsted, in Kent. As soon as he arrived, the doctor was told that Lord Stanhope, a fellow member of the Royal Society who had a home nearby, had invited both guest and host to call. "We accordingly waited on Lord Stanhope that Evening, who told me Lord Chatham desired to see me."

The account of the summons, set down presumably six or eight months later, reveals nothing of what the American had felt at the time before such a prospect. Lord Stanhope would oblige by picking Dr. Franklin up in the morning and conducting him to Hayes, Lord Chatham's estate not far off. With such a meeting before him, what kind of night did the doctor spend, lodged at Halsted, awaiting the carriage that would convey him to an interview so long desired and long despaired of, an interview that promised to hold so much to interest and gratify? Long ago, seventeen years before, when the Great Commoner was in his glory, the American had tried to gain just such an introduction on Pennsylvania business, unsuccessfully: "I afterwards considered Mr. Pitt as an Inaccessible: I admired him at a distance, and made no more Attempts for a nearer Acquaintance." Now finally, the moment of meeting was near.

Plans agreed on that August evening were carried out next morning. Franklin traveled to Hayes, and "that truly great Man Lord Chatham receiv'd me with abundance of Civility." We imagine them together in the spacious villa, its twenty-four bedrooms, its brewhouse, laundry, dairy, and stabling for sixteen horses, its pinery and peachery and fenced park of sixty acres and over a hundred acres beyond, its rich plantations, its tasteful pleasure grounds with seats and alcoves—imagine among such opulence the mutual admiring courtesies that those two extraordinary specimens of humanity would have exchanged in the gracious manner of the age. His lordship "inquired particularly into the Situation of Affairs in America, spoke feelingly of the Severity of the late Laws against the Massachusetts, gave me some Account of his Speech in Opposing them and express'd great Regard and Esteem for the People of that Country, who he hop'd would continue firm and united in defending by all peaceable and legal Means their constitutional Rights."

The American guest, confident that his countrymen would stay the course, said as much. That assurance pleased his lordship, coming from a source so well informed. During their interview Dr. Franklin did elaborate on one concern of his. The visitor found occasion to suggest to his host that, throughout history, great empires had begun disintegrating at their outer edges, in their distant colonies, which were usually badly managed by corrupt, self-serving governors. The genius of the British Empire had been its willingness in great measure to allow provinces at a distance to govern themselves, and thus be well governed, with the provincial populace satisfied. From that wise policy had arisen in America such encouragement to new settlement "that had it not been for the late wrong politicks, (which would have Parliament to be *omnipotent*, tho' it ought not to be so unless it could at the same time be *omniscient*) we might have gone on extending our Western Empire adding Province to Province as far as the South Sea"—clear to the Pacific Ocean.

Franklin told his host that he lamented the doom now apparently poised over so excellent a plan of governance, "so well adapted to make all the Subjects of the greatest Empire happy; and I hoped that if his Lordship with the other great and wise Men of this Nation would unite and exert themselves; it might yet be rescu'd out of the mangling Hands of the present Set of Blundering Ministers."

To all this Chatham responded with utmost politeness, appearing impressed by his guest's analysis of the situation, at the same time that he acknowledged the difficulty of forming a coalition out of the various parties opposed to the ministry in power. His lordship, like Dr. Franklin, earnestly wished for a restoration of the ancient harmony between colonies and mother country. Yet he was troubled, as he remarked near the end of their interview, by a current opinion, widely held, that America aspired to independence. Was it true?

Absolutely not. "I assur'd him," the doctor later recorded, "that having more than once travelled almost from one end of the Continent to the other and kept a great Variety of Company, eating drinking and conversing with them freely, I never had heard in any Conversation from any Person drunk or sober, the least Expression of a Wish for a Separation, or Hint that such a Thing would be advantageous to America."

An opinion could hardly be offered more forcefully. True, Franklin had last seen America ten years before, but he had remained in frequent, extensive correspondence with colonial leaders ever since; and this was his firm, informed judgment as late as August 1774. Lord Chatham was gratified to hear it: "He express'd," as their meeting ended, "much Satisfaction in my having call'd upon him, and particularly in the Assurances I had given him that America did not aim at Independence, adding that he should be glad to see me again as often as might be."

To such exceptional cordiality, Dr. Franklin responded that he would not fail to avail himself of the permission given to wait upon his lordship occasionally, "being very sensible of the Honour, and of the great Advantage and Improvement I should reap from his instructive Conversation, which indeed was not a meer Compliment."

The spirits of the American must have lifted after such a promising exchange of views. He would indeed meet with Lord Chatham again, and more than once, as the crisis grew worse. As for now, matters looked guardedly hopeful. If his countrymen would but stand firm, would decline to purchase English goods, and would respectfully identify their grievances in the congress assembling overseas, their cause should prove irresistible. Letters in American newspapers might be representing that Chatham had deserted that cause, but Dr. Franklin was soon proudly assuring Speaker Cushing in Massachusetts, of his own personal knowledge, that such was not the case, and that the great statesman's "Sentiments are such as you could wish." Moreover, as August ended, and with the doctor's return to London, he was able to report from Craven Street that "the Tone of publick Conversation, which has been violently against us, begins evidently to turn." Adhere to your present wise course in the province and this outlandish ministry must be ruined, with the English friends of America soon succeeding them in power.

Adhere to your present course. But three thousand miles from his native town, the agent for the Massachusetts Assembly could not have known how drastically Bostonians had already deviated from that course. For only now, only in August, was a correspondent in the blockaded American port writing the first of the letters that would inform the London agent of all the surprising, defiant changes that summer had brought to New England.

10

A SECRET MISSION

DATED AUGUST 15, 1774 (weeks, obviously, before its receipt in London), the letter describing changes in and around Boston was written by Dr. Samuel Cooper, longtime minister of the Brattle Square Church and one of those original privileged six Whig leaders to whom Franklin had earlier wanted the Hutchinson letters shown. On the present occasion, the cleric had been moved to write to thank Dr. Franklin for a recent generous gift of books to the library of Harvard College—though tardily, because, as he explained, he had spent most of this past spring and summer in the country. Now back in town, Dr. Cooper went on to describe conditions that he had found inside the blockade on his return.

"We are indeed in a most critical Situation," he wrote, "and what the grand Event may be Heavn only knows. All Arts have been employ'd to terrify, cajol, divide, and mislead us; they have had some Effect, I wonder they have had no greater."

Still, the clergyman remained hopeful. "Our Rights may perhaps yet be redeem'd, and prove a Means of saving the Liberties of Britain." Liberties, in his mind as in the minds of many of his countrymen, were what finally was at issue. Liberties were what Bostonians had been struggling and suffering for. If a handful of wicked placemen in London could manage to enslave a free people in America, as Ireland had already been effectively enslaved, tyranny would soon triumph back home as well, so that the contest on New England soil, far from having independence as its goal, was being waged for the liberties of all within the empire. Arts, as Dr. Cooper termed them, were being employed to rob

Americans of those liberties—first in New England, doubtless afterward in the other colonies—but his letter made clear that the efforts of the royal governor, chief instrument for exercising those
arts, had been encountering local resistance.

Early in the summer, Governor Gage and Admiral Samuel
Graves in Boston Harbor had set about enforcing the blockade
more strictly than even the parliamentary framers of the Port Act
had envisaged. The act had banned all goods from leaving or entering the port by water, with two exceptions. Fuel and victuals were
to be admitted if on vessels that had first put in and been searched
at Salem. But Gage was insisting that even those commodities must
be unloaded, then made to negotiate the slow, awkward, expensive
journey from Salem by land, twenty-eight miles on rough roads
through Roxbury and over the Neck to Boston. Moreover, local
skiffs were not allowed so much as to move hay from islands within
the harbor or to transport goods from dock to dock in town. Of
course, such rigorous enforcement made for difficulties, as the governor willingly conceded when townspeople complained; but it
was not his intention, Gage said, to lessen difficulties.

Boston must suffer until it paid for the tea. In addition, after much
delay and rumor and surmise, and only days before Dr. Cooper was
writing his letter in mid-August, texts of the various additional coercive acts had arrived in Boston at last, as late as August 6, aboard the
man-of-war *Scarborough*. Those outrageous acts (as Cooper per-
ceived them, their stench fresh in the air) were aimed at no less than
"vacating the Charter, and . . . encouraging the Soldiery to murder
us." They vacated the charter—rendered meaningless the charter
under which the colony had been benignly governed for nearly a
century—by decreeing (to repeat) that formerly elected councillors,
members of the upper house of the legislature, would now be ap-
pointive: tools of the king to serve at his majesty's pleasure. In addition, the acts diminished local freedom by limiting town meetings to
once a year; and even such rare meetings as those were to be brief, in
performance of routine business only, with politics a subject not to
be introduced among the assembled citizens. Besides that, as colonials read the terms of the new acts, soldiers (who now could be billeted in any empty building around the town) were being encouraged to murder, assured that the jury trial for such murder, as long
as performed in the line of duty, would take place outside Massa-

chusetts, in some other colony or in the accommodating environs of loyalist courtrooms in England.

With the arrival of those doleful measures—the Massachusetts Government Act, the Administration of Justice Act, and the Quartering Act—had come as well a list of thirty-six local gentlemen selected by the ministry back home, on the advice of certain Americans in London (Mr. Hutchinson, shown the list, had belatedly added his voice of approval)—a list of loyal Massachusetts worthies chosen to serve as councillors of a new, more tractable colonial legislature. Governor Gage had been instructed to notify the gentlemen so honored, gather them at once in Salem, and swear them in.

The governor had proceeded promptly to carry out his instructions. Or had tried to. Seven of those selected declined outright to serve. Of the others, one appointee was dead, another was in Surinam, another asked for time to think about it, another did not return an answer, so that, in fact, only twenty-five of the thirty-six had actually agreed to accept the honor that the king had seen fit to bestow upon them.

By agreeing to serve, those same twenty-five hardy American souls had filled their late summer days with turmoil. Ever since the arrival of the acts, this month of August in which Dr. Cooper was writing to Franklin had been witnessing rambunctious behavior among numerous townspeople and villagers, bent on persuading the newly appointed councillors to resign their office. Persuasion was taking various forms, some rather more intimidating than others, all directed first against councillors, soon against Crown-paid jurists and any other government sympathizers. Hymns that such loyalists led in church were met with stony silence by patriot congregations. Loyalist cattle were driven off; loyalist houses were fired into; loyalist outbuildings were burned. Merchant loyalists were deprived of trade when admonitory signs singled out their shops as places for lovers of liberty to avoid. Country loyalists had their grist mills destroyed, their horses painted, tripe thrown in their faces. Loyalist ladies were "pelted and abused with the most indecent Billingsgate language." Hopeful loyalist youths were treated insolently, and ancient loyalist gentlemen were driven into the woods, where (it was reported) they like to have died.

But that was by no means all. The fractious province had been perpetrating additional forms of insubordination for Governor

Gage to deal with. When not gathering threateningly before some Tory residence, New Englanders had been coming together in Concord, Acton, Littleton, Worcester, and elsewhere, under the direction of colonial veterans of the French and Indian wars, to mold themselves into a more formidable militia, exercising with firelocks once or twice a week while their women and children watched encouragingly along the edges of the green. Not much could be done about that: Since the earliest settlements, a militia had been part of colonial life, to protect against the Indians and French, although its drills in these present crisis-ridden days—of military evolutions and target practice and the rest—were becoming more regular and disciplined, and ever more numerously and faithfully attended.

Meanwhile, in Boston, blockaded for two months and longer, the mood of the townspeople had remained, from Governor Gage's viewpoint, exasperatingly calm, cheerful, and resolute. Since June, there had been no further talk of paying for the tea—and (what might have encouraged them to pay) less suffering perhaps than the governor, humane though he was, could have wished for.

If Bostonians were surviving the rigors of the blockade, it was in part because of contributions from surrounding villages and from colonies at a distance. That last, from Gage's point of view, should have appeared particularly ominous: Distant provinces, moved by the plight of the Yankee port, had over the summer set their numerous differences aside in order to join in a common effort. In early July, donations of food, livestock, and money had accordingly begun arriving over the Neck for the deprived and suffering: from Windham, Connecticut, 258 sheep; flour from Charlemont; rye from Farmington; 224 quintals of fish from Marblehead; 3,000 bushels of corn from Maryland; rice from the Carolinas.

And in much of this resistance to authority, Josiah Quincy, ardent patriot, had been deeply involved. Earlier, on the last day of May, Quincy's *Observations on the Boston Port-Bill* had appeared in Boston, and thereafter the young attorney had raised his eloquent voice regularly in meetings called to protest current English policy. At a crowded, impassioned town meeting in late June, for instance (before such assemblies were forbidden by law), his flourishing oratory had joined with that of like-minded defenders of the so-called Boston Committee of Correspondence, the local patriot group now corresponding regularly with other provinces to rally support from a distance for the beleaguered town.

Support was all very well, but when the Committee of Correspondence had proceeded as far in June as to prepare on its own and disseminate a Solemn League and Covenant for every man and woman in Massachusetts to sign, a document that pledged its signers to purchase no English goods until the Port Act was repealed, many influential Bostonians had balked. In addition to zealous loyalists, moderates—local merchants (and there were many of them) with goods from England already ordered and on the high seas, merchants likely to lose heavily by the boycotting covenant—had concluded that the Committee of Correspondence was exceeding its authority and should disband. Let the trouble-makers disband, they cried. Enough was enough. Let the tea be paid for, let his majesty be humbly petitioned for redress, and get on with the business of business.

Townspeople had assembled yet again, vociferously, and speeches were hurled back and forth over the indignant crowds in the Old South, in a tumultuous meeting that had stretched on until dusk of a late June day and resumed the following morning, when finally a vote was called for.

The "better Sort of People," as Governor Gage would interpret the result of that vote, had proved to be outnumbered by "a great Majority of the lower Class." However explained, the committee advancing the covenant was comfortably exonerated of any wrong-doing—an indication, perhaps, of which way local sentiment was tending in the heated aftermath of Parliament's recent statecraft.

Quincy, high in patriot councils, had been from the start a member of the now-vindicated Committee of Correspondence. With its existence successfully reaffirmed, the young lawyer was able briefly to leave agitated Boston before the end of June and make his way to Maine, answering the summons of professional duties by following the eastern circuit of the superior court. At York, he caught up with his brother Samuel, the solicitor general, and his brother's friend John Adams, two other lawyers accompanying the court with legal cases to dispose of. To those gentlemen, the traveler fresh from Boston delivered mail and reported on the interesting events unfolding back home in their absence.

And here a glimpse from John Adams's colorful correspondence, on a Sunday, July 3: The lawyers had traveled together with Samuel Winthrop from York to Wells that morning, to attend while a Harvard classmate of Adams's, a Reverend Moses Hemenway, preached. After church service, Quincy, "allways impetuous and vehement," had pushed ahead, Adams noted, "I suppose, that he might get upon the Fishing Ground before his brother Sam. and me." Only the briefest of observations concerning the "impetuous" younger Quincy, yet it vividly conveys the impression that Josiah made on one who had been intimate with his family for years.

The following evening, July 4, the same two traveling attorneys—John Adams and Josiah Quincy, who had earlier shared in the conduct of the defense after the Boston Massacre—were together in Falmouth (now Portland), at Mrs. Huston's spotless rooming house. Desks and tables shone like mirrors, and floors were white and clean and sanded. "Quincy and I, have taken a Bed together," Adams mentioned in the course of one of his numerous affectionate reports to his wife Abigail, back home in Braintree.

The lodging-house image, familiar enough in eighteenth-century travel prose, anticipates another, comical bedding-down two years afterward, in 1776. On that later occasion—with war in progress—this same John Adams, traveling in company through New Jersey, would share a bed with Benjamin Franklin. Adams wanted the one small window of the room in the country inn closed against the pernicious night air. The elderly Franklin wanted it open ("Oh! . . . dont shut the Window")—and insisted upon overwhelming his companion, who had reluctantly left the window ajar before leaping into bed, with his reasons: "An harrangue, upon Air and cold and Respiration and Perspiration, with which I was so much amused that I soon fell asleep," Adams recorded drily, "and left him and his Philosophy together."

Now it was with Josiah Quincy that a bed was shared, in Falmouth, at Mrs. Huston's. John Adams, thirty-eight at the time, had on his mind that summer evening much that his fretful journal and letters reveal. He was brooding about the fate of his country, and was overwhelmed with having recently been selected as one of the five Massachusetts delegates to the congress assembling in Philadelphia at summer's end (must he buy new linen, "a Suit of new Cloaths"? and how would he travel: on horseback, in a phaeton, a curricle, or with the others in a stagecoach? "I feel myself unequal to this Business"); was feeling annoyed, moreover, at the number of lawyers and divines encountered in these parts who were Tories, and at the notion here in Maine that it was "politest and genteelest to be on the Side of Administration, that the *better Sort*, the *Wiser Few*, are on one side, and the Multitude, the Vulgar, the Herd, the Rabble, the Mob only are on the other."

Well, Adams himself was finally, during this same interval, to settle irrevocably which side he was on, during this tenth and last journey of his following the circuit court into Maine. One early morning within days of his reunion with Quincy, he would be invited on a walk on Munjoy's Hill, overlooking Casco Bay, in company with his dearest friend, Jonathan Sewall. What Sewall, attorney general of the province (Maine then was a part of Massachusetts), would seek to do during the walk was persuade his companion not to go to the Philadelphia congress. England was too powerful, Sewall reasoned, was irresistible, "and would certainly be destructive to . . . all those who should persevere in opposition to her designs." Adams must not commit himself to a course certain to doom his every future prospect.

The delegate to the congress heard the argument out, and—as he remembered years later—solemnly answered his loyalist friend: "I see we must part, and with a bleeding heart I say, I fear forever; but you may depend upon it, this adieu is the sharpest thorn on which I ever sat my foot." Forty-five years afterward Adams would vividly recall the anguish of so valued a friendship's ending, remember his final words: "I had passed the Rubicon; swim or sink, live or die, survive or perish with my country, was my unalterable determination."

That same momentous summer and fall, others who had wavered were making a similar hard choice at the water's edge, unable longer to avoid commitment. Adams and Josiah Quincy, both firmly in opposition to the English ministry, both with loved ones remaining loyal to the Crown, had returned to Boston by mid-July. There they were selected to serve on various important patriot committees, a Committee of Safety and a Committee of Donations, the latter to distribute, among laborers whom the blockade had thrown out of work, food and grain that the town was continuing to receive from nearby villages and provinces farther off.

And soon, at eleven o'clock on the bright summer morning of August 10, John Adams and his cousin Samuel, Speaker Cushing and Mr. Robert Treat Paine (at the last a fifth, Mr. Bowdoin, had felt obliged to stay home), all delegates bound for the general congress, had set out from Mr. Cushing's in Bromfield Street in a coach and four, "preceded by two white servants well mounted and arm'd," as a townsman reported, "with four blacks behind in livery, two on horseback and two footmen," all passing directly alongside the British regiments quartered on the common, before proceeding down Tremont and Orange Streets over the Neck to the mainland. Fifty or sixty enthusiastic Bostonians had followed behind the coach the eight miles all the way to the dinner stop at Coolidge's in Watertown. There, "amidst the kind wishes and fervent prayers of every man in the company for our health and success," the delegates bade fellow citizens good-bye, before resuming their journey in midafternoon westward and south toward Philadelphia.

By then, delegate Samuel Adams had been informed of a sudden decision of Josiah Quincy's to take passage for England. This older Adams, at various times a failed brewer and inept tax collector, had only in midlife found his true calling, as leader of local resistance to Crown policies through the late 1760s and into the present. Now, in 1774, Samuel Adams, in his midfifties, was among the four representing Massachusetts at the general congress in Pennsylvania; and in his absence, his lieutenants, the young physician Dr. Joseph Warren and the young attorney Josiah Quincy, were to guide the patriot cause back home.

But the plans of the "allways impetuous" Quincy had abruptly changed. He, too, would be gone from Boston before long. "At the urgent solicitation of a great number of warm friends to my country and myself," he was writing a trusted correspondent August 20, "I have agreed to relinquish business, and embark for London."

Why? "I am flattered," Quincy went on to explain vaguely in the same letter, "by those who perhaps place too great confidence in me, that I may do some good the ensuing winter at the court of Great Britain. Hence I have taken this unexpected resolution. My design is to be kept as long secret as possible, I hope till I get to Europe"—for should the fact that he was undertaking a mission abroad become known, "our public enemies here would be as indefatigable and persevering to my injury as they have been to the cause in which I am engaged heart and hand."

Whatever the event, the patriot meant to dedicate himself wholly to the service of America. Pursuing that dedication through days that followed, Quincy made his secret plans to leave, gathering letters of introduction, arranging his passage.

They were frenzied days, as August gave way to September. The present changes overwhelming New England are nowhere more urgently conveyed than in Governor Gage's dispatches, regularly forwarded to his superior, Lord Dartmouth, back at Whitehall. Early on, in the weeks immediately after his arrival in Boston in mid-May to relieve Mr. Hutchinson, the new governor had felt encouraged by what he had found. As soon as troop reinforcements already on the high seas should enter the harbor and debark, he was assured that loyalist citizens, friends of administration, would begin speaking out in ever increasing numbers against the rowdy so-called Sons of Liberty. Moreover, Gage had noted with satisfaction, "No Design has appeared of Opposing the Execution of the [Port] Act, Nor do I see any Possibility of doing it With Effect."

A month later, the governor was still optimistic, despite the effort of local "Demagogues" to stir up resistance against fulfilling the conditions of the act and thereby opening the port. True, Bostonians were being flattered with promises that the other provinces would help them subsist through their ordeal and were told that the proposed congress would have the happy effect of forcing Great Britain to come to terms. Nevertheless, Gage had assured his superior in late June that several influential gentlemen, formerly tyrannized by the Sons of Liberty, felt encouraged by the firmness of government's response to step forward and speak at last, "endeavoring to persuade the People to comply with the Act of Parliament, as the only Means to save their Town from Ruin." As for the congress, "I believe a Congress of some Sort may be obtained, but when or how it will be composed is yet at a Distance; and after all, Boston may get little more than fair words." Meanwhile, the Fourth and Forty-third Regiments had arrived to inspirit friends of government, and additional troops from Ireland were daily expected.

Late in July, "Affairs continue here much in the Same Situation." South Carolina had sent some rice, and a few sheep had been driven into town; but all such efforts to maintain resistance, the governor felt certain, "are too precarious to be depended upon, and must fail them." Yet one unpleasant fact had to be acknowledged: "The Opposers of Government may be called only a Faction in the Province, [but] they are at least a very numerous and powerfull Faction. I hope the Acts"—those additional coercive acts, long rumored and so long delayed—"may soon arrive, which will be a Kind of Test of People's Conduct."

The acts that Gage was hoping to receive did come soon after, on August 6; and an enraged populace rose at once to the test that the measures imposed, so that by the end of August the governor was sounding a different note entirely, a note of alarm struck repeatedly in dispatches that followed into September. Dartmouth was to learn that all at once a frenzy had spread far beyond Boston, into Rhode Island, into Connecticut. "In Worcester they keep no Terms, openly threaten Resistance by Arms, have been purchasing Arms, preparing them, casting Ball, and providing Powder, and threaten to attack any Troops who dare to oppose them." The people had risen up, would not let the legislature meet, would not let the courts convene, would not serve on juries. "Nothing but general Phrensy can make the Province suffer the Inconveniencies, that must arise from the Want of a Legislature and Courts of Justice, therefore hope it's only a Fit of Rage that will cool."

Meanwhile (this on August 27), "It is agreed that popular Fury was never greater in this Province than at present, and it has taken it's Rise from the old Source at Boston," from the same set of Boston demagogues: the Adamses and Dr. Warren and Hancock and Quincy and suchlike, some of whose names were already too well known to the ministry in London. And on September 2, with unaccustomed promptness, another fevered dispatch from the governor, opening with the ominous news that "the State, not of this Province only, but of the rest is greatly changed since Mr Hutchinson left America." Recent events had moved Governor Gage to call for additional troop reinforcements from New York and Halifax, the situation having turned perilous. His majesty's chosen councillors from around the province had been frightened into seeking the shelter of Boston, behind the security of the peninsula's fortified isthmus—"amongst others Messrs Ruggles, Murray, Leonard and Edson, who have abandoned their Dwellings to the Mercy of the People, as have lately Messrs Loring and Pepperell. Civil Government is near it's End, the Courts of Justice expiring one after another."

Suddenly beset, Governor Gage was determined nevertheless to move cautiously, "to avoid any bloody Crisis as long as possible,

unless forced into it by themselves, which may happen." His
majesty must judge what is best to be done, of course, but Gage as
commander in chief of British forces would urge that if government should decide to meet the present resistance with armed
might, "a very respectable Force shou'd take the Field"—many
more troops than were on hand; for what troops were here now
sufficed only to irritate, not terrify. But to repeat: "Nothing that is
said at present can palliate. Conciliating, Moderation, Reasoning is
over, Nothing can be done but by forceable Means. Tho' the People
are not held in high Estimation by the Troops, yet they are numerous, worked up to a Fury, and not a Boston Rabble but the
Freeholders and Farmers of the Country."

More followed rapidly, all of it alarming: another letter on the 2d,
a letter on the 3d, a letter on the 12th ("I learn by an Officer who
left Carolina . . . that the People of Charleston are as mad as they
are here . . . even Places always esteemed well affected have caught
the Infection, and Sedition flows copiously from the Pulpits").

What had caused so distressing a transformation? The coercive
acts of early August, obviously: Parliament's plan was proving a
failure. "I hoped to have made some Progress," the governor wrote
almost plaintively, "when the Arrival of the late Acts overset the
whole, and the Flame blazed out in all Parts at once beyond the
Conception of every Body."

These, then, were the disheartening reports that Dartmouth, all
innocent in Whitehall, would in time be reading. "I trust my
Dispatches"—thus the distraught Gage, September 25—"to the
Care of Mr. Oliver, a Son of the late Lieutenant Governor's, who
embarks in a Ship from Salem, and I understand that a Person
whose Name is kept secret, goes in the same Vessel, and that there
is something misterious concerning the Object of his Voyage."

The passenger whom Gage's adept informers had been unable to
identify—still masking his purposes—was Josiah Quincy. At ten
o'clock Wednesday morning, September 28, the young patriot,
with Mr. Oliver and others, would depart Salem aboard the Boston
packet for England, leaving behind a province shaken with sounds
of tumult, a province bearing no resemblance to the contrite, obe-
dient colony bent on restoring itself to royal favor that its restive
well-wisher Thomas Hutchinson had longed to hear news of from
across the Atlantic.

11

Mr. Hutchinson's
Autumn

A MONTH EARLIER, AT THE END OF AUGUST, Governor Hutchinson at his desk in London had been brooding yet again on his countrymen's perverseness. "The payment for the Tea," he was writing an American correspondent, "and a little further advance towards an orderly state than what had been made before I came away, would most infallibly have enabled me to obtain the desired relief for the town of Boston: but all our advices since"—all news from overseas—"have been discouraging."

At that point, on the threshold of autumn, what the governor would know of discouragement was for the most part still out of view, over the western horizon, his Boston letters in hand dating only from the end of June. At that point, he knew only that the Assembly, convened in Salem, had refused to consider paying for the tea, had instead defiantly named delegates to a continental congress summoned to meet in September, and for its recalcitrance had been angrily dissolved by Hutchinson's successor, Governor Gage.

All sorts of Englishmen with whom Mr. Hutchinson conferred this late summer had become convinced that by flouting authority thus, Massachusetts was choosing a course destructive of its welfare—and in so acting had placed itself entirely in the wrong. The unanimity of opinion, among English friends of America as well as America's opponents, "causes the Ministry to give themselves but little concern about what you are doing," Hutchinson explained in writing home. "When they know what it is, they say they shall know what, or whether anything will be necessary to be done on their part. In consequence, I am therefore now altogether inactive, and strolling about the country for meer amusement."

This New England visitor, even with access to high officialdom, could do nothing more for his fellow provincials until they had come to their senses. Pay for the tea; restore order. Until that happened, the governor must amuse himself as best he could.

To pass these trying days, he paid his unending calls, kept up his correspondence, visited museums, ambled about the streets and parks, played the occasional game of quadrille, traveled into the countryside. A letter dated as late as July 20, from his son Elisha's wife back home in Massachusetts, reported "no remarkable occurrence"; and thus reassured, on the following morning, September 1, Mr. Hutchinson and his daughter Peggy set off in a chariot on a fortnight's visit to Norwich, beyond Cambridge northeast of London. In the course of the journey, Elisha and his brother Billy joined them. Talk with English hosts during the two weeks' excursion was much about Boston, naturally, and when the tourists were not speaking of it, wherever they went they were led to think of home. A public hall, for instance, reminded them of the Concert Hall in Boston's North End, and the landscaping of a country seat suggested alterations that the governor might profitably undertake once returned to his own lawns in Milton: He would install a ha-ha fence at the bottom of the garden.

By midmonth the tourists were back in London, where they promptly and gratefully availed themselves of New England news. The *Scarborough*, they learned, had reached Boston August 6, and a respectable number of the Massachusetts councillors appointed by the king had agreed to serve, with signs that "most of the rest would probably accept." So favorable an account was more than Governor Hutchinson had allowed himself to hope for. His spirits lifted. In a more sanguine mood, he was assured yet again during new conversations with influential Englishmen that the ministry had no intention of taxing the colonies further and would remove existing taxes as soon as the tea was paid for. Better and better. Perhaps the governor might even hope, as others were hoping, that some basis for reconciliation would emerge from the deliberations of the congress, now presumably in session in Philadelphia. Lord Dartmouth, in any event, felt that government must wait for word from the congress before knowing what next might be done.

While waiting, in late September Hutchinson set forth on another outing from town, a visit of four days with his son Billy to Aylesbury, thirty miles off; and on October 1, he was departing yet again for Norwich. But this time he lingered no longer than a week before abruptly cutting short his stay. Distressing reports, just arrived from overseas, brought the governor hurrying back to the metropolis, pressing forward over sixty-five miles in a single seven-hour leg of a two-day journey that landed him at his London home after dark on Sunday, October 9.

The following morning, with a new week opening, he appeared promptly at the colonial office in Whitehall. There, Hutchinson was shown news from Boston as of September 6, news suddenly all bad. In these most recent dispatches a disheartened Governor Gage had revealed that the New England courts, obstructed by mobs, no longer functioned, that the legislature was refusing to sit, that the king's frightened councillors had been driven into the fortified safety of Boston, and that outlying communities were amassing arms and uttering threats amounting to treason. More troops from home, many more troops, must be sent if order was to prevail.

What had happened? The colonial secretary, the gentle Lord Dartmouth, seemed, as Hutchinson spoke with him about Gage's latest dispatches, despairing. More troops? With winter coming on, it was too late in the year to send reinforcements from Ireland. Gage must wait for reinforcements until spring. Dartmouth did finally locate three guard ships and two companies of marines—no more than that, maybe six hundred men in all—to order to America at once. That took a number of days, which the governor for his part, agitated and powerless, spent in paying calls around London, encountering discouragement everywhere. English friends were dejected, at a loss as to what could be done.

Perhaps the colonial congress would lay a foundation on which peace might yet be built. A few clung to that frail hope. As for Mr. Hutchinson: "My thoughts day and night are upon New England." For a week, two long weeks, nearly three weeks, no further word arrived. As October advanced, all was silence from overseas.

It had been in Norwich on October 8 that the governor had first got wind of calamitous rumors from America. Hurrying back to

London, he had had the dismal truth of the rumors confirmed on Monday morning, the 10th. Then no further news until the 28th, two weeks and more of perplexity and apprehension to live through. On the 22nd, for instance, "Colo[nel] Skene, Mr Livius, Mr Green, and Mr Clark, dined with me. I felt but little inclination to discourse on any subject except America, the state of which distresses me, and we are all anxious to hear from thence, having nothing from Boston since the 6th of September."

One document from America before them as they waited described an event that sounded particularly disquieting. Governor Gage had sent the document along, and Mr. Hutchinson was given leave by his friend the secretary of state to read it. What he read were six small pages in the hand of a worthy American named Thomas Oliver (no relation to Hutchinson's late friend Andrew). This Mr. Oliver, esteemed citizen of Cambridge across the river from Boston, had in August received notice of his appointment as councillor and lieutenant governor of the province. On September 2, mobs (so they would have appeared to Oliver and Hutchinson both, even with freeholders and patriot gentlemen numerous among them)—mobs had descended and surrounded Mr. Oliver's fine Cambridge home. Harrowing hours that followed were the subject of Thomas Oliver's account, now in Mr. Hutchinson's hands. It spoke of villagers and countrymen pouring into Cambridge from all quarters in the early afternoon, great throngs of them, including many "of the lower class":

> I was just going into my carriage to proceed to Boston when a vast crowd advanced and in a short time my house was surrounded by 4000 people and one-4th part in arms . . . I waited in my hall, when 5 persons entered with a decent appearance who informed me they were a committee from the body of the people to demand my resignation as a Councillor . . . I absolutely refused to sign any paper. They desired me to consider the consequences of refusing the demands of an enraged people. I told them they might put me to death but I would never submit. The populace, growing impatient, began to press up to my windows, calling for vengeance against the foes of their liberty. The five persons appeared anxious for me and, impressed with some humanity, endeavoured to appease the people; but in vain. I could hear them from a distance swearing they would have my blood. At this time the distresses of my wife and children,

which I heard in the next room, called up feelings, my lord, which I confess I could not suppress. I found myself giving way . . . I took up the paper, and casting my eyes over it with a hurry of mind and conflict of passion which rendered me unable to remark the contents, I wrote underneath the following words "My house being surrounded with four thousand people, in compliance with their commands I sign my name Tho. Oliver."

One official had thus been terrorized into resigning his position on the council board. Governor Hutchinson would have been able to imagine the horrific scene to the last excruciating detail; it was at Hutchinson's recommendation, in fact, that Oliver had been appointed lieutenant governor. September 2, now fifty days and longer into the past, the poor man had been made to endure his ordeal. What other outrages were gentlemen of Boston and their families being forced, perhaps even at this moment, to submit to? Like everyone else, the governor could only wait and wonder.

Through this same long interval, although discouraged, Hutchinson sought to spare his daughter Peggy what worry he could. Her letters of the time only occasionally reflect the concern that was her father's constant companion. On October 13, the young woman did write her sister-in-law Polly of how anxious she was for those left behind, "nor do I see any prospect of relief for you." But much else that she wrote was lighthearted: of calls paid and received, of walks with her brother Billy in St. James's Park, "which, by the way, does not answer my expectations; nor do I think it much superior to our Boston Mall." And on one such outing, on the 19th: "Who do you think I see? Why, the King and Queen, as you are alive, carried through the Park in a couple of chairs! I have not seen them before but at Court. The Queen looked very pretty: I insist upon it she is handsome, but nobody will join with me."

As for young English gentlemen whom the writer might likewise judge handsome, "the men do not please me here; and Miss Murray and I both agreed on our first arrival, that New England was the only place for pretty fellows. I am still of the same mind when I think of them at all; but indeed they do not engross much of my attention. You say I enter into public places secure of conquest. O spare me my friend!" the lady protested good-naturedly. "Those I studied to please are many leagues distant from me."

One public place where a privileged twenty-year-old might enter and shine was at court, to which Peggy had returned, this time (with the formal presentation to their majesties behind her) more at ease, so that she had found herself at one point comfortably in the royal nursery, allowed to kiss the "pudsey little hand" of adorable Prince Ernest, age three. And there were plays to attend, despite dismal rainy weather all fall: *Alexander the Great, The Grecian Daughter,* that latter providing such a lively, affecting representation of devotion between daughter and father that Peggy had been obliged rapturously "to get as much out of sight as I could, and give full vent to my tears."

And dinners at home. A friend from Boston, self-exiled like Hutchinson, dined with them October 29, as he had often done of late. The elderly Mr. Richard Clarke (father-in-law of John Singleton Copley) had as a tea agent been in the thick of Boston tumults the preceding November, windows of Clarke's home on School Street shattered, mobs ranting at his doorway as they would rave later at Thomas Oliver's. Now the gentleman, all that fury behind him, was dining with the Hutchinsons. "We had a dispute after dinner," so Peggy reported to Elisha's wife, over "which was the best country—New England, or Old? Papa, your husband, and myself, were for the former: Mr C. and Billy for the latter. I own I still feel a partiality for my native country. Papa could not help expressing his in very strong terms. Mr. C. said he never should lose the idea of the last winter: that the injuries he then received were too strongly impressed upon his mind ever to be erased."

It had surprised the young woman to hear an American admit to feelings so alienated from his country. Peggy's feelings were not alienated; neither were her brother Elisha's; neither were her father's. O, my dear Polly, "how happy should I be to see that country restored to a state of peace and quiet!"—less for her own sake, she insisted, than for Papa's, who would be so much more contented returned to his native land.

But a voyage home looked more and more distant, as of October 29. A day earlier, Hutchinson had received fresh news at long last, though news anything but reassuring: "by a vessel from Philadelphia, advice of certain Resolves of a Committee of Towns in the county of Suffolk, which had been adopted by the Congress at Philadelphia." At once the governor had recognized and recorded that this latest turn of events was "more alarming than any thing which has yet been done."

Boston is in Suffolk County. When the coercive acts, with their prohibition of town meetings in Massachusetts, had arrived, citizens were prompt in devising means to circumvent the ban, one of which was by removing themselves from Boston to neighboring villages and inviting others in the county to join them, calling the resulting gathering a *county* meeting. Town meetings might be forbidden, but the law said nothing about county meetings.

Such a county meeting had assembled early in September in Hutchinson's cherished Milton, where seventy delegates from twenty communities had drawn up a set of uncompromising resolves that followed a prologue unusually eloquent. The prologue to the Suffolk Resolves recalled the blood and valor of ancestors, persecuted and driven from England, who had come to the uncultivated desert of the New World, there with their toil to purchase a dear-bought inheritance that they had bequeathed to the care and protection of their descendants; "and the most sacred obligations are upon us to transmit the glorious purchase, unfettered by power, unclogged with shackles, to our innocent and beloved offspring. On the fortitude, on the wisdom, and on the exertions of this important day"—Friday, September 9, 1774—"is suspended the fate of this new world, and of unborn millions." If we, the prologue continued, successfully resist the usurpations of unconstitutional power that have robbed Boston of the means of life, have thronged Boston's streets with military executioners, have lined our coasts with ships of war, have mutilated our charter—"that sacred barrier against the encroachments of tyranny"—and have through a murderous law sheltered villains from the hand of justice; if we succeed in resisting those wrongs, "the torrents of panegyrists will roll our reputations to the latest periods, when the streams of time shall be absorbed in the abyss of eternity."

Nothing in there about paying for the tea, or assessing funds for the support of the empire, or bowing to the sovereignty of Parliament. Nor were any such concessions made in the nineteen resolves that followed. The first was a pro forma expression of "cheerful" allegiance to the king, but the other stern resolutions! One removed citizens from any obligation to obey the coercive acts. A second denied the authority of local courts, the officers of

which had recently become king's appointees and paid by the
Crown instead of by the Assembly. A third proclaimed councillors
who declined to resign their office to be "obstinate and incorrigible
enemies to this country." Yet another urged provincials to acquaint
themselves with the art of war by regularly exercising in military
skills. Another advocated suspending all commercial intercourse
with Great Britain until local rights were fully restored. Still another called for the summoning of a congress of the province, a local *provincial* congress, "to concert such measures as may be
adopted and vigorously executed by the whole people."

But worst of all, the *Continental* Congress, with delegates assembled at Philadelphia from virtually all of the American colonies—
that other congress on which some in England had been pinning
their hopes for a conciliatory gesture—had as an early order of
business seen fit to approve those same seditious resolves from
Massachusetts, thereby throwing its continental weight, right from
the start of its sessions, behind the contumacious resisters foment-
ing rebellion in Boston and Suffolk County.

At that grim news, just arrived from overseas, Lord Dartmouth
was, in Hutchinson's word, "thunderstruck." Perhaps the account
of the congress's action was not genuine? But the governor knew it
would not be printed and attested to by their clerk if spurious.
Well, it was impossible in any event for government to give way.
That much Dartmouth was certain of, and repeated. Others high in
administration whom Hutchinson saw in surrounding days confirmed the fact: England could not pull back. Only a change of
ministry could alter the present measures, and such a change was
most unlikely.

What had gone so wrong? The governor mulled it over and over.
His rather circuitous prose expressed the only consolation he could
find. "I can never be thankful enough," he wrote, "for having been
enabled so to conduct myself during the time of my being in
Administration, as that in all the controversies I have had with the
people of the Province, I have never contended in any instance for
what I did not think perfectly right, and for the real advantage of
the men who were endeavouring my ruin. Without this reflection I
should not be able to support myself."

The reflection sufficed to invest him with a strange tranquillity.
New England was written strongly on his heart, whatever hap-

pened. The hope—"which I am determined not to part with"—that he would return there, together with the certainty that his enemies would be forced to admit that he had always meant the best by his country, supported the governor's spirits through these present anxious times. "I have not known more tranquility for many years past, than since I have been in England."

This on November 1, in a letter home (although Hutchinson's private journal contains numerous agitated entries hardly reconcilable with such professed serenity). In the same letter, to his younger brother Foster back in Massachusetts, the writer disclosed the extraordinary nature of his thinking at this time. Should his fellow provincials reassume their first charter (as rumored) and under its terms set up a new administration and choose him governor—choose *Hutchinson* governor?—"I am determined," he wrote, "not to serve." Choose for governor Thomas Hutchinson, by this time generally loathed in Massachusetts as few Americans have been loathed before or since? Yet he must cling to his illusions. On the 2d, placidly referring to the site of the Suffolk Resolves: "I bear not the least ill will to my Milton neighbours for the share they have at last taken in the general confusion. I know the nature of the contagion. . . . I shall yet live and die among them, and I trust recover their esteem."

The gentleman was out of touch, but hardly more so than were most others in England. November 8 brought news that the Continental Congress had defiantly recommended ceasing all commercial intercourse with Great Britain. On the 12th, Mr. Hutchinson was with the prime minister. Lord North, equally defiant in his own complacent way, judged that "the case seemed desperate, Parl[iamen]t would not—could not—concede. For aught he could see it must come to violence. He had the Kingdom with him. There was no danger of a change in Parliament. There was no danger of a change in Administration."

Into such intransigence were matters settled when word came November 14 of the Boston packet's having six days earlier put in at Falmouth, at the far western tip of England. Letters would be aboard, more news from America. On the 17th, Mr. Sylvester Oliver, passenger aboard the packet, recent graduate of Harvard College and son of Lieutenant Governor Andrew Oliver, called in London on his late father's dear friend. But Mr. Hutchinson was, unsurprisingly, out dining at the time. Rather than surrender his letters from America, young Oliver chose to return next morning with them, "having promised, as he said, to deliver them with his own hand."

Thus, November 18, as the governor noted in his diary, "S. O. came with a great number of my letters from my friends, and also General Gage's letters to Government. The latter I sent immediately to Mr Knox, Lord D. being in the country. Soon after I had sent them, Mr Pownall"—undersecretary at the foreign office, Mr. William Knox's colleague and as such privy to the information that the new dispatches contained—"desired, by a card, that I would come immediately to Lord D.'s office, upon an affair of very great importance."

12

JOURNEY OVERLAND

So urgent a summons from Whitehall must be answered at once.

At what point, one wonders, did Governor Hutchinson realize—he who all his adult life had played central roles in public affairs, had been consulted with, deferred to, honored, waited on—when, during these fall months, did it first dawn on the governor that the passing days had moved him to the margin? On his arrival in London his advice had been eagerly sought, up to the very king himself, and Hutchinson's mere presence (so Lord Dartmouth had insisted) had served as reassurance in times so unsettled. At first, ministry had shown the American lists of appointments to approve or disapprove, had considered his wisdom in forming policy, had seemed gratefully to accept his recommendations. But now, with all changed in the New World since Hutchinson's departure from Boston, less and less often did government seek out his counsel. Fewer and fewer were such summonses to the seats of power on "very important" matters as this, to which he was responding now.

The governor dropped what he was doing, of course. "My coach being out, I immediately took a hack," and arrived at Whitehall to find that the present important affair was not so very important after all, "was nothing more than to acquaint me General Gage had wrote that there was a person unknown, supposed to be going over in Lyde [that is, in the Boston packet, Captain Nathaniel Lyde], upon a bad design, some said to Holland, and that young Mr Oliver, who was a passenger in the same ship, would probably be able to give some account of him; and therefore Ld North had desired Pownall to examine Mr O."

If that was all, Mr. Hutchinson knew already who the mysterious passenger was, having learned this morning from his caller Sylvester Oliver the identity of those aboard the packet. No need to query young Oliver about the matter. "I determined it must be Quincy."

And Josiah Quincy it was. As to the reason the excitable young attorney, Samuel Adams's lieutenant, had come to England, people back home knew little more about the matter than did those in London now pondering his arrival. "Your leaving this country so privately," a friend in Boston had written the traveler after his departure, "has been matter of general speculation. Some say you went away through fear; others that you went to make your peace; others that you went charged with important papers from the continental congress; many conjectured you were gone to Holland; upon the whole it was a nine days' wonder."

Holland might serve as a source of gunpowder and suchlike materiel in the event of war. But whatever his motives, Quincy had landed at Falmouth ten days ago and from there made his way overland to the very heart of the empire. The time at sea had proven to be a restorative. At the start of his journey, when boarding ship in Salem back in September, the young man had felt in low health, and despite fine weather setting out, had been obliged within an hour of departure to take to his cabin and stay there. But mercifully, Quincy's seasickness had proved neither so violent nor so unremitting as in his voyage to the southern colonies a year earlier. Now after a few days, the invalid had started to feel better; and within three weeks on the high seas, the symptoms of the tuberculosis that had plagued him ashore had disappeared.

Of this present voyage, "five and twenty days," he would write to his wife shortly before landing in England, "rolled away with much of the uninteresting vacuity and sameness of a sea life." There had been ample time to feel the benefits of ocean air, for though the winds had been favorable throughout the passage, favorable beyond the memory of anyone aboard, the vessel itself was deep laden, "and as bad a sailer as was ever navigated by a Dutch commander; not a sail on the ocean but what passed by us as if we had been at anchor." Add to that a vexatious shift of wind, strong to the southeast, at the far side of the voyage, to delay their landing; so that what in even a tolerable ship would have been a smooth, speedy passage of twenty-one or twenty-two days, given the auspicious conditions, stretched out to more than forty, before land was near and the pilot boat at Falmouth was finally sighted approaching.

"But as for myself," Quincy wrote, "I had less reason than any one on board to be uneasy." Daily, this tubercular had felt his health and zest returning. Concerning those other passengers, eager to be ashore after the drawn-out voyage, the patriot wrote cryptically. Indeed, he wrote cryptically throughout his stay overseas, in a suspicious age when letters might well be opened and read by one's enemies. (Many were cryptic then. Quincy: "If I should write under a new signature, you must not be surprised." Hutchinson: "If I knew what was to be done here, I would not tell you in a letter." Franklin: "The uncertainty of safe Conveyance prevents my being more particular.") Discretion in corresponding—even in keeping a journal—seemed ever called for, as in such a fuzzy passage at the end of Quincy's present voyage as this:

"I found," the young journal-keeper hinted of his fellow passengers, "considerable advantage by attending to my companions, and often collected much information of men and things, that from the political jealousies and cautions prevalent in America, I could not there so readily attain. One of the first convictions I received, was touching the source of many American injuries, and one of my first emotions was indignation against public conspirators."

That would seem to mean the following: Among his shipmates aboard the packet, Mr. Sylvester Oliver and the others—old Mr. William Hyslop, Timothy Paine, Rufus Chandler, Stephen Higginson—were loyalists who spoke their minds more freely at sea than at home. Young Oliver's father, the late Lieutenant Governor Andrew Oliver, had with Governor Hutchinson been the object of the Assembly's sensational petition for removal from office last summer. Now Quincy, overhearing the son's unguarded talk among other passengers to beguile the time as days at sea stretched on, was moved to new-felt indignation against, precisely, Mr. Hutchinson and the late Mr. Andrew Oliver, "public conspirators" both. And referring perhaps to another subject of conversation among those traveling colonials, the patriot added, "I find that there was very great doubt whether I was going to embark for Europe; but certain Americans were very sure I should never dare to go up to London."

Such doubts were based on a presumption that authorities in London would take this agitator into custody, as they had been threatening to bring over for punishment such like-minded incendiaries as Hancock and Samuel Adams. Yet London was exactly where Adams's protégé would be heading, once ashore. Moreover, along the way Quincy meant to improve his time sightseeing; and in doing so, on this—the young man's first—venture outside America, his impressionable nature would often enough be astonished by what he encountered.

At the start, he took a walk of a couple of hours around Falmouth, happy to find himself on solid land, all his impressions heightened by an uncommon feeling of health and high spirits. "This place is in situation delightful," he wrote; "the country and cultivation surpass description." What impressed him most, about Pendennis Castle and everything else he gazed upon, was the antiquity of it all. But the sightseer had soon got his hands on the latest London newspapers and was devouring no fewer than twenty of them, all filled with the resolves of the American congress concerning the proceedings in Suffolk County. "They also seem to breathe a spirit favourable to America," Quincy observed, feeling cheered, despite troubling accounts of reinforcements having sailed for Boston in late October. And promptly, this first day ashore, the new arrival found himself conversing with a number of sensible Englishmen: "I have not yet met one, but what wishes well to the Americans. And one or two expressed great veneration for *the brave Bostonians*."

Next morning, he set out on his way east, proceeding by coach the twenty-two miles from Falmouth to Bodmin, "the roads hilly and good, affording agreeable riding, and delightful land prospects." Such prospects amazed this "mere American," as he called himself: Cornish fields cultivated to a wonderful perfection. He had seen nothing like it at home. "The first reflection upon the immense labour that must be bestowed on these fields was, where the men lived, who did the work. Extensive fields, highly tilled, without a house." Villages when met with along the way seemed dismal affairs, with miserable accommodations for honest labor—

merely huts of small stones and clay. "The lower orders of people," Quincy was able already to conclude this first day out, "are servile in their obeisance, and despondent in their appearance." A paradox: So little liberty had yet given so beautiful a face to nature. What if liberty were more general? Could perfection be improved upon?

The following day, another thirty-three miles, to Plymouth, and more surprises. The weather was cold and stormy, and yet the traveler made his way to the docks and went aboard a warship, the *Royal George,* two hundred guns, a first rate. "The rope-walks, buildings, armory, arsenal, naval and warlike stores, exceed the power of the human mind to conceive, that doth not actually behold." This, then, would be the potential and altogether formidable enemy in war. Quincy boarded other docked ships, boarded an Indiaman just arrived and laden with Orient wealth, toured the shipyards and saw vessels being built, from the laying of a keel to the finishing of a hundred-gun ship, all of it provoking "an astonishment I never before experienced. . . . I will not attempt to describe what I could scarcely realize to be true, while I was actually viewing. My ideas of the riches and powers of this great nation are increased to a degree I should not have believed, if it had been predicted to me."

The susceptible traveler lingered another day in Plymouth before pushing on, to Exeter the following afternoon, where he marveled at its cathedral, "surprisingly grand and antique;—amazing work of superstition!" as it appeared to a descendant of Puritans. He attended a service, appalled at the high mass, though relishing the procession of aldermen, bishops, archdeacons, the mayor, deans, and the like, in that age of frequent processions that delighted and awed the multitudes. On, then, to Salisbury on the 14th, where the traveler sought out Stonehenge, "which the learned and the virtuosi call one of the greatest wonders of the island. It is a wonderful piece of antiquity." And yet another cathedral to view, "called (and perhaps justly) one of the finest in the kingdom."

Quincy had his eyes open and was everywhere impressed by England's power, by its natural and cultivated beauty, by the antiquity of the island, by the "ruddy bloom" of its women, by their health and cleanliness, by the art and architecture, the statuary:

"The statue of George the First is very elegant and beautiful." On November 16, he lodged on the banks of the Thames. Nearing the metropolis, "the number of delightful seats &c. increases very much": country homes of the aristocracy, the earl of Pembroke, the earl of Portsmouth.

Then on the 17th, having traveled almost the width of the southern part of the island from west to east, "proceeded to London, where I arrived about eleven o'clock A.M." And once again the American was to be astounded. "The extent, numbers, opulence, &c. of this great city, far surpass all I had imagined."

London was, of course, the greatest city in the world, here at the very heart of the greatest empire in all of history to that time. What a contrast to Quincy's Boston, little provincial port of eighteen thousand souls far off at the empire's edges! This vast, sprawling, imperial metropolis alongside the cluttered Thames boasted a population of eight hundred thousand. Its imposing public squares, among them Hanover, Portman, Soho, and Bloomsbury, and all the grand mansions in town—Berkeley House, Burlington House, Devonshire House, Chesterfield House—as well as the vast parks and public buildings, including the Guildhall, the Royal Exchange, Lincoln's Inn Fields, the broad thoroughfares and multitudinous crowded byways, the Christopher Wren churches everywhere, the cathedrals: All were calculated to dazzle and overawe itinerant colonials who had left behind them nothing comparable in a new and chaster world.

And the wealth of the place, pouring in from America, from the sugar isles of the West Indies, from India—nabobs so conspicuous that virtually every traveler remarked on their extravagances, every moralist bemoaned their excesses. Evidences of wealth and the corruptions that wealth breeds were everywhere from the first day on, in public and in private, on the streets with the doxies that so held James Boswell's interest, in Parliament with its rotten boroughs and its seats routinely bought and sold, at race tracks and pleasure gardens, theaters and gaming tables, amid the talk in the numerous coffeehouses, in the counting houses of the great mercantile enterprises: the East India Company, the Bank of England. Americans seeing London for the first time were sure to be amazed, as the godly arriving from New England were as sure to find much to disapprove of in what they saw.

Quincy now in London would reasonably have felt one other emotion: concern about the reception awaiting him. His pamphlet, *Observations on the Boston Port-Bill,* was making the gentleman's name known to government; and some in America—like the anonymous Boston Tory who had written in the spring to warn him of the dangers of his conduct—were convinced that his speeches against Great Britain had put the young man's very life in jeopardy. Friends and family back home were, as Quincy's father wrote, waiting eagerly to hear how this traveler reaching London would be welcomed to the city and the court: "whether your enemies are to be gratified by ministerial persecution, or your friends by the esteem and honour with which they hope to hear you are received and entertained."

Among those friends, it was his family, more especially his dear wife, whom Quincy first thought of, settled snugly that initial evening in lodgings at Mrs. Lawrence's, Arundel Street, conveniently near the Haymarket. To Mrs. Quincy he wrote again before the long day in London had ended: "This is my third letter to you. Not a line yet from America." They had been married five years, and at home in Boston were a son two years old and an infant daughter. Abigail Quincy's father was William Phillips (brother of the founder of Exeter Academy), affluent Boston merchant and active patriot himself; Hutchinson cites Deacon Phillips as a radical leader, and his name appears on lists of committees furthering the Whig cause throughout the period. Thus, if Josiah Quincy's brother, the loyalist attorney, was one with whom politics was to be avoided in speech and writing, Quincy's wife and father-in-law assuredly were not, all the less so because the writer expected his lengthy letters from England to be shown widely among their many interested and sympathetic Boston acquaintances.

Yet although full of politics, as was all his correspondence, this present letter of November 17 to his wife, to "My amiable and D[ea]r Friend," reported at the beginning on the writer's health and spirits, "the first object and inquiry" of all who cared for him: "In one word (for just now I am a man of too much business to use many) they are both surprisingly fine,—rather bordering upon extravagance, than under par. Indeed, how could they be otherwise? From sea, I landed in fine health, and have now finished a most delightful journey of three hundred miles." What the marveling traveler had seen along the way—Plymouth Docks, Stonehenge, Wilton House, Exeter and Salisbury cathedrals—"exceed all description: nay, I will venture to say, that the imagination stretched to its utmost limits, cannot form any idea of their grandeur, without a view."

But why was he going on this way, he asked himself, and broke off. "Why do I waste time upon any other subject, than my country?"

That would be Quincy's impatient attitude toward distractions, however marvelous, throughout his stay in England; any diversion from the public purposes of his visit he professed to deplore. There may have been one private purpose at the start—in the sea voyage that had proved so salutary to his well-being—but he had come so far and reached the heart of the empire not to gape about at curiosities. Rather, he was here in London on behalf of his country, his province, his native town. And having arrived at his destination, he felt that "a large field is opening to me. I am preparing for the course with feelings, which render me careless, whether I shall be pursuing, or pursued."

Thus, again cryptically, in response to fears that others may have felt about his welfare here in the imperial capital, he expressed his own plucky indifference to whatever price in health or safety the days ahead might exact of him.

He did seem to be enjoying himself, with much already happening and much to be done. On his arrival this morning, he had been greeted by various residents in the city, Americans or those sympathetic to Americans: "Messrs Thomas Bromfield, C. Dilly, and J. Williams, from all of whom I received many civilities." Mr. Bromfield's sister was married to Mr. Phillips, Quincy's father-in-law. That welcoming gentleman greeted the newcomer with the information that he had thus early been the subject of gossip at a loyalist coffeehouse in Threadneedle Street (attention that Quincy was obviously relishing, as he relayed it to his wife at once). "A certain gentleman in the coffee-room, said,—'Yes, Quincy has been blowing up the seeds of sedition in America, and has now come to do the same here.' I," the subject of the gossip wrote, "returned my compliments"—through the bearer of the report—"and sent word, that, 'if I had done nothing but blow up seeds, they would probably be very harmless, as they would never take root; but if I should have the good fortune to sow any here, and they should afterwards ripen, he, or the ministry might blow them about at their leisure.'"

But what *was* his purpose in coming, after all? Likely a part of it concerned Benjamin Franklin. Franklin and Josiah Quincy's father had been friends for twenty years, ever since Quincy Sr. had appeared in Philadelphia in 1755 and, with Franklin's help, gained local backing for a Massachusetts military campaign in the French and Indian War. And Quincy the younger bore with him, besides his father's goodwill, a letter from Franklin's sister in Boston, as well as letters of introduction from other Boston friends of Franklin, including Dr. Cooper and Mr. Bowdoin. But the young attorney also brought to London a memory, less cordial, of what he himself had heard about the doctor a year and more ago in Philadelphia: that Franklin was a trimmer and a courtier, had even—so it was charged—earlier proposed the Stamp Act to government as a way of raising revenue in the colonies (a charge untrue, of course, but in some American circles still firmly believed).

For that matter, Quincy's famous patron back home was no admirer of Franklin's. Samuel Adams would not even correspond with the London agent for the Massachusetts Assembly, so doubtfully did Adams regard the philosopher's loyalty, for all the reasons that had accumulated over a decade: Dr. Franklin's long residence in England, his and his son's Crown offices, the ambiguity of his behavior regarding the Stamp Act, his recently expressed alarm over the destructiveness of the Tea Party. No, Samuel Adams chose to learn what he needed to know about affairs overseas from the doctor's London associate Arthur Lee, who earlier, privately, had gone as far as to suggest to the Boston leader that it was "hardly in the nature of things" to suppose that Franklin as agent could be "faithful to his trust." The doctor's involvement in governmental matters, his post office job, his son's royal position, his need to cultivate the ministry to advance Pennsylvania business, his generally temporizing conduct, all (Lee had written Samuel Adams three years earlier) "preclude every rational hope that in an open contest between an oppressive administration and a free people, Dr. F. can be a faithful advocate for the latter; or oppose and expose the former with a spirit and integrity which alone can, in times like these, be of any service."

Had Quincy come to England, then, in part to determine whether the agent for the Massachusetts Assembly, so long a resident among the British, could be trusted? If so, the newcomer would be given an opportunity promptly to delve into the matter. This very first day, before the sun had set on his arrival in the metropolis, Quincy was taking tea with the agent himself, so that on that same evening, he was able to write his wife, "I have spent about two hours to-day with Dr Franklin."

13

FIRST DAYS IN
THE CAPITAL

ALTHOUGH WHERE IS NOT SPECIFIED, the two Americans—one
nearing seventy, the other just thirty—would reasonably have
taken tea at Franklin's quarters in Craven Street, because one of the
gentlemen who had met Quincy on his arrival this November
morning was well connected with the doctor. Mr. John Williams,
an absentee Massachusetts customs inspector, was the brother of a
gentleman married to a niece of Franklin's; the latter gentleman's
son was even now living with Dr. Franklin in Craven Street, helping to settle the post office accounts and other affairs before the
doctor's return to America.

Inspector Williams had passed on to Quincy a flattering bit of information. When he had earlier reported to Dr. Franklin the news of
the young Bostonian's coming to town, the Great Person had
wanted to know "if it was the author of the 'Observations' &c; and
being answered in the affirmative, he replied, 'I am very glad of it.'"

Quincy had been well enough pleased with that response to forward it promptly to his wife, gratified no doubt to have been recognized first for his authorship, instead of merely for being his
father's son. And the good augury of Franklin's initial reaction to
the name Quincy was borne out by the two hours over tea that the
gentlemen shared before the day had ended. Doubts about the
agent's reliability, about his devotion to the American cause, could
hardly survive even one meeting with the politic philosopher. "He
appears," Quincy wrote enthusiastically this same evening, "the
stanch friend of America, and confident of the ultimate success of

its friends. He has promised me his patronage, and I have reason to believe him sincere. He inquired particularly after 'his old friend,' my father"—and rejoiced to hear that the elder Quincy was comparatively well and happy.

Despite the rejoicing, the agent into whose counsels an old friend's son was being admitted November 17 had passed a worrisome autumn. For one thing, the slow but relentless progress through chancery of the Whately case had been giving Franklin cause for concern: that business about bringing the agent to court to force him to reveal who had furnished him with Hutchinson's letters. The matter was not to be made light of; if Dr. Franklin lingered in England and was summoned before the bench and there refused to divulge his source (and his word of honor required that he remain silent), jail might await him. Under such circumstances, it would seem wise to wrap up his affairs at once, as he had been talking of doing for nearly a year now, and embark for home.

All the more so because of a concern for his wife. "It is now nine long Months," he had written to Philadelphia on September 10, "since I received a Line from my dear Debby." Did her silence arise from her presuming that her husband was in transit? Was she ill? What was the reason for her not writing? "I have imagined any thing rather than admit a Supposition that your kind Attention towards me was abated. And yet when so many other old Friends have dropt a Line to me now and then at a Venture, taking the Chance of its finding me here or not as it might happen, why might I not have expected the same Comfort from you, who used to be so diligent and faithful a Correspondent, as to omit scarce any Opportunity?"

Guilt may have tinged the gentle reproach, from this husband of forty-four years, absent from home a decade. (How delicately does he phrase his concern, however, in a line anticipating the grace of Jane Austen: "I have imagined any thing rather than admit a Supposition that your kind Attention towards me was abated.") "This will serve," Franklin went on, "to acquaint you that I continue well, Thanks to God. It would be a great Pleasure to me to hear that you are so."

Wistful reminder in September; yet November had arrived and was more than half over, with still no spousal word to reassure him.

And his only son troubled an old man's ease as well. Franklin's son William, an English-trained lawyer in his early forties, who for the past decade and longer had been the royal governor of New Jersey, had written his father over the summer and inevitably got on the knotty problem of Boston. In early July, Governor Franklin had felt obliged to comment on the extraordinary behavior of the Massachusetts Assembly and the town of Boston in not having yet "so much as intimated any Intention or Desire of making Satisfaction to the E. India Company and the Officers of the Customs" for losses sustained in last December's rampage with the tea. If town or province would only pay for the tea—would do what was simple justice, after all—they could have their port opened in a matter of months. But if they waited for the congress to meet, and for all the issues dividing colonies and mother country to be settled, the younger Franklin foresaw that they might as well abandon Boston altogether; for by then trade would have flowed into other channels—into Salem, Marblehead, Newport, New York—and Boston merchants and artisans must either be ruined or of necessity have taken their industry elsewhere. "Besides they ought first to do Justice before they ask it of others, and the Business of the Congress may be carried on as well after the Port is opened as it can be when it is shut."

All of that seemed self-evident to his excellency Governor Franklin, as it had to thousands of other Tories and moderates up and down the seaboard, at least in July, before the August arrival of the remaining coercive acts.

But for his part, the royal governor's illustrious father had found nothing perplexing about Boston's behavior, in July or any time later. "I do not, so much as you, wonder that the Massachusetts have not offered Payment for the Tea," the father had taken time to reply from London on September 7, in dealing with William's midsummer letter recently received. The elder Franklin itemized the reasons, as he saw them, for Boston's unresponsiveness. For one thing, the measure closing the port had been so vaguely stated as to provide no assurance that the blockade would be lifted even if the tea were paid for. Even then, other terms might be insisted upon: that the populace must first reestablish its loyalty, say, persuading the powers in London of a devotion to peace and order. Again, no specific sum of money had been demanded. Further, "No one knows what will satisfy the Custom house Officers; nor who the 'others' are that must be satisfied, nor what will satisfy them." And finally, when all was said, the king—not the East India Company—had the last word; his majesty too must be satisfied, in ways left unclear.

"As to 'doing Justice before they ask it,'" Franklin wrote, "that should have been thought of by the Legislature here," by Parliament, which instead of behaving justly had chosen to pass unconstitutional acts extorting many thousands of pounds from America and had sent armed troops to assure that the revenues were collected. The English ought to give that money back. Let them take from the amount whatever payment would cover the cost of the tea and return the rest. "But you," Franklin ended impatiently, in words that betrayed his exasperation, "you, who are a thorough Courtier, see every thing with Government Eyes."

Earlier, the father had been close to this only son, had felt great pride in him, had in some measure come to depend on him. Now the two were separated, an ocean apart, and their former closeness rent so far asunder that the love once shared would never be felt again.

And as though that were not sufficient, Franklin in London had still another matter to trouble him this fall. If the Whately case in chancery did not land him in jail, the old man might see the inside of a cell another way. All those soldiers in Boston—brightly uniformed, up to six thousand of them by year's end, in a town of fewer than twenty thousand civilians: one in four walking the Boston streets a hated lobsterback—no more was needed than another such incident as the Boston Massacre of four years earlier, and Franklin knew what would follow. "I am in perpetual Anxiety," he had written in early October, "lest the mad Measure of mixing Soldiers among a People whose Minds are in such a State of Irritation, may be attended with some sudden Mischief: For an accidental Quarrel, a personal Insult, an imprudent Order, an insolent Execution of even a prudent one, or 20 other things, may produce a Tumult, unforeseen, and therefore impossible to be prevented, in which such a Carnage may ensue, as to make a Breach that can never afterwards be healed."

One personal addendum to such a disaster he noted a few days later to yet another correspondent in America. "My Situation here is thought by many to be a little hazardous," he wrote, "for that if by some Accident the Troops and People of N. E. should come to Blows I should probably be taken up, the ministerial People affecting every where to represent me as the Cause of all the Misunderstanding; and I have been frequently caution'd to secure my Papers, and by some advis'd to withdraw."

Nothing was more likely than that troops and civilians, crowded together on the little peninsula across the globe, would sooner or later be at each other's throats. Here, for example, is what Franklin's sister Jane Mecom would witness on the spot a mere month later, in November (before the doctor's letter just quoted would have even arrived), that same November during which Franklin and Quincy were meeting over tea in London. In Boston, the devoted Mrs. Mecom wrote her brother with idiosyncratic vividness, made all the more energetic by the suggestive ambiguities of her misspellings:

> We were much surprised the other day upon hearing a Tumult in the street & looking out saw a soulder al Bloody damning His Eyes but He would kill Every Inhabatant He mett & Pressing into a shop oposite us with His Bayonet drawn bursting throw the Glas Dore & the man of the house pushing Him out & he to do what mischeif He could Dashing the chiney & Earthen were which stood on the window threw the sashes with the most terrable Imprecations. The case it seems was He Percved they sould liquer & went into the House Demanding some but being refused He went into the closet & took out a gon & said His comanding officer tould Him he might take any thing out of any house He had a mind to upon which the batle Ensued & the man & His servant were boath very much wounded. There were to of them soulders but I saw but won, a Gaurd with an officer came & careyed Him away & I have heard nothing of Him since but this has made me more Timerous about what may be before winter is out.

With such alarming episodes a fact, Franklin three thousand miles from there might well worry about some fracas getting out of hand that would send him to prison as cause of it all. He ventured to presume that his innocence would prevent anything more serious befalling him than imprisonment on suspicion—not, certainly, execution as a traitor: appalling image of the old gentleman, the benevolent "Mr. Fatsides," "the Great Person," ending a distinguished life dangling from a rope at Tyburn, the hangman's bloody hands in his bowels (some in England longed to serve Messrs. Hancock and Adams and all other traitors thus). But even the lesser punishment "is a thing I should much desire to avoid," the elderly gentleman confessed, "as it may be expensive and vexatious, as well as dangerous to my Health."

His concern was genuine, and yet with all that, Dr. Franklin retained his optimism, continuing his busy life undeterred, lingering in London dutifully for the results of the American congress's deliberations, and assuring Josiah Quincy at the first of their many meetings that he remained "confident of the ultimate success" of the American cause.

During his stay in the metropolis, young Quincy became Franklin's almost constant companion, seeing the agent virtually every day, made to feel promptly at home in his extensive circle, introduced at the Royal Society, welcomed at the Club of Honest Whigs that met alternate Thursday evenings in the London Coffeehouse on Ludgate Hill. And within ten days of his arrival, Quincy would express an unreserved admiration to his wife and others back home. "Dr. Franklin," he wrote fervently on November 27, "is an American in heart and soul. You may trust him;—his ideas are not contracted within the narrow limits of exemption from taxes, but are extended upon the broad scale of total emancipation. He is explicit and bold upon the subject, and his hopes are as sanguine as my own, of the triumph of liberty in America."

Partly because of Franklin's patronage, Quincy's welcome in London had been entirely gratifying. These early days were packed with activity. The young man's health continued robust; and within a week of his arrival, he had even gained, through Mr. Inspector Williams's interest, access to the highest levels of administration. Quincy was received privately, and at their requests (so he maintained), by figures no less exalted than the prime minister, Lord North, and—upon his return from the country—the colonial secretary, Lord Dartmouth.

The interview with the former had taken place as promptly as the second day after Quincy's reaching London, perhaps a sign of the significance with which government regarded this friend of the wily Franklin, disciple of Samuel Adams, and effective pamphleteer in his own right. In fact, his very first day here, Quincy had learned that *Observations on the Boston Port-Bill* had been reprinted by Mr. Charles Dilly, the London bookseller, and (he had been assured) been much approved of by those sympathetic to the American cause. Two mornings later, at nine-thirty, the author of that noteworthy polemic was to find himself seated in the prime minister's levee room, a new arrival already being treated as a figure of some consequence.

He was not kept waiting long. Lord North welcomed the visitor into his apartment politely, "and with a cheerful affability his Lordship soon inquired into the state, in which I had left American affairs."

To the point at once. This, surely, had been high among the purposes of Quincy's coming to England: if he could, to lay before the ministry the colonial case, shorn of falsehoods and misrepresentations. For the case of Boston and Massachusetts and America had been grievously misrepresented, of that the emissary felt certain. And if for their part, the ministry chose to regard Benjamin Franklin "as the cause of all the Misunderstanding" between colonies and mother country, Josiah Quincy knew better. One man lay at the root of the difficulties all right, but it was not Dr. Franklin. The man to blame was Thomas Hutchinson.

Already, within hours of his arrival, Quincy had learned— Inspector Williams had told him that first day—of Hutchinson's continued, baleful meddling in American affairs. "He informed me, that Governor Hutchinson had repeatedly assured the ministry that a union of the colonies was utterly impracticable; that the people were greatly divided among themselves, in every colony; and that there could be no doubt, that all America would submit, and that they must, and moreover would, soon. It is now not five minutes, since Mr Williams left me, and these I think were his very words." Moreover, that same first evening in town, Dr. Franklin had confirmed the truth of what Mr. Williams had reported.

What use would the ministry make of such apparently knowledgeable advice as Mr. Hutchinson's? America to remain divided. America soon to submit. What behavior on the part of government would such assurances as those likely encourage?

Thus, in his interview with Lord North, the gentleman just arrived from Boston was forthright in identifying what he took to be the origin of the current regrettable differences between the two countries: "gross misrepresentation and falsehood." Quincy, this confident young attorney, spoke explicitly to the prime minister, "with much freedom," through two hours, and would have said more, "had not," as he put it quaintly, "his lordship's propensity to converse been incompatible with my own loquacity." What the garrulous North enlarged upon, among much else, was the propriety of the Port Act. "He said they were obliged to do what they did; that it was the most lenient measure that was proposed; that if administration had not adopted it, they would have been called to an account; that the nation were highly incensed, &c."

And his lordship went on. He "more than thrice spoke of the *power* of Great Britain, of their determination to exert it to the utmost, in order to effect the submission of the Colonies."

That was candid enough. "He said repeatedly, 'We must try what we can do to support the authority we have claimed over America. If we are defective in power, we must sit down contented, and make the best terms we can, and nobody then can blame us, after we have done our utmost; but till we have tried what we can do, we can never be justified in receding. We ought, and we shall be very careful not to judge a thing impossible, because it may be difficult; nay, we ought to try what we can effect before we determine upon its impracticability.' This last sentiment," Quincy adds, "and very nearly in the same words, was often repeated,—I thought I knew for what purpose."

The purpose doubtless was to send the young ambassador forth with advice for colonial incendiaries that England would not back down, that the full might of England—a bit of which the traveler had seen for himself in Plymouth Docks—would be brought to bear upon rebellion.

But for all that, Quincy felt that the interview had gone well. Two hours it had lasted—as long as Hutchinson's earlier with the king—while messages and letters were being delivered to the busy prime minister throughout. "I several times rose to depart, telling his lordship I was afraid I should trespass on his patience, or the concerns of others." But the amiable North had urged his young caller to stay and "continued his conversation with his usual spirit. Upon my departure he asked me when I should leave England. I told him it was uncertain,—but imagined not this twelvemonth. He hoped the air of the island would contribute to my health, and said he thought the most unhealthy months were past; and then saying, 'I am much obliged to you for calling on me,' we left each other to our meditations."

All very civil and, from Quincy's viewpoint, profitable. He had said what Lord North had needed to hear and had listened to what the obliging first minister had had to say as well. In fact, everyone was behaving obligingly to this young visitor, whose arrival the morning papers had announced as the author of the *Observations* (even as, in reading the announcement, "several at the coffeehouses wondered how 'I dared to come'"). Especially obliging was Commissioner Corbyn Morris, whom Quincy dined with November 22, two or three days after his interview with Lord North.

Mr. Morris was, as the American noted, "supposed framer of the annual ministerial budget, being a choice friend of the ministry." They dined together at the commissioner's request, precisely in order to consider American affairs. Quincy's present host struck him as "sensible, intelligent, and very conversable," although what he had to say was much like what Lord North had said not long before. "Mr. Morris expatiated largely upon the infinite resources of commerce, wealth, and power of the English nation. I heard him."

Yet his lordship had earlier only implied what Mr. Morris now made explicit. "'Mr Quincy,'" he said, "'you are a man' &c. (flummery.)"—that is, you are a gentleman of discrimination and influence and perspicacity and so on. Then Morris got down to business. You have talked to administration. You have discovered here no wish to injure, much less oppress the colonies. Government wants only to see America free and happy. "You must be sensible of the right of Parliament to legislate for the colonies, and of the power of the nation to enforce their laws. No power in Europe ever provoked the resentment, or bade defiance to the power of this island, but they were made to repent of it. You must know your countrymen must fail in a contest with this great and powerful people. Now as you find how inclined administration are to lenity and mildness, you should, you ought, to write to your friends this intelligence, and endeavour to influence them to their duty. I do not doubt your influence would be very great with them, and you would by this means be doing a lasting service to your country."

Thus, the sensible commissioner sought to show a way around the present deadlock. And soon afterward, Lord Dartmouth took his turn. Nothing that Dartmouth said (his lordship back in town and meeting with the American visitor two mornings later, November 24) varied substantially from what Mr. Morris or Lord North had told Quincy earlier. And like those others, the colonial secretary was all cordiality. "Lord Dartmouth," Quincy recorded of their interview, "being called out for a few minutes to attend the physicians of his lady, made his apology, and taking up a pamphlet that lay on his table said, 'I would entertain you with a pamphlet ("Observations on the Port Bill"), during my absence, but I fancy you have seen *this*. I think you know the author of it.' His lordship bowed with a smile, which I returned, and he retired for a few minutes."

Their conversation, when it resumed, continued through an hour and a half, during which Quincy again reverted to his dominant theme. "I was convinced," he told his lordship frankly, "that the American and British controversy would be much sooner, and much more equitably settled, if it were not for the malevolent influence of a certain Northern personage now in Great Britain."

That person, of course, was Dartmouth's new friend Hutchinson. In succeeding days Quincy found fresh confirmation of his opinion regarding the former governor of Massachusetts Bay. One informed observer, with access to Whitehall and Parliament, had "confirmed me," as Quincy wrote his wife, "that the people of Boston are not mistaken in the man whom they have most reason to curse of all others." More specifically, Hutchinson, according to the same reliable source, had been responsible for all the measures that England had taken against America. "I do assure you, America has not a more determined, insidious, and inveterate enemy than Governor Hutchinson. He is now doing, and will continue to do, all he can against you." Accordingly, when a "great officer of state" with whom Quincy soon found himself in conversation vouchsafed that the newcomer's presence in London would be of service to both countries, Quincy had been moved grimly if circumspectly to reply: "'There is a certain *influence* which will counteract all I can possibly do.' I was understood," he adds, "*not* to mean a *British* influence."

And yet with much about English attitudes to deplore and almost frantically busy as he was, the young man was having the time of his life. Scarcely an hour of these first days in the capital could Quincy call his own. "The friends of liberty," he wrote, "and the friends of the ministry, engross my whole time. I am in a delicate situation. I have a very difficult task. Each party makes great professions of friendship." Even so, "(save the concern I feel for my country) I have high pleasure. My health is good beyond example, and my spirits are truly American"—all his thoughts running faithfully on his homeland. "Tomorrow I am to see Lord Chatham [a meeting that, for whatever reason, did not take place]. In the afternoon I am to dine with Lady Huntingdon. On Tuesday I am to go to the House of Lords, at the opening of Parliament, and on the same day shall converse with Sir George Saville. My whole time," he exulted on the 27th, "is dedicated to the common cause. My heart and soul are engaged in it."

But through such days to be alive, to be of consequence, to be in London!

14

THE KING BEFORE
PARLIAMENT

THE EVENTS THAT PASSED during Quincy's reception at the seat of
power in Whitehall had been set promptly and fully before Mr.
Hutchinson, who was keeping close tabs on the young man's activities in any case. London was enormous, but the world in which
those two moved within the metropolis was small. Often their paths
crossed, even if (surprisingly) no indication survives that either laid
eyes on the other during the months that both Americans spent in
the city. "I visited Mr Keene in the morning," Hutchinson, for instance, noted on November 15 in his diary, one of several such entries, whereas Quincy, in his, noted on the 28th (the day that he had
expected to be with Lord Chatham): "Dined with Mr. Keen," secretary to the lord chamberlain, member for Ludgershall, and
Dartmouth's brother-in-law. That same morning of the 28th, Quincy
had gone "to Westminster Hall and heard Lord Chief Justice
Mansfield deliver the opinion of the court, in Campbell's case of the
4 1/2 per cent. duty." Hutchinson likewise that day: "This forenoon I
spent an hour most agreeably in the Court of King's Bench hearing
Ld Mansfield give judgment in the Grenada Cause" concerning a li-
ability "to a duty of 4 1/2 p ct upon sugars, &c."

Did they see each other—they who had been in courtrooms together before—and not mention it in their journals? Was the courtroom so crowded? Had one left before the other arrived?

Again, on the 19th, the very morning of Quincy's interview with
Lord North, Hutchinson had been conferring with that same minister. His lordship had "wished to know what he [Quincy] was. I

informed him," the governor explained, "he was a lawyer, as inflamatory in Town Meetings, &c., as almost any of the party: that I fancied his errand here was to inflame the people by his newspaper pieces, and in every other way possible; and to give information to those at Boston, of the same spirit and party, what was doing here, and whether they were in danger."

Armed with that verbal caution, North had gone forward, and Mr. Hutchinson was not long in hearing the results of the interview. Whatever Quincy may have thought of the prime minister, North thought Quincy "a bad, insidious man, designing to be artful without abilities to conceal his design." The young American had entered 10 Downing Street (according to what Hutchinson was later told) with the explanation that his business in London was the recovery of his health, "but as he was here, he wished for an opportunity of waiting on his Lordship, and assuring him that the people of the Massachusetts must have been much wronged by the misrepresentations which had been made from time to time to the Ministry, and which had occasioned the late measures: that there was a general desire of reconciliation, and that he thought three or four persons on the part of the Kingdom, and as many on the part of the Colonies, might easily settle the matter."

None of that about reconciliation appears in Quincy's account of the interview. But as for misrepresentations, Lord North (again, according to what Hutchinson was told) had flatly disavowed being motivated by any representations or misrepresentations at all. Not words but deeds had signified: It was what the colonists had done—"their own Acts and Doings"—in denying Parliament's sovereignty that had moved government. The young Bostonian should be clear on one thing: The authority of Parliament over America would never be given up. Administration was adamant on that. Lord North was adamant. If the prime minister "should yield the point, he should expect to have his head brought to the Block by the general clamor of the people, and he should deserve it. This must be submitted to, and then he would give the most favourable ear to every proposal from the Colonies."

That, Hutchinson insisted, was about all that Quincy had been able to get from his lordship.

The interview with Lord Dartmouth had gone no differently. Again, Governor Hutchinson had been consulted beforehand, on the 23rd, the day before the colonial secretary's meeting with Mr. Quincy. Dartmouth had just received a copy of *Observations on the Boston Port-Bill.* "He asked me the character of the book, and of the man," Hutchinson recorded, "which, when I had given"—had the governor then read the pamphlet?—"he said he had seen letters from persons in Boston to persons of respectable characters here, recommending him as a person well disposed to bring about a reconciliation between the Kingdom and the Colonies." Dartmouth would meet with the emissary. Very well, but Hutchinson took care that his lordship should know that the supposed peacemaker Quincy had called upon the scheming Dr. Franklin "the first day after he landed."

After the interview, Dartmouth himself "gave me," wrote Hutchinson, "a particular account of what passed between him and Quincy." Once more, the young man had professed that his health had been the cause of his coming, but while here, he wished to represent conditions in Massachusetts correctly: for instance, that the people would not soon become quiet and contented, that the councillors appointed had in general been persons the most obnoxious to the province, and more in that captious vein. In the course of their talk, Quincy did express the highest opinion of the illustrious Chief Justice Mansfield (whose court he would be attending with admiration in a few days), nor did the young man doubt that Lord Mansfield's was the sort of mind "capable of projecting a way to reconcile the Kingdom and the Colonies." The colonial secretary had responded dryly to that hint. "Lord D. asked if he"—Quincy—"had seen Ld Mansfield? He said No: he did not know how to be introduced to him, or to that purpose. Lord D. said he believed Lord M. was fully of opinion that the proceedings in Massachusetts Bay were treasonable." Treasonable? To that, all that "Q." could answer, weakly, was that "he knew the people in N. E. had no idea that they were guilty of Treason."

Here, as often, representatives of the opposing sides were speaking at cross-purposes. Yet they did speak, they and everyone else, English and Americans, with what on occasion seems almost too much cordiality, which may have served to obscure just how grave the crisis had become. All over London—in coffeehouses, dining rooms, drawing rooms, levees, taverns, assemblies, offices—people were using their shared language to express contrasting views about America through these late November days of 1774. The indifference of August was past. And by now, with many on both sides thoroughly engaged in the controversy, more than a few thought they knew precisely what ought to be done.

During two days immediately ahead, the 29th and 30th, a public event, spectacular and consequential, was to be enacted. Again, Mr. Hutchinson and Mr. Quincy would attend, and again with no indication from either of an awareness that the other was there. What they witnessed was the opening of a new Parliament.

In the summer and early fall, Benjamin Franklin had been writing his American correspondents repeatedly that firmness and patience among the colonists would bring about a new government in England, made up of legislators more friendly to America, legislators committed to repealing the extreme and futile measures of their predecessors. Law dictated that an election would have to be held by the spring of 1775; but what had happened abruptly, unexpectedly, the last day of September, was that the king had dissolved the present Parliament and called for elections six months ahead of time. "The chief motive," Horace Walpole, well-informed commentator on affairs in the city, had written when the news was fresh, "is supposed to be the ugly state of North America"; but whatever the cause, the surprise had caught the opposition ill-prepared. The political world was thrown into turmoil. "The first consequences, as you may guess, were such a ferment in London," according to Walpole, "as is seldom seen at this dead season of the year. Couriers, dispatches, post-chaises, post-horses, hurrying every way!"

The results of such bustling about were soon known. After the brief, intense campaigns for office, after the buying and selling of seats, after the balloting and counting of votes, the king's friends in the new Parliament had not only maintained but had strengthened their numbers. Henceforth, his majesty and his majesty's ministers could rely, even more confidently than before—and for up to seven years into the future—on parliamentary support for whatever policies they might determine to pursue.

Meanwhile, at the close of November, the king himself must open the new Parliament with an address. What would his majesty say? People wondered whether the troubles in the colonies would even be mentioned on so august an occasion. Walpole presumed the speech would be general in nature, as did Thomas Hutchinson: Friends in the know had told the governor that "the K. Speech will be very general, and will point out no measures." Parliament's authority was to be generally supported, and that was about as far in the direction of specifics as his majesty would deign to express himself.

For their part, Benjamin Franklin and his friends knew what the king *ought* to say. In the American Philosophical Society in Philadelphia is a brief work entitled "The intended speech for the opening of the first Session of the present Parliament viz. Novr. 29 1774." Scholars for two centuries have attributed the satire, reasonably enough, to Franklin: Though written in another hand, it is very much in Franklin's style, and rests among his papers. But David Hartley's was the hand that transcribed the document, and only lately has an author's rough draft, also in Hartley's hand, been uncovered elsewhere. Thus, the speech proves to have been the creation of David Hartley, parliamentary candidate for Kingston-on-Hull. That politician and Franklin were friends, however, and were seeing each other at this time. The doctor would surely have concurred with the good sense to which the speech gives expression.

Here, then, is what the king, if he were sensible, would say to the lords and gentlemen gathered before him. All of the recent enactments of the former Parliament, he would remind them—the Tea Act, the Port Act, the Government Act, the Justice Act, and the rest—have failed to produce in America what the ministers in Whitehall promised. "I therefore sent that Parliament apacking rather abruptly," his majesty would say, "& have called you in their place to pick a little advice out of your wise heads." An entirely new policy would be necessary. As for any program aimed at subjugating America, that would be "a seven or ten years job at least." Some were arguing that the colonies would soon be brought to heel, that Americans were "no better than a wretched pack of cowardly run a ways, & that 500 men with whips would make them all dance to the tune of Yankee Doodle." But the king knew better. The attempt to subject America to Parliament's will would cost not a farthing less than forty or fifty million pounds, and in imposing sovereignty, forty or fifty thousand Englishmen would "get knocked on the head and then you are to consider what the rest of you will be gainers by the bargain even if you succeed."

Even if you succeed, trade between the mother country and a ravaged land would be destroyed, and the expense of keeping America subjugated would be "certain & inevitable." However, should you lose the war, "should that connection which we wish most ardently to maintain be dissolved, should my ministers exhaust your treasures & waste the blood of your Countrymen in vain will they not deliver you weak & defenceless to your natural enemies"—to the ever covetous, ever dangerous powers of France and Spain?

In addressing Parliament, the king should reiterate that trade was where profits in the relationship between Britain and its provinces lay. Those who had advised against taxing America had been proven right. Attempting to shear colonists through taxes would not be worth the effort: "We should raise a cursed outcry & get but little wool."

Thus, the new Parliament must fashion an entirely different, more conciliatory approach to America, forgetting about taxes, furthering trade. Something like that would be the speech to his legislators of a statesman king. Yet Franklin's new friend Quincy could hardly have been expecting to hear such wisdom as he prepared to attend the opening, possessed of a rare ticket that influential acquaintances had managed to wrangle for him. In the event, this budding republican was able to keep his enthusiasm for what he did see and hear in check, as he briefly recorded two mornings of ritual:

"November 29th. Went to the House of Peers, saw the grand procession of the king, his reception of the new house of commons, in his robes and diadem, surrounded with his nobles and great officers. I was not awe-struck by the pomp." The spectacle reminded the Bostonian, in fact, of Milton's dour admonition: "The trappings of a monarchy will set up a commonwealth."

Next day: "November 30th. Went to the House of Peers; got to the foot of the throne, and saw the formality of presenting a new speaker by the Commons. Heard the king deliver his speech from the throne. Heard the Bishop of Litchfield and Coventry read prayers, as most bishops do," badly (in the opinion of an American dissenter), "without *grace* in the heart or expression."

Mr. Hutchinson's account of the same mornings is, by contrast, altogether more sympathetic. On the first of the two days, the governor had called on Mr. Keene yet again and heard further particulars about what the royal speech would contain, then had walked awhile in St. James's Park before proceeding to Lord Dartmouth's colonial office, with its windows overlooking Whitehall. From that comfortable vantage point, the governor had watched "the King go to the Parliament House, the parade of which was much less than I expected; but little appearance of state except the State Coach itself, and the ordinary Guards."

Of pomp, Quincy was seeing too much, Hutchinson too little. Next morning, the 30th, the governor with a friend called upon Lord Barrington, secretary at war, and spent nearly an hour in conversation on American affairs with that durable official. "He detained us so long that we had scarce time to dress to go to the House of Lords to hear the King's Speech." Dartmouth had given Mr. Hutchinson a card to show the usher, so that the American and his friends and daughter Peggy and son Elisha soon found themselves positioned advantageously—in fact, like Quincy, close to the throne. Thus, the two American adversaries could hardly have been standing more than a few yards apart in the throng.

"As I had not been present on such an occasion when I was before in England," Hutchinson wrote, "except once in a great crowd at the lower part of the House, and as I now stood near the Throne to great advantage, and had a pretty good view of the King upon the Throne, and the two Houses of Parliament, and saw the formality of the Speaker's presenting himself, and heard his Speech, and the King's acceptance signified by the Chancellor, and then the Speech in return by the Speaker, and after that the King's Speech from the Throne to both Houses, delivered with admirable propriety—upon the whole, I have received greater pleasure than I have done from any other publick scene since I have been in England."

Even more satisfied had been Hutchinson's son Elisha, writing his wife afterward in praise of the whole elaborate spectacle, the handsome figure that his majesty had made, the very tone of the royal voice—though neither Elisha nor his father had commented immediately on the words that the royal voice had uttered. In fact, what George III said on the occasion belied predictions, for the king spoke of public affairs altogether more bluntly and consequentially than had been anticipated.

He was addressing a nation uninformed about recent events overseas. Not for weeks had any news come from the colonies. Six days earlier, Walpole had reported that "the world is in amaze here that no account is arrived from America of the result of their General congress." Now, a week later, as his majesty was speaking before the new Parliament, still no word about what the American congress at its secret deliberations had decided to do, and apparently nothing for weeks and weeks had been heard from Boston. Troops, it was known, had been sent to reinforce Governor Gage's regiments, but that was about all that the public could learn of such matters. What would the colonial congress recommend? And what had been happening in Boston meanwhile?

Among much else, what remained undisclosed was that the king for his part had already made up his mind about the course he meant to pursue. Not two weeks earlier he had written privately to Lord North: "the New England Governments are in a State of Rebellion; blows must decide whether they are to be subject to this Country or independant."

"Blows"—that hearty, vacuous euphemism. But his majesty was in a mood to brook no compromise. The colonies must back down. Accordingly, addressing the new Parliament at the end of November, George III did not shrink from pronouncing publicly and specifically that "a most daring Spirit of Resistance and Disobedience to the Law still unhappily prevails in the Province of the Massachusetts Bay." Moreover, the rebellious spirit had infected other colonies. All the more reason, then, that the coercive acts must be enforced, all of them. The king's listeners, whoever and wherever they were, "may depend upon My firm and steadfast Resolution to withstand every Attempt to weaken or impair the supreme Authority of this Legislature over all the Dominions of My Crown."

The maintenance of parliamentary authority was essential to the welfare of the empire. The House of Lords and the House of Commons were therefore instructed to "proceed with Temper in your Deliberations, and with Unanimity in your Resolutions. Let My People, in every Part of My Dominions, be taught by your Example to have a due Reverence for the Laws, and a just Sense of the Blessings, of Our excellent Constitution." Whatever a wise monarch might have said, that is what this monarch did say. His colony of Massachusetts Bay was disobedient. Such unruliness allowed of only one remedy. Addressing this high forum, with the world's eyes on him, the sovereign had solemnly affirmed that the coercive measures enacted earlier against the colony were to be implemented to the full and that the authority of Parliament, at whatever cost to the empire, was to be upheld.

"The King's Speech, as it appears in print, is strong," Mr. Hutchinson was assuring an American correspondent soon afterward—and went on to add approvingly: "If you had heard him deliver it, with infinite propriety, you would have thought it much stronger."

15

A STRANGE SILENCE

ON THE AFTERNOON OF THE DAY of George III's appearance before the new Parliament—Wednesday, November 30—the House of Lords set about considering the customary vote of thanks for his majesty's gracious address. Moving for the address was Lord Hillsborough, a nobleman whom patriots among Americans had long ago learned to detest, Dartmouth's predecessor as secretary of state for the colonies. Hillsborough spoke for an hour and a quarter, finding occasion to read a letter of Mr. Hutchinson's anonymously in support of one opinion, and, in passing, to voice another dark opinion in the following terms: "There were," he said, "then *men* walking in the streets of London, who ought to be in Newgate, or at Tyburn"—in Newgate Prison or on the Tyburn gallows.

With that, a duke in opposition rose to observe that "he was surprised that his Lordship should cast such a heavy reflection on his Majesty's ministers, by suggesting a matter, which, if true, proved they were guilty of a gross neglect of duty" in not pursuing such criminals. Lord Hillsborough should make clear whom and what he meant. "Upon which"—the account of the exchange comes from Mr. Quincy himself, passed along proudly some days afterward to his wife back in Boston—"Lord Hillsborough rose, and pointed out, though not by name, yet so as every body knew whom he meant,—Dr Franklin and Mr Quincy. The latter gentleman he mentioned as *author* of a late publication, called 'Observations on the Boston Port Bill.'"

That would have identified well enough one of the two to be jailed or hanged. Incidentally, none of the three Americans of this present account—neither Dr. Franklin nor Mr. Quincy nor Governor Hutchinson—had been on hand to hear Lord Hillsborough's remarks that afternoon. Dr. Franklin was just now all unwittingly approaching the threshold of secret, fascinating negotiations that would occupy him through December and into the new year. His friend Quincy, after attending the king's speech that morning, had left the Lords and "spent the afternoon and evening with Mr Pearson and his friends." The following day, December 1, Quincy would dine with Mr. Rogers of the treasury, "in company with a commissioner of the treasury, two members of Parliament, and others." Then: "Went at six o'clock with Dr. Franklin to the seat of Samuel Vaughan Esq. at Wanstead, where we spent our time very happily till Saturday night."

As with Quincy, so with Hutchinson, who had also left the House of Lords after the king's address on the 30th and before Lord Hillsborough had risen to speak. Returning home, the governor learned that that same Hillsborough, addressing his peers in the afternoon, had earlier sent a servant "to desire to speak with me." Accordingly, Hutchinson called next morning on his lordship "and found that he [had] wanted my leave to read one of my letters to the House of Lords, and not seeing me had ventured to read it without leave. It gave me concern until I heard what letter it was, and I think it would have been better to have omitted even that, especially as both Ld North and Ld Dartmouth had seen it, and must know where he had it."

We understand the governor's reluctance to have more of his private correspondence made public. Yet Hutchinson's intimate involvement with ministers and other officials in administration, whether confirmed by his letters or not, was widely taken as fact around London these days. Quincy heard reports of it everywhere he went. Commissioner Morris, over dinner December 6, assured the American that the governor's advice had been closely attended to "in the late measures against the colonies," though the commissioner did go on to say that "government had found that many things had turned out different from Mr Hutchinson's representation, and that things had not been at all conformable to what he foretold." Calling on Quincy the following day, Mr. Williams repeated his conviction (as the former recorded) "that Governor Hutchinson was the sole cause and presser-on of the measures against Boston and all America. 'It is his advice that dictated the steps of administration, and it is his present opinion and assurances that keep up the spirits and measures of the ministry,' were his very words." A few days later, Quincy noted that Lord Shelburne, friend of America, "confirmed my former intelligence of Governor Hutchinson's assiduity, assurance, and influence."

By now all doubt had been removed, so the patriot could write about the matter confidently (if, to foil the censors, guardedly) to those back home:

"Will you believe me," he submitted, "when I tell you, that your letting a certain character escape from your justice is imputed to you on all hands as a fault. Your enemies impute it to your cowardice; your friends to your want of political sagacity. Certain it is, that from one man,—from one man, I say, and he neither a Bute, a Mansfield, a North, or a Bernard [each a Briton], are all your miseries supposed to flow. . . . 'It was his [an American's!] advice that dictated the steps of administration, and it is his present opinion and assurances, that keep up the spirits and measures of the ministry,'—were the very words uttered to me, not twenty minutes ago."

In fact, such an evaluation considerably overestimates Mr. Hutchinson's influence. These days the governor knew little more about administration's plans and purposes than Quincy did. As far as Hutchinson could tell, there hardly seemed to be a plan at all. What with the holy days looming, and still no word from Boston and no word from Philadelphia, the plan, if it could be called such, appeared to be to wait. Wait to hear, and even then do nothing until after the Christmas holidays, during which time the new Parliament would be recessed in any case, not to convene again until late January.

In Hutchinson's tentative phrasing, December 10: "A general plan, I have reason to think, is forming to provide for all events; but the completion of it I suppose is deferred for want of news from Philadelphia and Boston."

In the meantime, if hard news was scarce and plans put off, there was abundance of gossip and rumor in drawing rooms or over dining tables to fill the interval until facts could arrive from beyond the sea to set a response in motion. Rumors, as always, flourished where news was suspended. Quincy had been complaining November 27, "Not a line yet from America; judge of my impatience to hear of your welfare." Eight days later, Governor Hutchinson noted, December 5: "It's now nine weeks since we have heard from Boston." And Quincy again, to his wife on the 7th: "I have had no tidings of you since I sailed"—since way back in September, two and a half months and not a breath of news from family and friends. Nor would it be until yet another full week had passed, not until December 14, that the patriot could finally write of receiving letters at last, months out of date, from his wife and father.

But in the absence of news before mid-December, Quincy and Hutchinson both had heard rumors galore. There was talk of a proclamation to be issued that would declare recent proceedings in Massachusetts treasonable and would offer pardons to all who took an oath of loyalty within a specified time, "except such persons as should be named"—Samuel Adams, of course, Hancock, and one or two others whose excesses may have put them beyond forgiveness. There were rumors of high dissatisfaction with Gage's tameness in the execution of his office; rumors of British merchants planning to meet to petition government to conciliate; rumors that the Americans had formally expressed a willingness to accept a settlement of present differences on the basis of a restoration of the empire to its status before the Stamp Act. Most alarmingly, Quincy heard a rumor that peremptory orders had been issued to General Gage in mid-autumn instructing him to proceed to extreme measures: "BOSTON WAS NOW IN ASHES." Relaying that appalling word westward into the silence, "You will not think," he wrote, "my own bosom free from anxiety!"

And still nothing certain arrived, while gossip swirled as well through London. Hutchinson learned that Mr. Quincy had tried to secure an introduction to Lord Mansfield, only to be rebuffed; the distinguished jurist had not cared to speak with the young man from Boston. Everyone, it was said, even the last holdouts, had given Dr. Franklin up, after his astonishing public statement a year ago admitting responsibility for forwarding the letters. Lord Chatham was pronounced alert, his partisans mustering—he meant to make a bustle when Parliament reconvened. Franklin's post office accounts were in shameful disarray. Quincy had been giving it out that he had not asked to see Lord North; rather, the prime minister had asked to confer with *him*, whereas in fact, the American had simply appeared impertinently in his lordship's anteroom, in place of the messenger supposed to have been sent for North's negative reply to the earlier request for an interview.

Rumor and gossip, gossip and rumor, and unwearying social calls, unflagging dinings in company fill the relevant diaries of these tense days. Finally, however—"This kingdom never saw a time in which the minds of all ranks were more upon the rack with expectation"—hard news did arrive from over the ocean to give rumor and gossip pause. December 13 brought the eagerly awaited results of the general congress's deliberations in America. "The long-expected sloop is arrived at last," Horace Walpole pronounced, "and is indeed a *man of war!*"

The American congress had voted defiance, and on a continental scale.

If government in Westminster had no plan, delegates in Philadelphia had fashioned a plan to follow that was forthright and unequivocal. This was the congress's plan, as the English people were now to learn. After a certain date not far off, and until all of the coercive acts were repealed, no more British goods would be imported anywhere in America. No British goods were to be consumed. No American goods were to be exported to England, Ireland, or the West Indies. In every colonial town and village were to be formed so-called "associations," of citizens committed to making sure that their fellow townspeople complied with the embargoes. Moreover, if in the future British troops in Boston should commit any hostile act, the other provinces were agreed instantly to come to the aid of that embattled port. And, Walpole reported, congressional delegates had prepared statements setting forth their case, to be forwarded to London. One, "in the nature of a petition of rights, shall be sent to the King; another to the House of Commons; a third to the people of England."

To General Gage in Boston—as to many in the mother country—the congress's secret work, at last made public, seemed a "piece of Insolence," an insult, a calculated provocation. Dartmouth regarded it as such. The day after word from Philadelphia had finally reached Whitehall, Mr. Hutchinson called on the colonial secretary there. His lordship "gave me the result of the Congress to read and to return, and asked me what could be done? but added, there was no doubt that every one who had signed the Association, was guilty of Treason: and if he was to be directed by the resent-

ment natural upon the first news of such an insult, the most vigorous measures would immediately be pursued in order to punishment; but it was an affair to be well considered, and deliberated
upon."

The governor was moved to wonder aloud whether the arrival
of the news might mean that Parliament would act before adjourn-
ing for the Christmas holidays. Although unsure, his lordship
rather thought not.

That was regrettable; Hutchinson was longing for government to
move decisively. Why delay longer? "Since," as he put it in his
diary a few days afterward (in the limp prose of which he was
sometimes capable), "the last accounts are so full that there can be
no doubt of the intentions of America to refuse submission to the
late Acts, it is a matter of speculation for what reason American
matters are deferred until after the holidays." This expatriate
wanted the Boston incendiaries put down, the empire saved, peace
restored over there, so that he and his family might return home to
a province where friends and addressers could flourish as of old.
Government should act at once to bring those desirable ends
about.

Yet when it came to it, what could government do? The secretary
for the American Department might well wonder, might well—on
receipt of the congress's resolutions—have asked his friend
Hutchinson "what could be done?" Since as long ago as mid-
October, confronted with the earliest of Governor Gage's bleak,
alarming dispatches, Lord Dartmouth had been wrestling with
that question. Gage had written that the coercive acts could be enforced only by conquering New England; but his call for vast numbers of troops—twenty thousand of them!—to effect such a conquest could not be answered from ill-equipped Britain, certainly
not before spring, even in part.

What else might be done then? In casting about for something to
recommend, Dartmouth had suggested in a secret dispatch that
Governor Gage might disarm the inhabitants of Massachusetts,
Connecticut, and Rhode Island. But only picture the impossibility
of it: all those farmers and militiamen outward from Boston with
their muskets tucked away!—although his lordship did add:
"Whether such a Measure was ever practicable, or whether it can
be attempted in the present state of things you must be the best

judge; but it certainly is a Measure of such a nature as ought not to be adopted without almost a certainty of success, and therefore I only throw it out for your consideration."

As for that, in the current state of affairs, the governor-general on the spot must finally decide what to do. Dartmouth could offer little practical help. "I am sensible, Sir"—this as far back as October 17—"that in the present critical situation of The King's Affairs in North America, and more particularly in New England, every thing depends upon your fortitude, & discretion. Your conduct must be governed by occurrences as they arise; for you must be sensible that it would be very difficult, at this distance, to add any thing to the Instructions you have already received."

Yet those instructions, the essence of them, had been contained in a letter dated as long ago as last April, delivered to General Gage before his departure from London to assume his new role as governor of Massachusetts Bay. By now, eight months later, the king's affairs in North America were transformed utterly from when the orders had been devised. In Boston now, as his majesty's ships held to their blockade of the harbor, the British general and his forces on land wore more the appearance of the ones bottled up, inside their peninsular garrison behind new fortifications at the Neck. Through what had mercifully proved to be a mild, long fall, Gage had barely been able to get his troops out of their thin tents on the town common and into barracks in time for winter, local carpenters having refused all help in erecting the housing. Supplies were in jeopardy: Scows transporting bricks had been mysteriously sunk, loads of lumber overturned, hay burnt. British troops were being urged persuasively to desert, so that numbers of them already had. Councillors and other loyalists had meanwhile continued fleeing into the troubled town, crowding to their only safety, and dared not risk venturing forth to the mainland again, where patriots—militias, mobs, freeholders—had matters their own way entirely.

On the mainland, beyond Gage's fortifications, colonial patriots over the autumn had formed a provincial congress—in Hutchinson's judgment more treasonous than was the Continental Congress in Philadelphia. The provincial congress had met first in Concord, then in Cambridge, and set itself up as an alternative local government, replacing the defunct legislative assembly and

inoperative council. It had named a treasurer to gather funds and a
Committee of Safety as directorate to make policy, and it had issued orders to the various militias around Massachusetts to form
into companies and elect new officers and gather military supplies—tents, cartridges, spades, and such—and perfect their fighting skills. And all the while, food and money were continuing to
arrive from elsewhere in New England and beyond, passing over
the Neck to mitigate the penal effects of his majesty's vaunted harbor blockade.

Faced with all that, the mild Gage had gone as far as to hint to
his superiors through a letter to Mr. Hutchinson that the coercive
acts might better be temporarily suspended, until additional
troops could be mustered on New England soil from elsewhere in
the empire. The spinelessness of such a suggestion had left government sputtering. Be assured that this time, unlike on earlier occasions—with the Stamp Act and the Townshend duties—there
would be no repeal or suspension of an act of Parliament. In that
connection, the colonial secretary, on December 10, forwarded
Governor Gage printed copies of the king's recent speech, wherein
was affirmed that colonial measures were to be enforced at whatever cost.

Forwarded as well were the supportive addresses of lords and
gentlemen in response to their sovereign, "which were passed in
both Houses by a very great Majority. . . . The Resolution,"
Dartmouth summarized in a passage rife with emphatic capitals,
"of both Houses to support those great Constitutional Principles
by which His Majesty's Conduct hath been governed, and their entire Approbation of the Steps His Majesty has taken, for carrying
into Execution the Laws passed in the last Session, will, I trust,
have the effect to remove those false Impressions, which have been
made upon the Minds of His Majesty's Subjects in America, & put
an end to those Expectations of Support, in their unwarrantable
Pretensions, which have been held forth by artful & designing
Men."

The king's address must serve as government's plan for now.
Make clear that the laws were to be enforced with firmness, at all
costs; and presumably colonial resistance would dissipate. To be
sure, before Parliament adjourned, Lord North as first minister did
rise to say that he would be presenting a plan himself—some de-

parture from what was currently passing for policy—for dealing with America "as soon as the Holidays were over." That was on December 16. Shortly thereafter, Westminster fell quiet, and London itself seemed to adjourn for the season.

"There's a strange silence upon American affairs," Hutchinson noted three days later, "to me unaccountable, considering the importance of them, unless it proceeds from amazement." Yet the silence deepened, and in time became all but tangible. The governor visiting Whitehall found every office inactive, the undersecretaries at the colonial office (as he wrote with dismay) "lownging." Dreary winter noontimes grew as dark as night, shop candles burning through the midday smoke from the thousands of chimneys. And traffic thinned, so that beyond Hutchinson's window the normally noisy street had become as quiet as Saturday evening in God-fearing Boston. By nine at night, he noted, coaches were done passing outside.

In all that new quiet, the governor did manage a talk with Lord North before the prime minister departed for the country. This was on the 22nd. A couple of days earlier, Hutchinson had heard that the petition to his majesty from the Continental Congress was now in Dr. Franklin's hands; from Lord North at his levee he was to learn more about that impertinent document. "He observed to me," the governor recorded, "that he had seen the Petition, and asked if I had seen it? and upon my saying I had not, he gave me an account of it." North explained that the American congress had set forth a number of so-called grievances and prayed his majesty for relief from them. However, nowhere, the minister was pleased to notice, did the document deny the right of Parliament to pass whatever laws were necessary to administer the empire. Hutchinson reminded his lordship that the congress had produced other documents besides the petition that did deny that parliamentary right. "Yes, he repeated my words, they accompany it with papers which deny the Right. He added, he thought it a poor composition. That, I thought might be owing to the amendments proposed by one and another of the many members."

The governor did sense, in talking with the prime minister, that his lordship would have been happy to have found something in the petition that might have served as a basis for accommodation between colonies and mother country; and that if it had not been for the various outrageous addresses and the illegal association to enforce the embargoes, "the Petition would have been attended to"—that is, answered favorably. For now, Hutchinson learned, the document was in Lord Dartmouth's hands, carried there by Dr. Franklin as agent for the Massachusetts Assembly.

What would come of this? Where was the way out? Mr. Keene had an idea. The governor had called on Dartmouth's brother-in-law the day before his talk with Lord North, and in the course of their conversation, Keene had ventured a simple suggestion for ending all the difficulties between America and England. He had "asked whether it was not better to give up to the Americans, than to be at the expense necessary to reduce, and afterwards secure them? And," Hutchinson adds incredulously in noting so extraordinary a thought, "he appeared to be serious."

Let them go in peace, and thus salvage the lucrative trading arrangements. But such a "solution" was preposterous. Year's end, December 31, saw a visit with the more sensible Dartmouth, whom the governor found to be "more free upon America than he has been of late. He read to me the long Petition to the King from the Congress. It is artful, and full of duplicity."

Congress's petition would be but one of numerous colonial matters left to deal with in the new year 1775. But for now London remained empty, the ministry idle, and Parliament in adjournment until January 19. Under those vexing circumstances, Governor Hutchinson and his family might as well venture on a change of scene themselves.

January 6: "About a quarter after nine we set out from St. James's Street, in a coach with four post horses for Bath: made our first stage at Hounslow, the next Maidenhead, then Reading, and a quarter after five put up at the Castle Inn in Speenham Lands, 58 miles, which is more than at the rate of 8 miles an hour for the time we were in the coach"—a good beginning on the way to the celebrated watering place in western England. Mr. Hutchinson and his family would reach Bath on January 7.

No more than a few days earlier, the governor's enemy Josiah Quincy had set out from London bound for the same destination.

16

PEACE PLANS

THE PETITION TO HIS MAJESTY, approved by the general congress in Philadelphia on October 26, was in London by December 17. Mr. Hutchinson, as we know, had learned of the contents of the document through the prime minister, Lord North, who had discussed it with him even as his lordship was adjudging the effort to be badly written. And by the colonial secretary, Lord Dartmouth, Mr. Hutchinson had been privileged, the final day of 1774, a week or so before heading off for Bath, to hear the document read aloud. What the governor had heard sounded "artful" to him and "full of duplicity."

Not everyone shared such negative opinions of the petition as did Hutchinson and Lord North. The great Chatham, for one, would rise in the House of Lords early in the coming year to venture his own passionate judgment of that and the various other publications of the American delegates, who until now had been hiding their deliberations behind an impenetrable veil of secrecy. "For genuine sagacity," Chatham would tell the peers, "for singular moderation, for solid wisdom, manly spirit, sublime sentiments, and simplicity of language, for every thing respectable and honourable, the congress of Philadelphia shine unrivalled."

Chatham had been shown the petition to his majesty through the good offices of Benjamin Franklin, who had remained in England all this while in part to receive the grievances of the Continental Congress and lay them before the appropriate authority. Lord Dartmouth as colonial secretary was that authority. Dartmouth, in turn, had received the petition from agent Franklin on December

21 and, after hesitating (the congress after all was an irregular if not illegal body), had consented to pass it on for his majesty's consideration and relay the king's response when it was given.

Reading now the words that Lord North's eyes rested on, the words that Lord Dartmouth would soon read aloud to Governor Hutchinson, one wonders how anyone could have faulted a manner of expression so clear and temperate. Nor are artfulness and duplicity at once apparent in what the American delegates had composed. The document, addressed to "the King's Most Excellent Majesty," at least begins respectfully enough: "MOST GRACIOUS SOVEREIGN, We your Majesty's faithful subjects" of twelve American provinces—all of the original thirteen but Georgia—"in behalf of ourselves and the inhabitants of those Colonies who have deputed us to represent them in General Congress, by this our humble Petition, beg leave to lay our Grievances before the Throne."

Specific complaints are then set down, sixteen of them. A standing army was being maintained in the colonies without the consent of the assemblies there. The commander in chief of that army had been appointed governor of a colony. Commerce had been burdened with new and oppressive restrictions. Many new administrative offices—of customs and the like—had been created. Judges were now receiving their salaries from the king rather than from the Assembly representing the people over whom they presided. Councillors were being appointed by his majesty rather than being elected by the Assembly. Assemblies had on occasion been injuriously dissolved. Agents of the Assembly had been "discountenanced," embarrassed and disapproved of in London. Government had ignored earlier humble and reasonable petitions. And in the last session of Parliament, other acts had been passed to block up Boston Harbor, unilaterally to alter the charter of Massachusetts Bay, and to empower the governor of that province to send people indicted for murder to another colony or to England for trial, thereby allowing offenders to escape just punishment.

To such a sovereign as now rules Great Britain, "the bare recital of these Acts must, we presume, justify the loyal subjects, who fly to the feet of his Throne, and implore his clemency for protection against them." The petition goes on to identify a "destructive system" of administering the colonies, "adopted since the conclusion of the last war," as the source of all the present "distresses, dangers, fears and jealousies, that overwhelm your Majesty's dutiful Colonists with affliction; and we defy our most subtle and inveterate enemies to trace the unhappy differences between Great Britain and these Colonies, from an earlier period, or from other causes than we have assigned."

The colonists were aspiring to nothing novel. Indeed, "so far from promoting innovations, we have only opposed them"—have sought only for a return to conditions before the Stamp Act—"and can be charged with no offence," the petitioners declared, "unless it be one to receive injuries and be sensible of them."

Hence, the present petition. Colonists were responding to injuries inflicted. What follows—whatever else may be said of it—is anything but badly written; yet Mr. Hutchinson would doubtless have heard these words as duplicitous. Circumstances have obliged the delegates to entreat the royal attention, "and as your Majesty enjoys the signal distinction of reigning over freemen, we apprehend the language of freemen cannot be displeasing. Your Royal indignation, we hope, will rather fall on those designing and dangerous men, who, daringly interposing themselves between your Royal person and your faithful subjects, and for several years past incessantly employed to dissolve the bonds of society, by abusing your Majesty's authority, misrepresenting your American subjects, and prosecuting the most desperate and irritating projects of oppression, have at length compelled us, as by the force of accumulated injuries, too severe to be any longer tolerable, to disturb your Majesty's repose by our complaints.

"These sentiments are extorted from hearts that much more willingly would bleed in your Majesty's service." Heretofore, the petitioners went on, we have lived in filial peace, devoted to our sovereign, venerating the state that gave birth to our ancestors. Thus, we "can derive no instruction in our present unhappy and perplexing circumstances from any former experience. . . . We ask but for Peace, Liberty and Safety. We wish not a diminution of the prerogative, nor do we solicit the grant of any new right in our favour. Your Royal authority over us, and our connexion with Great Britain, we shall always carefully and zealously endeavour to support and maintain."

The petition, in fact, had only one purpose: by obtaining redress of grievances to secure "relief from fears and jealousies, occasioned by the system of Statutes and Regulations adopted since the close of the late war, for raising a Revenue in America." Abolishing that system would restore the harmony between Great Britain and the colonies, "so necessary to the happiness of both, and so ardently desired by the latter. . . . In the magnanimity and justice of your Majesty and Parliament we confide for a redress of our other grievances, trusting, that, when the causes of our apprehensions are removed, our future conduct will prove us not unworthy of the regard we have been accustomed in our happier days to enjoy."

The delegates conclude pointedly by imploring a most gracious sovereign, whose glory can be advanced only in rendering his subjects happy and keeping them united, as the loving father of his whole people "not [to] suffer the transcendent relation formed by these ties to be farther violated, in uncertain expectation of effects, that if attained, never can compensate for the calamities through which they must be gained.

"We therefore most earnestly beseech your Majesty that your Royal authority and interposition may be used for our relief and that a gracious Answer may be given to this Petition." Then the signatures, of fifty-one delegates (Samuel Adams, John Adams, G. Washington, and the others), under a "sincere and fervent" prayer that his majesty may enjoy every felicity of a long and glorious reign over loyal and happy subjects, "and that your descendants may inherit your prosperity and Dominions till time shall be no more."

Franklin, having delivered the petition to Lord Dartmouth, had now to await the king's reaction to it. Meanwhile, as soon as he could find an unencumbered interval in what had become a particularly busy schedule, the agent set out into the country, to Hayes, two hours northeast of London, to transmit this latest news from overseas to Lord Chatham, as he earlier had promised he would.

Chatham, who received his visitor most cordially, read the petition and responded to it and the other proceedings of the American congress quite differently from government. The congress, his lordship assured Dr. Franklin, "had acted . . . with so much Temper, Moderation and Wisdom, that he thought it the most honourable Assembly of Statesmen since those of the ancient Greeks and Romans in the most virtuous Times. That there were not in their whole Proceedings above one or two things he could have wish'd otherwise. . . . The rest he admir'd and honour'd. He thought the Petition decent, manly, and properly express'd."

Clearly, opinions in England differed concerning America's response to the present crisis. If the differences could be exploited, if the various interests opposing government's policies could be united—and that hope in part accounted for the unusually active December that the always active Franklin was engaged in. Many, in government and out, were convinced that only firmness and force would serve Britain's ends in dealing with America at this late hour; yet some, outside government but perhaps within it as well, were persuaded that conciliation still offered plausible means for settling difficulties between the mother country and her colonies. And those who thought of conciliation thought often of Dr. Franklin, conversant with England and admired overseas, as the person best placed to mediate successfully between the opposing sides.

The doctor was often engaged thus in December, answering summonses to consider ways of averting the disaster of civil strife that threatened.

Yet he was not too busy to play chess. Back in November, in early November, an intermediary had approached Franklin asking if he would play a game of chess with a lady of distinction, a Mrs. Caroline Howe, eager to test her skills against the famous American's. She fancied, Franklin recalled later, that "she could beat me, and had requested him to bring me to her." Would the doctor be willing? Dr. Franklin was always willing to oblige a lady, but in the press of affairs he had thought no more of the matter until some weeks afterward, when the intermediary reminded him of his earlier acceptance of the challenge and reproached him for his negligence. He was urged to set a date when the match might take place. Accordingly on December 1, a Thursday, the doctor had appeared as invited at Mrs. Howe's home in Grafton Street.

The occasion turned out to be enjoyable. A widow in her fifties, his hostess proved to be "of very sensible Conversation and pleasing Behaviour"; so that after they had played several games together, Franklin most willingly consented to another chess party a few days later.

The second meeting occurred on December 4. This time, having played "as long as we lik'd, we fell into a little Chat, partly on a

Mathematical Problem"—in passing, Franklin noted that "this Lady, (which is a little unusual in Ladies,) has a good deal of mathematical Knowledge"—"and partly about the new Parliament then just met." What was to be done, the lady wondered, with the dispute between Britain and the colonies? "I hope we are not to have a Civil War."

In answering, her guest resorted to a bit of gallant language: that the two sides should kiss and be friends. Quarreling was of no use to either and could ruin both.

"I have often said, says she, that I wish'd Government would employ you to settle the Dispute for 'em, I am sure no body could do it so well. Don't you think that the thing is practicable?"

Indeed, Madam, it is—if, said Franklin, "the Parties are dispos'd to Reconciliation, for the two Countries have really no clashing Interest to differ about. It is rather a Matter of Punctilio, which Two or three reasonable People might settle in half an Hour." Yet the doctor could hardly serve as one such person. He thanked his hostess for her good opinion of him, but noted that "the Ministers will never think of employing me in that good Work, they chuse rather to abuse me"—remembering Wedderburn's hour-long invective in the Cockpit last winter and all the ministerial rage that had followed.

"Ay, says She, they have behav'd shamefully to you. And indeed some of them are now asham'd of it themselves."

Thus, the two chatted amiably on, all this the visitor taking to be no more than "accidental Conversation." In time he bade good afternoon to the lady and went about his business, thinking no further of the exchange. But on Christmas Day—exactly one year it was from the date of his costly note to the press that had revealed his role in the affair of the Hutchinson letters—Dr. Franklin was once more paying a visit to Mrs. Howe. And on this occasion, as soon as he entered, his hostess informed him "that her brother Lord Howe"—the lady had married a cousin, so that her married and maiden names were the same—"Lord Howe wish'd to be acquainted with me; that he was a very good Man, and she was sure we should like each other."

Franklin, of course, knew Lord Howe. Everybody knew Black Dick, Admiral Richard, Viscount Howe, head of a distinguished and powerful family, a favorite of the king's, an independent and moderate in politics, one of the most exalted of British naval officers. In his late forties, the admiral was nearing the summit of an already remarkable career, brave and resourceful enough to have won the admiration of the entire nation during the recent war. Franklin assured the hero's sister that "I had always heard a good Character of Lord Howe, and should be proud of the Honour of being known to him."

It happened that the admiral was nearby at the moment. "Will you give me Leave to send for him?"

By all means, if the lady thought proper. Mrs. Howe then rang for a servant, wrote a note, and within a few minutes Lord Howe himself appeared from his residence four doors away.

Introductions were made. "After some extreamly polite Compliments," Franklin recalled, "as to the general Motives for his desiring an Acquaintance with me," the admiral proceeded to say that "he had a particular one at this time, viz. the alarming Situation of our Affairs with America, which no one he was persuaded understood better than myself." Some of the admiral's friends—and they would, of course, be very high-placed friends—felt that no one could do more than Dr. Franklin to reconcile differences between the mother country and her colonies, if he would only undertake to try. The admiral of course was sensible of the ill-treatment that Dr. Franklin had received at the hands of the ministry, "but he hop'd that would not be consider'd by me in the present case." His lordship much disapproved of the ministry's conduct, and some ministers were themselves ashamed of it by this time "and sorry it had happen'd, which he suppos'd must be sufficient to abate Resentment in a great and generous Mind."

As an independent member of Parliament and a lover of the empire, Lord Howe for his part wished only to do what good he could in these difficult times, and toward that end he had sought this opportunity of learning Dr. Franklin's sentiments on how imperial differences might be settled. He hoped, wrote Franklin of the admiral—and in doing so illustrated the high level of civil discourse achieved in that social century—"he hop'd his Zeal for the public Welfare, would with me excuse the Impertinence of a mere Stranger, who could have otherwise no reason to expect, or right to request me to open my Mind to him on these Topics."

For obvious reasons, as the admiral went on to note, Dr. Franklin might not wish to have direct communication with the present

ministers or have it known that he was even in indirect communication with them. But Lord Howe was willing to serve as a means
of "conveying my Sentiments to them and theirs to me," thus
paving the way for negotiations that could later be acknowledged
publicly if they should prove successful.

At this point Mrs. Howe offered to leave the room, but Franklin
requested that she stay. He would have no secrets from her, "for I
had never conceiv'd a higher Opinion of the Discretion and excellent
Understanding of any Woman on so short an Acquaintance." The
three thereupon set about arriving at a way to proceed.

On the basis of the king's recent speech to Parliament, as well as
because of measures that government had talked of and already
taken, Franklin now professed himself skeptical of ministerial de-
sires for peace; yet he was prepared to be as useful in the present
instance as his "small Ability" permitted. Lord Howe assured the
American that "some of the Ministry were extreamly well dispos'd
to any reasonable Accommodation, preserving only the Dignity of
Government." Would Dr. Franklin draw up a list of conditions that
might serve as a basis for negotiations? They could meet again to
consider those conditions, say, on the Wednesday following, at the
admiral's house or the agent's—though (come to think of it) either
meeting place might occasion comment. That being so, it was
thought better that the three reconvene here at Mrs. Howe's, where
already "it was known we play'd together at Chess."

Such a list of conditions as the admiral asked for, which Mrs.
Howe was agreeing to disguise by transcribing into her own hand,
might appear redundant. Franklin mentioned that congress's petition provided just such matter to consider, and he even read aloud
some of the petition, the moving language of which "seem'd to affect both the Brother and Sister." Yet Lord Howe would be obliged
to the doctor for setting down acceptable terms as he himself understood them. Franklin agreed to try.

But when next calling by appointment at Mrs. Howe's a few
days later and again meeting with her brother, the doctor had still
to find time to do what he had said he would. "I apologiz'd," he
later recalled, "for my not being ready with the Paper I had
promis'd, by my having been kept longer than I intended in the
Country"—in part on his most recent visit with Lord Chatham. But
the two gentlemen, Admiral Howe and Dr. Franklin, found much

to talk of in any case, "and his Lordship told me"—words that affected the doctor profoundly—"he could now assure me of a Certainty that there was a sincere Disposition in Lord North and Lord Dartmouth to accommodate the Differences with America and to listen favourably to any Propositions that might have a probable tendency to answer that salutary Purpose."

Clearly, the admiral was speaking with authorization. The moment was an emotional one. Two years later, after the war that both would have averted had begun, Franklin had occasion in writing Lord Howe, then commanding the British fleet against America, to remind him sadly of "the Tears of Joy that wet my Cheek, when, at your good Sister's in London, you once gave me Expectations that a Reconciliation might soon take place."

For now, at least, if only for a moment, a way did seem opening that would circumvent calamity. And other faint gleams of hope had appeared as this present, stormy 1774 neared its end. Franklin had already earlier been asked by others to provide a list similar to the one that Lord Howe had requested. Two friends well connected, both peace-loving Quakers, had sought from the American terms on which the imperial differences might be adjusted in ways agreeable to both sides. Both gentlemen had access to individuals either high in government or of influence with those who were. One requesting such a list was Dr. John Fothergill, personal physician to both Franklin and Lord Dartmouth, who saw the colonial secretary virtually every day.

The agent had fashioned such a list in early December: "HINTS for *Conversation* upon the Subject of Terms that might probably produce a durable Union between Britain and the Colonies." For their part the colonies would pay for the tea destroyed a year ago and would agree to furnish requisitions to support imperial military efforts in wartime. Government for its part would repeal the various objectionable acts passed in the last Parliament. Moreover, any duties arising from parliamentary acts for regulating trade with the colonies would be paid into provincial treasuries for the public use of the colonies themselves. No troops would hereafter enter any colony without the consent of its legislature.

These and other such hints that composed Franklin's document had been taken by Mr. David Barclay and Dr. Fothergill to their unidentified contacts in or near administration—the whole affair, of course, shrouded in mystery, nor has time lifted the shroud very high off the corpse of such hopes. But after turning over his hints to the two intermediaries, Franklin had soon heard from an elated if circumspect Barclay that he had seen "a Person with whom he had been yesterday (before he call'd on Dr: F) and had the satisfaction of walking part of the way with him to another Noble Person's house, to meet on the *business*, and he told him, that he could say, that he saw some *light*."

Mysterious: Was the first "Person" referred to Barclay's diplomatic and well-connected friend Lord Hyde, and the other "Noble Person" Lord Dartmouth himself?

Franklin thought so. But one further matter, also promising, called for no guesswork on the American's part to interpret. This news was both encouraging and unequivocal. Promptly, on December 24, the busy agent for the Massachusetts Assembly had been able to report, by circular letter to the American colonies, that the colonial secretary had this day informed him of having brought the petition of the general congress to the king and "that his Majesty had been pleased to receive it very graciously, and to say, it was of so great Importance, that he should, as soon as they met, lay it before his two Houses of Parliament."

America's grievances were to be listened to at last.

17

Two Visits to Bath

DR. FRANKLIN HAD SPENT DECEMBER in part drafting conditions that might serve to resolve the quarrel between America and England. Josiah Quincy had been approached as well, early the same month, with that same purpose in mind: to help in specific ways to reconcile differences between the mother country and the colonies. On December 6, at ten in the morning, Mr. Commissioner Corbyn Morris had called on Quincy once more and stayed with him an hour and a half. "His conversation," the Bostonian recorded, "was much on the propriety of my laying down some line of conduct to which the colonies would accede, and by which the present controversy might be amicably adjusted." Mr. Morris had also urged his host to go wait on Lord North, wait on Lord Dartmouth again; further interviews with those two officials would be both proper and expedient. And meanwhile, know that the distress of our poor in England is formidable: the hedgers, the ditchers, the threshers. "'They are extremely poor, and wretched indeed,' Mr. Morris assured Quincy; 'every thing here is taxed to the utmost. The colonies must relieve us. They must ease us of our taxes,' &c. &c."

The patriot listened, recorded, but was unimpressed. He neither waited again upon Lords Dartmouth and North, nor did he, in any document that survives, set about "laying down some line of conduct to which the colonies would accede." Nevertheless, through these same days and nights of December, the young American was continuing to be tirelessly active. Writing his wife on the 7th, the evening after his talk with Commissioner Morris, "My whole time," the patriot assured her, "is taken up in my *duty*. I never was more busy. I never was more talkative." Three weeks he had been in London, with only two evenings given over to entertainment; only once had he taken time even to see David Garrick, though the great actor had been performing four nights recently on the London stage.

"You will wonder," he wrote, "how I spend my nights and days in serving my country; but in one word I find every body eager to hear, most people willing to be set right, and almost all grossly ignorant of the American world. I have been taught to believe that I have spoken conviction to many sensible minds."

All that exertion had, alas, within the last few days, brought about one alarming consequence, a "raising of blood again," a brief return of the tubercular symptoms that Quincy had been spared since boarding ship in September. He wrote his wife about it. "I have as yet had no symptom of taking cold since I have been in London, but incessant application,—incessant talking with several members of Parliament, and others, these four days past, has brought on a little fever, and some raising of blood. But otherwise I was never better in my life,—certainly I never was in better spirits. Do not be concerned about this circumstance. I would not have mentioned it but in fidelity to one, from whom I cannot conceal any thing which concerns my welfare."

Blood—however called forth—was on Quincy's mind as December advanced. Within a week, the patriot had come to feel, from all his conversing with friends of America and friends of the ministry, that England would never agree to terms until his countrymen had made clear that their very lives were committed to liberty. "Let me tell you one very serious truth, in which we are all agreed," he wrote Mrs. Quincy solemnly on the 14th; "*your countrymen must seal their cause with their blood*." But in forwarding home that somber thought, could the writer have been envisioning anything like the disastrous seven years of fratricidal warfare that loomed? Or did he rather foresee colonial determination demonstrated at some crossroads encounter, where a handful of patriots might be required to die for their beliefs, and in doing so conclusively persuade a repentant England to change course, replace the ministry, give in?

America must in any event, at whatever cost, hold firm. Quincy had learned that much from his conversations with Englishmen.

The many friends of the colonies among these English were reluctant to show their support until certain that America meant to hold firm. It was simple enough. Should they support the colonies prematurely, then learn that those same colonies had capitulated to England, such politicians in and around Parliament as had done so would find their careers ended, all advancement blocked—and not a public figure in England but was ambitious of advancement. Thus, even America's friends here planned prudently to wait and see. They needed to be sure: Were the colonies in earnest, or were they merely talk?

Foes were confident that the colonies were merely talk. Americans were too selfish, too greedy, too cowardly to stay the course. Quincy had heard those charges and read them repeatedly in the newspapers. The various provinces were too selfish to remain united. They were too greedy—too attached to "commercial leeks and onions"—to deny themselves comforts and amenities by observing the congress's boycott of English goods, any more than they had shown themselves able to maintain a similar boycott in 1770. And they were poltroons in any case, cowards and poltroons: That conviction about Americans, based on military ineptitudes in the French and Indian wars, was particularly and comfortingly widespread in England.

Yet liberty could be gained, Quincy insisted, if America only held firm, even to the point of spilling blood. Others corroborated his opinion. On December 12, he met with Lord Shelburne, Chatham's lieutenant and "a very warm friend to the Americans," who assured his Boston visitor that if the colonies "continued united they must have all they ask. He said the ministry would not be able to carry on a civil war against America; that they began to hesitate and would be obliged to give way."

Incidentally, how often through these months, and from all sides, is heard that same piece of wisdom: Hold fast in order to gain your heart's desire. General Gage had listened to the identical cry over the summer, from among the Tory side. Boston, he was told—and told Whitehall—was full of silent friends of government, delaying to declare their loyalty openly only until assured that the ministry meant to hold fast. Acts of Parliament had been repealed before. Might not they be repealed again? After government's friends among the Bostonians had declared themselves publicly, would this new Port Act and the other coercive measures be disavowed back in London, leaving those friends of a discredited ministry exposed high and dry in Boston, among their triumphant enemies?

Hold fast. Franklin through the fall had advised the colonies for whom he was serving as agent to persevere in *their* resistance, and they would win the support in England of merchants and manufacturers now silent but ready to speak out when assured of America's resolve—merchants sufficiently influential to have the present wretched ministry replaced. And the king just days ago had made it clear in addressing the new Parliament that he meant to hold to *his* course and see the coercive acts enforced at whatever cost, for the same reason: His majesty felt sure that when England's determination became clear, friends on both sides of the water would take heart and openly declare their support, while foes would be dismayed and their futile resistance would wither.

Each party was being urged, then, to believe that only adherence to its present course could lead to triumph—and the courses on which the two sides were set were dangerously angled toward a collision.

On December 16, Quincy was at the House of Commons to attend a last debate on American affairs before the holidays. There he heard Lord North explain what he had meant when earlier he had vowed to have America at his feet before he would deign to deal with the colonials. That notorious utterance had long rankled overseas, understandably; but what the prime minister had meant, he now explained, was merely that he would have the colonies petition properly for redress before he would consider their grievances.

The patriot Quincy found the explanation disingenuous. But Mr. Hutchinson also sat among the spectators in the gallery that day (and he and Quincy seeing nothing of each other?—again, neither mentions the other in his journal entry). Hutchinson heard Lord North likewise and thought he "spoke exceeding well: let them know the affairs of America were of that importance that they would force their way into the House, whether he inclined to bring them there or not." Accordingly, the first minister had promised on the occasion to return from the holidays at last with his own plan for settling the controversy.

Till then, all important questions were to be deferred. The holidays upon them, Josiah Quincy and two other Americans thus set out for Bath, on the other side of England, on December 29. Arriving at five the following afternoon, the sightseers went straightway that very evening to the famous Pump Room, and the last day of 1774 found Quincy uncharacteristically alone for two pleasant hours, walking the hills that encircled the splendid city, relishing a "most enchanting prospect" (as would walk Mr. Tilney and his sister with the innocent Miss Morland, all three young people equally absorbed a few years later, on the same site, viewing the same prospect, in the immortal imagination of an English spinster-novelist from Hampshire, sometime resident of this same Bath).

The present excursion of Mr. Quincy's to the west of England proved beneficial. There were visits with Dr. Joseph Priestley, Mrs. Catharine Macaulay, the Hon. John Temple, the colorful Colonel Barré ("I learned that he was once the friend of Mr Hutchinson . . . but that he had for a long time, and especially since his last arrival in England, wholly deserted him"). Quincy took a post chaise on January 3 and rode by invitation to nearby Bowood, at Calne, luxurious country home of the thirty-seven-year-old earl of Shelburne, that warm friend to America. "I met Lord Shelburne walking alone, at a considerable distance from his mansion-house, and alighted to walk with him over his grounds." The grounds proved extraordinary: an artificial lake, Roman ruins, sheep numbering a thousand. And inside the mansion, the elegant library, the beautiful paintings, "a very sumptuous table and very fine wines," two young sons most promising, one eleven, one seven, "very sprightly geniuses. They took leave of the company, on departing for bed, with much grace and propriety." Before such patrician hospitality, words failed this incipient republican. "Every thing," Quincy noted, "is great and truly noble; surpassing any idea that I can convey by my description."

On the 5th, returned to Bath, the sightseer ventured the twelve or fifteen miles to Bristol, second commercial city in the kingdom, where he arrived about noon. There Quincy visited the hot wells, the exchange, Radcliffe Church, and a coffeehouse within which he lingered, "surrounded by the intolerable racket of dice boxes, and the noise of party cabal," in order to write his wife yet again.

What he now had to tell Mrs. Quincy arose partly from conversations with Bristol merchants. He did not think much of them, did not think much of merchants in general, this lawyer. "You must know that I am a perfect infidel, in matters of mercantile virtue," doubting whether such types back home would forgo their profits to abide by any embargo. Perhaps they would. Perhaps America could obtain its ends peacefully after all, although the writer felt skeptical. One other matter, however, his recent talks had convinced him of. "The ministry, I am well satisfied, are quite undetermined as to the course they must take with regard to America. They will put off the final resolutions to the last moment." Unlike the colonies, the mother country still had no plan—nor would government devise a plan until some deadline or other forced it to.

On a personal note, the devoted husband could assure Mrs. Quincy with typical exuberance of his return to full health, after that single small quantity of blood raised and mentioned earlier. Since then he had had no symptom of the old disorder, "and at this time, and indeed ever since I have been in Britain, I never enjoyed greater health and spirits. This climate undoubtedly agrees with me much better than my own. Neither colds nor fevers have molested me, since sojourning in this land of my fathers."

Ending the January 7 missive, writing among the clatter of the Bristol coffeehouse, the patriot thought to attach a postscript: "Let our friend, Samuel Adams, be among the first to whom you show my letters."

That same date was seeing the arrival in nearby Bath, only a couple of hours away, of Samuel Adams's archfoe, and Quincy's, Governor Thomas Hutchinson, similarly diverting himself for the holidays. Hutchinson and his family entered Bath at four in the afternoon, found lodgings at Mr. Briton's in Milsom Street, and went to dine at the Bear. During their stay, these newly arrived Bostonians would unconsciously duplicate much of what that other Bostonian Quincy had done a few days before them, would call on some of the same people Quincy had seen: Mr. Temple, Lady Huntingdon (whom the patriot had recently visited in London), Colonel Barré (though the call, which Hutchinson made on his first free day in town, found the colonel out; Barré, who had assured Quincy shortly before of his and the governor's current coolness toward each other, is not recorded as having returned the courtesy).

But whatever sightseeing and visiting the Hutchinsons managed on their excursion had had to be delayed; for their first full day in

Bath proved altogether disagreeable. "8th.—A storm the whole day," wrote the governor, "so that I did not go out of the house. Billy, in the evening was taken very ill with, as I thought, a bilious cholick. I gave him a dose of Indian root, which, not working in an hour, and his pain being extreme, I sent for Dr Carleton"—a name recommended back in London—"who, by the help of camomile tea, set the vomit a-working, and afterwards prescribed a composition instead of castor oil, which I had prepared for him as a cathartick, which, after some 7 or 8 hours, had the intended effect."

The sojourn had gotten off to a bad start, and much in the days that immediately followed proved disappointing. Bath itself Mr. Hutchinson did find to be "perhaps the most elegant city in England, prodigiously improved within a few years, most of the buildings new," building stones uniformly and handsomely buff-colored, streets paved in the newest style, so that even after ex-tended rains "three or four hours of sun make them so perfectly dry, that you may walk about town in slippers." Ten thousand visitors were gathered in this watering place, "but nobody has the appear-ance of a stranger, and people who never saw one another before, are as familiar as those who have been intimately acquainted all their days."

One may wonder whether the governor found such familiarity to his liking. On the 9th—the day after Billy's bout with the colic—Hutchinson was taking time to answer a letter from his son Tommy back home, a letter dated September 15, more than three months in its passage. Three full months, nearly four: Not to have reached London till the evening of January 4! "I long," this absent father and American confided dejectedly to his son, "to return to you, which I say little about, and not only put on the best appear-ance, but take every method most likely to keep up my spirits, and chiefly for that purpose I made a journey here"—to Bath—"but I meet with no diversions or entertainments that are so agreeable to me as what I could find at home. Indeed, I had rather live in obscu-rity there, than in pomp and splendor here. I hope affairs will be settled this summer, and that the people will be convinced that their best friends are those who they have esteemed and treated as their greatest enemies. I hope the children will not forget me, or rather Peggy"—the governor's granddaughter—"for Tommy"—his grandson, born in Boston only two years before—"was too small to have any lasting impressions. Peggy"—their aunt here in England—"often wishes to see them."

These are not the thoughts of a contented man. "Elisha and I intend to go to Bristol to-morrow," continues the affectionate parent ("Yr Affect. Father," as he signs himself), "and the latter end of the week we all intend to go back to London. I had like to have said— to go home to London; but that I hope would have been a very improper expression."

With Elisha, then, the governor set out early next day in the post chaise to Bristol—as Quincy had done—arriving in time for breakfast at the American Coffeehouse. But the day provided little to lift the older traveler's spirits. The water at the hot wells was hardly even warm—not much different from Milton water, he noted—and consumptives all about. The cathedral offered "nothing worth observing." People at the exchange were dressed negligently, like ordinary tradesmen, "as different from the Londoners on 'Change as one city differs from another." Indeed, Bristol as a whole, with its mean houses and narrow, dirty streets, seemed to the governor "scarcely fit for a first-rate tradesman to live in."

He and his son got themselves on back to Bath that same evening. And all the time the father's thoughts fled overseas. By summer, he kept hoping, the present crisis would be settled; and meanwhile, of the day just ending: "The sun but little abroad to-day; the weather, notwithstanding, remarkably mild and soft, like an October day in New England."

Two or three more days of idling about Bath, making calls in the Crescent, attending at the Pump Room, looking in at the coffeehouses. Then on the evening of the 13th, Hutchinson learned that a vessel from Boston twenty-five days out had arrived in London bearing letters; nine letters and a large packet, he was told, had been left at his house. "I determined therefore to make all the haste I can to London."

Their holiday was cut short. The next morning about eight, the family was on the road precipitately eastward, getting as far the first day as Whitchurch, "where we lodged but tolerably."

Even lodgings disappointed. Little, in fact, about this venture had gone well. They got off the following morning again at eight, but not before the governor had left a tooth behind him. After the trouble it had caused, he was glad enough to part with it, "tho' with some additional pain; and I could not help a reflection as I was riding—that part of my body was gone, which I now felt no more affection for, than if it had been the tooth of a stranger. I could easily imagine the case to be the same with a finger, a hand, an arm, and so on to every part of the body, even to the brain, my thinking part still existing, and perhaps assuming some other better form, or the same materials moulded anew. In this reverie I remained for some minutes, the more easily from my situation at this time of life, so unexpected to me, three thousand miles from my country and friends, so that every scene has the appearance of a dream, rather than a reality."

The feeling may be recognizable yet—of days stretching into weeks of bemusement and wondering, of gazing vaguely about on city streets, in a line in a bank: Who are these people? Why am I standing among them? How did I arrive at this place?—

The travelers reached London about four. And after all their expedition, the letters that they had hurried back for held little of consequence. Governor Hutchinson took his, nevertheless, dutifully to the colonial office the next morning, January 16, and "shewed most of my letters to Ld Dartmouth, and afterwards I saw him at Mr Jno Pownall's, when Mr Pownall and Knox were present; but nothing very material passed."

Nothing much to the purpose could pass till Parliament reconvened three days hence. Meanwhile, January 18 was the queen's birthday. Mr. Hutchinson and his family, returned to the metropolis, went to court that day and found the place "crowded excessively." Lady Dartmouth graciously accompanied Peggy, and the loyal Elisha was in attendance.

In those celebratory crowds at court was also the high-spirited republican Josiah Quincy, he too back from his western travels. "Spent this day and evening," wrote Quincy irrepressibly on that same date, the 18th, "at St. James's in attending the celebration of the Queen's birthday at the drawing and ball room. The dresses were splendid and magnificent, much beyond any thing I had ever before seen. The Queen appears amiable and is very affable. The young Prince of Wales"—future regent, future fat George IV, now twelve years old—"resembles his mother in countenance and air very much. The *Bishop* of Osnaburgh"—another of the royal children, Frederick, age eleven—"is a very handsome *boy*. The little princes are comely enough."

Even in the sovereign's castle, in monarchy's very domain, the zest of this republican dissenter seems unquenchable. His life remains ever full of astonishments; words continue to fail him; one must see what he has seen to believe it all.

The very next day Quincy would take himself to Parliament House, to the House of Commons, in session again for the first time since December. Earliest on its agenda, the lower chamber was expected to consider the autumn petition of the American congress that the agent Franklin, through Lord Dartmouth, had laid before his majesty.

More wonders appeared to be beckoning.

18

IN THE HOUSE OF LORDS

RETURNED IN JANUARY from the holiday at Bath, Josiah Quincy had at once resumed his hectic London schedule of December, dashing about the town, meeting almost daily with Dr. Franklin and associates, conferring with politicians, writing at length to his numerous correspondents.

January 14, 1775, to Mrs. Quincy: "My best Friend, I was this moment closing my advices to you"—completing yet another long letter—"when I received from Mr Blowers," recently arrived from America, "your letter of October 15th, November 3d and 18th,—and my father's of November 3d. I am so fatigued with writing &c., that I *can write no more*. The person by whom I send this, goes in ten minutes. Thank my friends most heartily for their letters. Don't let them think I neglect their favours; they must consider my letters to you as addressed to them all. I am so hurried I have no other way."

But the busy patriot did take time to add reassuringly: "My health was never better. I have as yet had no symptom of a seasoning."

The following day Quincy dined with Mr. Dilly, the London bookseller and English publisher of *Observations on the Boston Port-Bill.* On the 16th: "Dined with Mr Brand Hollis, in company with Dr Priestley, Dr Franklin, Dr Price, and others." On the 17th, a happy occasion, an anniversary in Craven Street: "Dined with Mrs Stevenson," Franklin's London landlady of seventeen years, "with a number of ladies and gentlemen, in celebration of Dr Franklin's birthday, who made one of the festive company, although he this day enters the seventieth year of his age."

Would that such records had been more ample! (The group, by the way, would have reasonably assumed that the doctor's long, distinguished career was winding down, whereas in fact a full, eventful decade and a half of further glorious achievements lay ahead; young Quincy's was the career nearing its end.) On the 18th, Quincy ventured to court, as mentioned, for a different birthday, this time the queen's, on a date when troops in Boston as all over the vast empire were joining in toasting Queen Charlotte. And on the 19th, the Boston patriot was among the privileged spectators who saw Parliament recommence its legislative business after the holidays.

Again, however, Quincy's journal entry is brief and noncommittal: "January 19th. Attended the House of Commons and heard debates between North, Burke, and Mr. Eden, &c. Spent the evening at the London coffee-house with Dr Franklin, Priestley, Price, Calder, and many others."

No more detailed an account than that; the diarist provides not a hint that what had gone on in the Commons that day had proved disheartening to the American cause.

His friend Dr. Franklin wrote of the day's proceedings more fully. The doctor, with other agents for the colonies, had earlier been assured by Dartmouth, the colonial secretary, that his majesty had considered the petition from the general congress that the Americans delivered of such importance as to order it laid before Parliament as soon as the legislators reconvened in the new year. "We flatter'd ourselves from the Answer given by Lord D.," Franklin would write one Philadelphia correspondent after the fact, on February 5, "that the King would have been pleased to recommend it to the Consideration of Parliament by some Message; but we were mistaken." In the event, nothing was attached to the congress's petition to distinguish it from among a host of other American papers submitted at the same time that first day back in session: "a great Heap," as Franklin described those papers, "of Letters of Intelligence from Governors and Officers in America, Newspapers, Pamphlets, Handbills, &c from that Country." The petition was in fact the last listed, the very last—"No. 149. Petitions of sundry persons, on behalf of themselves and the inhabitants of several of his Majesty's colonies in America; received 21st December, 1774"—and laid on the table indiscriminately with the rest.

Nothing was done with item No. 149; no particular attention was paid to it.

Little was done in that opening day in the Commons in any case, so that when Mr. Hutchinson, for his part, was made aware of the routine inactivity of the session, he determined, to his later regret, to forgo attending the opening of the Lords the following day. "I lament," the governor noted in his journal for the 21st, "my not being at the House of Lords yesterday, imagining, as there had been nothing said in the Commons, there would not in the Lords, until a day was assigned."

But unlike in the Commons, a great deal concerning American affairs had transpired in the upper chamber on its first day back, January 20. That such would be the case had been communicated in advance to Benjamin Franklin, who had taken care accordingly to be on hand when the peers convened. His young protégé Quincy was at the Lords that day as well.

Franklin's English friend—and Chatham's—Lord Stanhope, had sent the American a note on the 19th, "acquainting me, that Lord Chatham having a Motion to make on the Morrow in the House of Lords concerning America, greatly desired that I might be in the House, into which Lord S. would endeavour to procure me Admittance." (The rule was that no peer, not even a Chatham, could introduce more than one friend to that august assembly.) The following morning, another note from Stanhope requested that Dr. Franklin be in the lobby of the house at two that afternoon; "Lord Chatham would be there about that time, and would himself introduce me."

Franklin met the earl on the premises of Parliament House at the hour appointed. After an exchange of courtesies, his lordship took the American's arm and led him along the corridor toward the door that entered the legislative chamber near the throne.

But a doorkeeper barred their way. Only the eldest sons or brothers of peers were permitted to enter the house through that door. Whereupon his lordship, wracked as he was with illness, "limped back with me to the Door near the Bar, where were standing a Number of Gentlemen waiting for the Peers who were to introduce them, and some Peers waiting for Friends they expected to introduce, among whom he deliver'd me to the Doorkeepers, saying aloud, this is Dr. Franklin, whom I would have admitted into the House."

With that announcement, the lower door was opened at once, and the crowds clustering around it stared; none had known that the celebrated, not to say notorious, American agent and Lord Chatham were even acquainted, much less that they had been conferring as allies and friends. Indeed, Chatham's appearance inevitably occasioned notice in Parliament House. Franklin observed that his lordship's presence in the lobby "caus'd a kind of Bustle . . . something of Importance being expected when that great Man appears, it being but seldom that his Infirmities permit his Attendance."

The agent for Massachusetts was thus this day admitted to Parliament under the most distinguished auspices. Josiah Quincy had gained admittance as well, by the more conventional means of a ticket to the gallery, and the younger man found himself advantageously stationed up there, "in one of the best places for hearing, and taking a few minutes," or notes, of what was said. Speeches in Parliament were not then officially recorded, but Franklin later judged the notes that the accomplished Quincy set down this January 20, of the various speeches that both were hearing, by far the best account of that day's debate.

No mean public speaker himself (the Boston Cicero, John Adams called him), Quincy on this occasion was to find himself utterly in thrall to the greatest orator of the age. In speaking, Chatham exhibited—through language, voice, and gesture—more emotion than his listener from overseas had ever seen or heard displayed publicly before, either in legislative assemblies or in courtrooms, here or at home. "He seemed like an old Roman senator," Quincy wrote, "rising with the dignity of age, yet speaking with the fire of youth," a "great and astonishing character," punctuating his successive thoughts with now a hand stretched forth with "decent solemnity," now a smiting of the breast "with the energy and grace of a Demosthenes."

It was, of course, an age that relished oratory. Never afterward, though the children of that generation, and their children's children as well, adored oratory (in America, too, where would thunder the voices of Daniel Webster and Henry Clay and Stephen A. Douglas), never again on either side of the water were so many superlative English speakers to gather together under the roof of a single edifice: among them Edmund Burke, Lord Camden, Charles James Fox, but above all the incomparable Chatham.

Now, in his premature old age, Pitt—the Great Commoner, Lord Chatham—had risen once more to speak on the American question, his first address before the Lords in eight months. Quincy recorded it, rapturously. The statesman began with some general remarks on the gravity and magnitude of the present quarrel between colonies and mother country. His lordship alluded to the dangers that the nation faced because of that quarrel, and with (said Quincy) "great severity and freedom" arraigned the policies of his majesty's ministers that had brought on those dangers.

Then Chatham addressed the tardiness with which the crisis was being met. "My Lords, these papers from America," he said, "now laid by administration for the first time before your lordships, have been, to my knowledge, five or six weeks in the pocket of the minister. And notwithstanding the fate of this kingdom hangs upon the event of this great controversy, we are but this moment called to a consideration of this important subject. My Lords, I do not wish to look into one of these papers. I know their contents well enough already. I know that there is not a member in this house but is acquainted with their purport also. There ought therefore to be no delay in entering upon this matter. We ought to proceed to it immediately. We ought to seize the first moment to open the door of reconciliation."

Yet such a door did not even lie along the path that government was currently pursuing. "I know not who advised the present measures: I know not who advises to a perseverance and enforcement of them; but this I will say, that whoever advises them, ought to answer for it at his utmost peril.

"I know that no one," Chatham elaborated, "will avow that he advised, or that he was the author of these measures; every one shrinks from the charge. But somebody has advised His Majesty to these measures, and if His Majesty continues to hear such evil counsellors, His Majesty will be undone. His Majesty may indeed wear his crown, but, the American jewel out of it, it will not be worth the wearing."

The current policies, his lordship went on, are utterly unjustified. "What foundation have we for our claims over America? What is our right to persist in such cruel and vindictive measures against that loyal, respectable people? They say, you have no right to tax them without their consent. They say truly. Representation and taxation must go together; they are inseparable."

Lord Chatham recalled that, in the last Parliament, all was anger
and rage. "The Americans were abused, misrepresented, and traduced, in the most atrocious manner, in order to give a colour, and
urge on the most precipitate, unjust, cruel, and vindictive measures
that ever disgraced a nation." And how had the colonials behaved
under their grievances? "With," his lordship adjudged, "unexam-
pled patience, with unparalleled wisdom." Without bribery, without
corruption, they chose delegates to a general congress. The delegates
met and spoke the sense of the continent. And when they speak,
said Chatham, these wise people "do not hold the language of
slaves; they tell you what they mean. They do not ask you to repeal
your laws as a favour; they claim it as a right—they demand it. They
tell you they will not submit to them; and I tell you, the acts must be
repealed; they will be repealed; you cannot enforce them."

The ministry are checkmated. They have, said his lordship, a
move to make on the board, and yet if they make that move, they
are ruined.

"My Lords, deeply impressed with the importance of taking
some healing measures at this most alarming, distracted state of
our affairs, though bowed down with a cruel disease, I have
crawled to this House to give you my best counsel, and experience." And what Lord Chatham would counsel, the motion that
his experience had urged him to lay before the house was this:

The Americans will never be in a temper or state to be reconciled—
they ought not to be—till the troops are withdrawn. The troops are a
perpetual irritation to these people; they are a bar to all confidence,
and all cordial reconcilement. I therefore, my Lords, move, "That an
humble address be presented to His Majesty, most humbly to advise
and beseech His Majesty, that in order to open the way towards an
happy settlement of the dangerous troubles in America, by beginning to allay ferments and soften animosities there, and above all, for
preventing in the mean time any sudden and fatal catastrophe at
Boston, now suffering under the daily irritation of an army before
their eyes, posted in their town, it may graciously please His Majesty
that immediate orders may be despatched to General Gage for removing His Majesty's forces from the town of Boston, as soon as the
rigour of the season, and other circumstances indispensable to the
safety and accommodation of the said troops, may render the same
practicable."

A simple, dramatic gesture. But by making it—by removing British forces from Boston to other localities, by calling some home—government will convince the colonies that it means to try the American cause not by codes of blood but by the laws of freedom and fair inquiry. As for Boston, "how can she now trust you, with the bayonet at her breast?" Treat the Americans as subjects, Chatham pleaded, before you treat them as aliens or rebels or traitors.

His lordship moved toward his impressive conclusion. "Thus entered on the threshold of this business," he said, "I will knock at your gates for justice without ceasing, unless inveterate infirmities stay my hand. My Lords, I pledge myself never to leave this business. I will pursue it to the end in every shape. I will never fail of my attendance on it at every step and period of this great matter, unless nailed down to my bed by the severity of disease. My Lords, there is no time to be lost; every moment is big with dangers. Nay, while I am now speaking, the decisive blow may be struck, and millions involved in the consequence."

Vatic utterance: Even now at some village green in New England—

But in closing, Lord Chatham hoped to be understood. "I would not by any thing I have said, my Lords, be thought to encourage America to proceed beyond the right line. I reprobate all acts of violence by her mobility"—by those menacing mobs in the streets of American towns and villages. "But when her inherent constitutional rights are invaded, those rights she has an equitable claim to enjoy, by the fundamental laws of the English constitution, and which are engrafted thereon by the unalterable laws of nature; then I own myself an American, and feeling myself such, shall, to the verge of my life, vindicate those rights against all men who strive to trample upon or oppose them."

That phrase of Chatham's: "I own myself an American." Mr. Hutchinson might well have regretted missing the opportunity of attending at such an oration, from such a source, however much he would have disagreed with the substance of what was uttered. As for Dr. Franklin, who did attend, he was delighted with what he heard. "I had great Satisfaction in hearing his Motion and the Debate upon it," and took pains to send copies of Chatham's speech to America, "and was the more pleased with it, as I conceiv'd it had partly taken its Rise from a Hint I had given his Lordship in a former Conversation."

The doctor is modestly alluding to a point made on his recent visit to Hayes over Christmas, when he had mentioned to Chatham, as he recalled, "the very hazardous State I conceiv'd we were in by the Continuance of the Army in Boston; that whatever Disposition there might be in the Inhabitants to give no just Cause of Offence to the Troops, or in the General to preserve Order among them, an unpremeditated unforeseen Quarrel might happen between perhaps a drunken Porter and a Soldier"—one recalls the account of a similar altercation recorded by Franklin's sister in November—"that might bring on a Riot, Tumult and Bloodshed, and in its Consequences produce a Breach impossible to be healed: that the Army could not possibly answer any good purpose there, and might be infinitely mischievous; that no Accommodation could properly be propos'd and entred into by the Americans while the Bayonet was at their Breasts: that to have any Agreement binding all Force should be withdrawn. His Lordship seem'd to think these Sentiments had something in them that was reasonable."

His lordship thought so assuredly—and had made the hint the basis of his motion. Yet it was all, the doctor said later, as the sound of the wind. The wisdom of Franklin, of Chatham, and of Camden and Shelburne and Rockingham and Richmond, who also spoke to the measure that January day in the House of Lords, "avail'd no more than the whistling of the Winds. The Motion was rejected." A dead majority, as Franklin termed it, of king's friends and bought votes made debate superfluous. Chatham's motion to remove the troops went down to defeat, 68 to 18.

In the aftermath, his lordship saw that his friend Dr. Franklin received promptly, as a mark of esteem, the notes from which the speech had been delivered, a gift that in turn elicited its own gracious acknowledgment. Lord Stanhope had transmitted the papers, and Franklin, thanking "his Lordship and Lord Chatham for the Communication of so authentic a Copy of the Motion," went on, in the third person that was conventional in such correspondence: "Dr. F. is fill'd with Admiration of that truly great Man. He has seen in the Course of Life, sometimes Eloquence without Wisdom, and often Wisdom without Eloquence; in the present Instance he sees both united, and both as he thinks, in the highest Degree possible."

Yet all that eloquence, all Chatham's wisdom had not changed governmental policy one whit; and indeed, during the debates in the Lords, supporters of the administration had made light of the readiness with which opposition felt free to censure when not obliged to offer detailed alternatives. Chatham had said at the time—and Franklin had heard him say—that he would not be one of those idle censurers, that he had thought long and hard about America and meant soon to lay before the house the results of his meditations, in a plan—an alternative policy—designed to heal the differences between colonies and mother country, and thus restore peace to the empire.

Franklin had wanted very much to know what Chatham's plan was, but in succeeding days of late January the American's time was so taken up "with Daily Business and Company" that he was unable to find ways to gratify his curiosity. Not until the 27th was he able at last to take a post chaise at nine in the morning into Kent, reaching Hayes, Chatham's vast estate, about eleven, there to meet with his lordship by appointment.

At their meeting, Chatham took Franklin entirely into his confidence, explaining his new plan in detail, reading parts of it aloud. Lord Camden had been consulted, but no other person was to know before the plan was presented to the House of Lords. Chatham "requested me to make no mention of it," Franklin wrote later, "otherwise Parts might be misunderstood and blown upon, beforehand, and others perhaps adopted and produc'd by Ministers as their own. I promis'd the closest Secrecy, and kept my Word not even mentioning to any one that I had seen him. I din'd with him, his Family only present, and return'd to town in the Evening."

Two days afterward, a Sunday, January 29, Lord Chatham in turn deigned to call on his confidant Franklin in Craven Street. For two full hours his lordship's resplendent carriage with its celebrated blue-and-silver livery stood at the curb before the American's doorway, "and being there while People were coming from Church it was much taken notice of and talk'd of, as at that time was every little Circumstance that Men thought might possibly any way affect American Affairs. Such a Visit from so great a Man, on so important a Business," the philosopher was human enough to admit, "flattered not a little my Vanity; and the Honour of it gave me the more Pleasure, as it happen'd on the very Day 12 month, that the Ministry had taken so much pains to disgrace me before the Privy Council."

What the two determined in conferring together that Sunday morning was that his lordship's plan must be presented promptly. The English statesman's health was, as always, precarious. News might arrive any day to make the plan "less seasonable." Or government might proceed along its course and later claim that if the plan had been produced sooner, it would have been attended to. Accordingly, Chatham determined to lay his bill before the Lords no later than this coming Wednesday, February 1.

But by now, and well before the end of the present month, a dark shadow had fallen over the days of Franklin's friend Josiah Quincy. Quincy, who on January 14 had been able to write his wife that his health had never been better, was scarcely a week beyond that date forced to note in the privacy of his journal, on the evening of January 23:

"This night, for the first time since my arrival, I was taken very ill with a fever and spasms."

The entry is portentous. The previous summer, in Boston, Quincy's affectionate loyalist brother had set down in writing a hope that God would preserve the ebullient young patriot "in health and longevity, the friend and patron, and at length the father of your country." Arresting phrase to appear so early: the father of your country. But on a cold January night in London these eight months later, any such hope was abruptly doomed. From now to the end of the few weeks remaining to him, Josiah Quincy, thirty years old, would never know health again.

19

MR. HUTCHINSON'S
WINTER

QUINCY HAD FALLEN ILL on the evening of Monday, January 23. That day the young man had spent once again at Parliament House: "Attended a long debate in the House of Commons on American affairs."

Thomas Hutchinson had attended the same debate and had recorded his impressions at length, in a style rather more sprightly than was the governor's custom. Hutchinson had noted the hostile Burke's flowering away "in an oratorical strain, with great verbosity; half his speech was aimed at Ld North, for suffering the Parl[iamen]t to go over so long, to eat his mince pyes." Captain Luttrell had spoken, professing that he knew Massachusetts well "and knew them to be destitute of money; scarce a man could command 100£," whereas, the knowledgeable Hutchinson remarked parenthetically, "it is the most flush of money of any Province in America." Mr. Innes had made "a short blundering speech," his odd manner "keeping the house in a roar"; Charles Fox "spake with fire, but nothing more than had been said"; and the well-fed North in addressing the Commons had sought to excuse the long adjournment while matters so important were pending.

By this time Mr. Hutchinson had come to feel that the resolution of those matters was, at any rate, out of his hands. The governor clung to the belief that summer must resolve the crisis one way or another; but for himself, as he had repeated to an American correspondent on the 19th (the day after the queen's birthday, with

Parliament finally reassembling): "I have despaired of being instrumental in bringing about the relief of Boston ever since the re-
fusal to pay for the tea."

Even so, the suffering of his native town continued to haunt him.
He had friends in Boston, friends loyal to the kingdom, innocent
merchants and tradesmen and lawyers with whom he corresponded; and those innocents, who had had nothing to do with the
Tea Party, were the ones being made to suffer by Parliament's measures, their businesses interrupted or in ruins, their lives in fearful
disarray, their Tory deprivations unrelieved by donations from patriots in the other provinces. During these weeks early in the new
year, Hutchinson in London accordingly spoke about what he
called the "ineffectiveness" of the Port Act to whoever among his
distinguished callers would listen.

Listeners might grant the justice of what the American was telling
them, but most were persuaded that any concessions offered now—
moderating the terms of the Port Act, for instance—would only encourage colonials to demand that all their other grievances be addressed. No, those to whom Hutchinson spoke were not in a mood
to make any adjustments whatever. The solicitor general this very
day, January 19, treated the governor, a guest in his home, to his own
quite different recipe for handling the controversy. Secure the heads
of the congress, Mr. Wedderburn advised; bring them to justice, declare them aliens. And another thing: Gage should use his troops to
disperse the mobs. If that led to bloodshed, why (this Scottish jurist
blithely concluded), a little bloodletting was not a bad thing. Had
not Scotland been better humored ever since some of its blood had
been spilled in the rebellion of 1745?

More and more people with whom the governor spoke these
days sounded like that. Hutchinson was aware of what a fellow
Bostonian was advising his constituents back home: "I doubt not,"
he said, "that Franklin will still write, encouraging his deluded
correspondents, that a strong party are in their favour." But the
governor's observations disclosed no such party: rather, only a few
opposed to the present ministry, a few divided among themselves
and ambitious of seizing power for their own purposes, which had
nothing to do with gratifying colonials.

It kept coming back to this, as Lord Dartmouth was assuring Mr.
Hutchinson on January 30: Whatever gestures government might

propose to placate the Americans would be "excepted to" in Parliament "as tending to encourage them in their claim of Independency by concession, of which they had always been ready to take advantage." England had given in before, and look at the consequences. England did not mean to give in by granting concessions now.

Possessed of that confirmatory opinion from the colonial secretary, the governor proceeded this same January morning, a Monday, to call on the earl of Hardwicke and heard that nobleman, whose public career reached back to the 1730s, lament that the present "was the most difficult time he had ever known."

It was difficult assuredly for Mr. Hutchinson, in large ways and small, suffering at the moment from a cold made worse by having attended yesterday, a windy winter day, at services in the drafty abbey. The governor's body was suffering, as was his mind. Tomorrow, the final day of January, on an excursion from Westminster into the city, that persistently anxious mind was to be apprised, through news off the packet just arrived from New York, of a recent and appalling patriot outrage in New Hampshire, news that would add to the governor's sense of just how hazardous the present times had become.

Last fall, the king, alarmed by information that colonials were acquiring gunpowder from Holland and elsewhere, had issued an order in council prohibiting any further such imports into America. General Gage had meanwhile moved to secure stores of powder in and around Boston, to the anger of New Englanders, who insisted that such supplies were the property of the provinces and the local militias. Now Mr. Hutchinson was to learn from the American newspapers that in mid-December last, "a mob of several hundred people" had stormed the lightly manned Fort William and Mary at the entrance of Portsmouth Harbor, New Hampshire, had secured the surprised fortifiers, and had made off unhindered with a hundred barrels of powder. Unlike the disguised Tea Party vandals before them, these rioters were well known, yet too numerous for the ill-armed authorities in New Hampshire to apprehend.

Bolder and bolder had grown colonial acts of defiance.

Yet in the face of news just arrived of such rebellious carryings-on overseas, on the very next day, February 1, Lord Chatham would rise in Parliament and propose what Hutchinson, learning of it, described as "an unexpected motion . . . in order to introduce a strange Bill, more like a News-paper or Declamatory Speech, as I heard one of the Lords say, than like a Bill, in which the measures of late years were condemned."

This, then, as it seemed to Governor Hutchinson, was Chatham's precious plan for settling the troubles in America: Ignore rebel outrages and condemn all the acts that Parliament had passed so far.

On the first day of February, the English statesman did indeed stand before his peers once more, as promised, to tell them what they should do. They should, said Chatham, suspend all thirteen measures enacted in recent years that concerned the colonies. Repeal all of the coercive acts, the whole lot of them, and henceforth respect the charters of the various provinces. No taxes should be levied without the consent of those taxed, as expressed through their representative bodies. Chatham's proposal did recognize Parliament as supreme in the empire, but Parliament should acknowledge the American congress at Philadelphia to be a lawful assembly under that supremacy. In turn, the Continental Congress should agree to provide his majesty with a perpetual grant to pay the colonials' part of the cost of administering the empire. And though the king might maintain a standing army in the colonies, the army must never be used "to violate and destroy the just rights of the people."

All this his lordship offered and explained in what Benjamin Franklin (his judgment differing sharply from Hutchinson's informant's) termed "a most excellent Speech"—nothing strange or newspaperish about it—before a House of Lords crowded for the occasion. Brought by Lord Stanhope once more at Chatham's request, Dr. Franklin had been on hand to hear the plan presented. The doctor had watched Chatham take his seat at the end of the presentation, then watched as Lord Sandwich rose in opposition and proceeded, "in a petulant vehement Speech," to give his opinion that the plan "ought to be immediately REJECTED with the Contempt it deserv'd. That he could never believe it the Production of any British Peer. That it appear'd to him rather the Work of some American; and turning his Face towards me"—toward Franklin himself—"who was leaning on the Bar, said, he fancied he had in his Eye the Person who drew it up, one of the bitterest and most mischievous Enemies this Country had ever known."

The charge had turned all lordly heads craning in Dr. Franklin's direction; but as he had done a year earlier, when standing accused before the Privy Council, the philosopher had caused his countenance to remain as immovable "as if my Features had been made of Wood," as though Lord Sandwich had been referring to somebody else entirely.

Others had gone on to speak to the measure. Then Chatham rose once more, this time to take notice of Sandwich's "illiberal Insinuation that the Plan was not the Person's who propos'd it."

Well, it *was* his lordship's plan, entirely so. Lord Chatham felt all the more reason for declaring his sole responsibility for the proposal because many in the chamber "appear'd to have so mean an Opinion of it; for if it was so weak or so bad a Thing, it was proper in him"—Chatham—"to take care that no other Person should unjustly share in the Censure it deserved. That it had been heretofore reckon'd his Vice not to be apt to take Advice. But he made no Scruple to declare, that if he were the first Minister of this Country, and had the Care of Settling this momentous Business, he should not be asham'd of publickly calling to his Assistance a Person so perfectly acquainted with the whole of American Affairs, as the Gentleman alluded to and injuriously reflected on, one," Chatham specified, "whom all Europe held in high Estimation for his Knowledge and Wisdom, and rank'd with our Boyles and Newtons; who was an Honour not to the English Nation only but to Human Nature."

Imagine what the often vilified object of such praise, in such a public forum, and from such a source, was feeling. But we need not imagine, for Franklin tells us: "I found it harder to stand this extravagant Compliment," he wrote, "than the preceding equally extravagant Abuse, but kept as well as I could an unconcern'd Countenance, as not conceiving it to relate to me."

The truth was, Chatham had shown his American friend the plan and had sought his response to it in detail. Franklin had duly set down his thoughts and arrived at Hayes ready to share them. That was just the day before, at the end of January, and the two gentlemen had stayed together four hours. But later the doctor recalled of their conference that his lordship, "in the manner of I think all eloquent Persons was so full and diffuse in Supporting every particular I question'd, that there was not time to go thro' half my Memorandums; He is not easily interrupted, and I had

such Pleasure in hearing him that I found little Inclination to inter-
rupt him." Anyway, if the plan were seriously considered, there
would be abundant opportunities to offer objections and amendments later. "I therefore ceas'd my Querying; and tho' afterwards
many People were pleas'd to do me the Honour of Supposing I
had a considerable Share in Composing it, I assure you, that the
Addition of a single Word only was made at my Instance, viz.
'Constitutions' after 'Charters.'"

Thomas Hutchinson had missed the drama in the House of
Lords that first of February: Chatham's unheralded proposal of a
way to settle the American controversy, Sandwich's virulent opposition with his charge of Franklin's complicity, and Chatham's spirited response to the insinuation. But having missed so much, the
governor made sure to be on hand at Parliament House for what
might transpire on the morrow. Next day, February 2, Hutchinson
gained admission to the Commons. However, the crowds in the
lobby beyond the legislative chamber proved so numerous and
noisy as to impede the work of the members. "Lord George
Cavendish not being able to introduce his friend," the governor
records in his journal, "and being vexed to see so many in the
Gallery, introduced by other Members, moved the House might be
cleared; and it is a rule of the House, that upon any Members moving, the House shall be cleared without any question."

Hutchinson and the other spectators must leave.

It was moments later, on his way out, that the governor got a
glimpse finally of one who had played so prominent a role in his
life of late. "While I was in the Lobby," he noted with a reticence
and good breeding that were typical—almost never, in public or in
private, revealing his personal antipathies—"Doctor Franklin
passed by, and seemed in great agitation, but returned without getting into the House. This is the only time I have seen him since I
have been in England."

Seven months—and what had been Hutchinson's feelings at that
instant, the bulky figure of his enemy finally in view? "What has
that man to answer for!" an unnamed gentleman had remarked to
the governor just the other day. "If it had not been for that most
wicked proceeding about your letters, England and the Colonies
would now have been reconciled. He saw the probability of it, and
therefore ruined his own character to prevent it."

That was how a number of friends of government were viewing Benjamin Franklin by this time, as an inveterate schemer reduced to venturing everything in order to secure the independence of America, even going as far as to destroy his own good name if such was required. Gossip that the governor had set down (like much gossip, untrue) included what he had heard from gentlemen members of the Royal Society, that Dr. Franklin had "never shewn his head among them, nor in any other company that they could hear of, for a twelvemonth past, nor had he ever appeared at any public office, or on any public occasion, except when he went a little while ago to Lord Dartmouth with Bollan and Lee to deliver the Petition to the King." Persuaded of such pariahdom, perhaps Mr. Hutchinson, who was capable of considerable feats of magnanimity, felt little besides pity at the sight now of an agitated old man scurrying about the lobby of Parliament House, his reputation demolished among people who counted, here at the end of a long life not without some earlier glory.

Chatham's proposal, like his recommendation to remove the troops from Boston, went down promptly to defeat in the Lords, 61 to 32. Such an outcome had been all the more predictable, given that statesman's regrettable penchant for confiding in so few—in Franklin and only one other in the present instance—sharing nothing of what he was thinking with the various leaders of opposition groups in Parliament who might have been persuaded to join forces with him. But the sound defeat of the current proposal was good news for all friends of empire committed to policies that would deal sternly with rebellion. And as February unfolded, the wisdom of such policies, to which administration had determined to adhere, seemed to gain further support in word arriving from Governor-General Gage in Boston.

"21st.—At Lord Dartmouth's," noted Hutchinson, "who I found in high spirits upon a letter from Gage, of 18 Jan. which he afterwards sent me to read."

What the governor read in the general's most recent dispatch was in truth encouraging. Gage had written that the frenzy seizing Americans had needed a steady supply of "New Events" to be maintained; any tranquillity would allow "Leizure for Reflection," time to think "seriously of their Danger." And in the depths of winter, just such tranquillity had come, so that the general had been pleased to hear "from Several parts of the Country" that "the People's Minds are greatly cooled, and many begin to want Courts of Justice; and that the Friends of Government have shewed themselves openly in many Places." Tory pens in Boston had lately been writing to good effect in the press, laying out the perils of resistance to government as well as the rewards of dutiful submission. And eloquent Tory arguments had been set forth in the papers to expose in masterly style "the Absurdity of the Resolves of the Continental Congress ... which has served to lower that Impression of high Importance, which the Congress had made upon People's Minds."

But there was even more good news from New England. The general wrote of word reaching him that the New Hampshire rebels "concerned in the rash Action against Fort William and Mary ... are terrifyed at what they have done, and only anxious to obtain Pardon for their Offence." Moreover, Gage had reason to believe that before long "many considerable People" in Boston would convene to make an open declaration of loyalty to the king in Parliament; and if such people were hesitating, it was only until they were sure that "the Mother Country will not relax, but resolve to pursue her Measures." Those consequential people's coming together would have beneficial results. "If they begin to associate in the Town, it's likely they will also fall on Means to pay for the Tea, for as they are mostly Traders, it would be very advantageous for them to have the Port open, in the present Conjuncture of their Commercial Affairs."

Finally, Governor Gage wrote, "the Eyes of all are turned upon Great Britain, waiting for her Determination; and it's the opinion of most People, if a respectable Force is seen in the Field, the most obnoxious of the Leaders seized, and a Pardon proclaimed for all other's, that Government will come off Victorious, and with less Opposition than was expected a few Months ago."

On every count a highly gratifying report; the dispatch did appear to confirm the statesmanlike wisdom of England's present policy. Yet with all that, Mr. Hutchinson found himself in the aftermath of reading it unable to share Lord Dartmouth's elation.

During these late days of February, the governor's reveries had continued to dwell on home. He thought apprehensively of the future, longingly of times past, of happy times when his beloved wife was alive, she who had appeared always to be something more than human in his eyes. He remembered days in Boston and Milton with his wife alive and his family young, his own position honored in town. He recalled a present, now so distant, that had been rewarding and full, when a future shone bright before him and his family. "The uncertainty of human affairs"! Here in "my situation at this time of life, so unexpected to me, three thousand miles from my country and friends, so that every scene has the appearance of a dream, rather than a reality." How different it all was then. Who could have foreseen the way that matters would work themselves out?

"My Dear Son," in one such mood, February 22, the day after reading Gage's sanguine message, this exile wrote to Tommy back home, "I hope peace and order will return to you before the summer is over, and that I shall return before winter,—I am not anxious in what station." Return as governor ("which I have no doubt I may do if I chuse it"), should there seem a prospect of his being of service; or, if the populace persevere in their animosities, and friends should advise it, return in a private station. In the latter case, the more obscure the better.

But this letter to a dutiful son soon passed to a different subject, going on to broach a project of a morose and delicate nature, one that, Hutchinson confessed, had been some years on his mind. What the exile was requesting was that a tomb be prepared in Milton—so somber were his current thoughts—to which the remains of his wife, now twenty-one years in her grave, would be removed from Boston. A space should be left beside her for himself. Have the tomb built (the governor even included directions as to where appropriate stone might be procured); defer any inscription or ornamentation for the widower's return; then speak to Wolleston, sexton of the Old North Church, in the grounds of which Mrs. Hutchinson lay buried. Do everything at nighttime, so as not to awaken the curiosity of idle gapers and passers-by. "I am sensible," the father, the widower, admitted, "this fond fancy will not bear examining upon meer rational grounds; but it is not criminal, and I am countenanced by the like sort of fondness in the old Patriarchs."

He ended: "I cannot write upon any other subject after writing upon this."

And sent off his letter—bound on an errand that would at the last come to nothing. Over these recent months, Hutchinson's native province, to which his instructions would be making their slow way, had changed beyond what he might have recognized, had altered too much to permit of any such personal accommodations as the exile here was soliciting. He had written from London on February 22. Four days earlier, on the 18th, on the other side of the ocean, a relative by marriage had been drafting a letter of his own, to Hutchinson's son Elisha. Dr. Peter Oliver's distraught report to his brother-in-law depicts a Massachusetts town and countryside transformed.

"I am at last drove here by the mob"—this uprooted resident of Middleborough writes with grim breathlessness from Boston— "The times are got to be very serious. Great preparations on both sides for an engagement . . . such times as I never expected would come to pass in America. . . . Such an enthusiasm and madness of the people never was before in any part of the globe."

With catastrophe thus preparing, Mrs. Hutchinson's remains must rest for now where they lay.

20

THE MINISTRY
COMMITS ITSELF

THOMAS HUTCHINSON JR., to whom a father's somber letter of February was directed, had taken refuge in Boston since before the start of the new year, caged up with all those other loyalists who now included Tommy and Elisha's brother-in-law, Dr. Peter Oliver, the husband of Governor Hutchinson's elder daughter Sarah.

Last summer, Sarah's brother Tommy had been named one of his majesty's new legislative councillors and from Milton had dutifully accepted the king's appointment like other stout souls so honored, although (like others) only briefly. He had been sworn in August 16, 1774; but by month's end, a mere two weeks later, young Mr. Hutchinson had felt moved to write Governor Gage resigning his commission.

May it please his excellency, the writer was fully sensible of the honor that the appointment as a member of his majesty's council had conferred upon him. Moreover, he would be happy to contribute in any way he could to restoring peace and good order in the province. But here in Milton, as in surrounding villages, a spirit had been enkindled in the breasts of the people that would oblige young Hutchinson either to resign his office or to quit his present domicile; and "it would be exceedingly inconvenient for me to change the place of my residence, or submit to any kind of restraint of my person, being the only one of Governor Hutchinson's family now in the country, and having the care of his affairs here, as well as those of the late Lieut. Governor Oliver, both of which I apprehend will suffer greatly by my being under any personal restraint."

The late Andrew Oliver—married to the sister of Governor Hutchinson's wife—had been Tommy's father-in-law as well (and uncle of Dr. Peter, Tommy's brother-in-law, so remarkably intertwined were these two families). To be sure, the reasons that young Hutchinson was offering now for resigning his post were personal, "but as they relate to the concerns of others more than my own," he wrote, "I hope Your Excellency will think them sufficient to induce you to accept the Resignation of my trust as one of His Majesty's Council for this Province."

Yet even as a private citizen, the young merchant had found living in Milton—site of the Suffolk Resolves of September—increasingly trying as the fall advanced. A newly erected liberty pole stood obnoxiously within view of the Hutchinson home, and numerous patriots among the villagers were active. Accordingly, the former governor's son had left Milton for good in November (so expeditiously that all his father's furnishings and personal belongings remained behind)—to join those swarms of Tories who had abandoned their residences on the mainland and put themselves under the protection of his majesty's troops beyond the fortified Neck.

By January, the peninsular port of Boston had been blockaded by sea seven months and longer, though access to the mainland across the Neck remained grudgingly open. How were the people crowded behind the wall of warships in the harbor faring by then? A traveler visiting January 21 wrote to gratify the curiosity of colonials elsewhere up and down the seaboard. He had been impressed, he reported, to find the town peaceable still, after all the deprivation, despite the absence of a legislature, of magistrates, of courts, of executive officers. Gage's army of bloodybacks, everywhere about the streets, appeared to him sickly, and addicted to desertion. "Do you think," this Whig correspondent mused in closing his newspaper account, "such an Army would march through our woods and thickets, and Country Villages, to cut the throats of honest people contending for liberty?"

Honest, English-speaking people, whose ancestors had themselves come over from England? The thought seemed preposterous—and from such a feeble, demoralized force as this that he observed in any case. That, of course, was a patriot's view of the situation, which looked different from the vantage point of loyalists. As Governor Gage saw it, for instance, the new year appeared finally to be bringing relief after the strains of fall, with desertions down and with the first clear signs of a return to reasonableness, to order.

Having already dispatched a hopeful report to Whitehall on the 18th, the governor wrote Lord Dartmouth again toward the end of January, on the 27th, in part to relay agreeable information that had reached him from the surrounding countryside. Tories in towns and villages of Massachusetts were (how often we seem to have heard this) starting to speak out at last. Moreover, "the Tyranny and Oppressive Acts exercised against Persons deemed Friends of Government, has driven them in Several Places to combine together for their Mutual Defence." In Marshfield in particular, a village south of Boston, loyalists, having formed an association among themselves and having then been harassed by their patriot neighbors for doing so, "applyed to me for Protection; and I have sent a Detachment of one hundred Men to their Relief." This was the first such instance of an appeal for government's support, "which the Faction has ever tried to perswade the People they would never obtain, but be left to themselves."

Government had no intention of leaving its colonial friends to themselves or of disregarding their appeals, for by reinforcing local supporters, as at Marshfield, it might hope soon to hear of other towns standing up to patriot demagogues. Not that all was suddenly smooth sailing, of course. In Portsmouth, to the north, the magistrates were now letting General Gage know that they wanted sufficient means to apprehend those concerned in the attack on Fort William and Mary a month ago or to keep them safely in jail if they did apprehend them. Accordingly, the New Hampshire governor was asking that two of the king's regiments be stationed nearby, even though Portsmouth lacked quarters to house the troops, and Gage could hardly spare two regiments in any case.

The situation in New Hampshire was vexing, but perhaps additional reinforcements would soon be on their way from England. "People are waiting Determinations from home," Gage once more informed the colonial secretary before closing, "which will probably make great Alterations in Proceedings here."

Two weeks and more passed, and the wait continued. On February 17, the governor-general prepared another dispatch, reminding Lord Dartmouth that until he heard how the proceedings of the congress in Philadelphia had been received in London, he must bide his time here in Boston. His most recent official message from home had been contained in Dartmouth's brief word of December 10, which had merely acknowledged receipt of Gage's September dispatches and enclosed the king's address opening the new Parliament at the end of November. His majesty's insistence, on an occasion so high and public, that the coercive acts were to be enforced and that Parliament's supremacy throughout the empire would be maintained "has Cast a Damp upon the Faction," the governor was able now to assure his superior, from here in Boston in February. Indeed, patriot spirits were sinking for more than one reason. "The Sending a Detachment to Marshfield has had a good Effect in that Quarter of the Country," he wrote, "and I hope will encourage other Places where Oppression is felt, to make Applications of the same Nature." And Gage found himself able by this time to speak in the past tense of the "Phrenzy" of autumn, as something behind them at last: "The Fury into which People were thrown and which spread like an Infection from Town to Town and from Province to Province is hardly to be paralleled where no Oppression was actualy felt, but they were stirred up by every Means that Art could invent."

By late winter, that fury appeared spent, even if annoyances persisted. For one, there seemed little hope any longer of punishing the people in Portsmouth involved in the attack on Fort William and Mary, "unless they were sent to England for Tryal." And the demagogues were still at work, deceiving the locals by distorting the king's speech and all that government had done, although "Your Lordship's Dispatches by the Falcon will probably undeceive them."

For Lord Dartmouth had promised, in this his most recent note in Gage's hand of December 10, that the ministry and Parliament would soon be considering the state of the province as described in the general's letters (letters dated no later than September and early October, recall, when the patriot frenzy had been at its height); "and the Falcon sloop of War lies ready at Spithead," his lordship had written, "to convey to you such orders & Instructions as shall be judged necessary thereupon."

It was those orders aboard the *Falcon*, promised from London in December, that the governor was awaiting in February. As it happened, not until mid-April would the orders finally and very tardily arrive. But consider what the long delays of the times had effected. Gage's dispatches from Boston early last fall, in September, had been filled with alarms that verged on panic. On September 12, for instance, he had reported: "The Country People are exercising in Arms. . . . They threaten to attack the Troops in Boston, and are very angry at a Work throwing up at the Entrance of the Town . . . there is no Security to any Person deemed a Friend to Government in any Part of the Country; even Places always esteemed well affected have caught the Infection, and Sedition flows copiously from the Pulpits." Again, September 25: "It has been suggested," Gage had written, "that it was highly necessary to apprehend a certain Number of Persons"—Adams, Hancock, Warren—"which I believe wou'd have been a very proper Measure some Time ago, but at present it wou'd be the Signal for Hostilities, which they seem very ripe to begin. . . . The new Council appointed by the King who have taken Refuge in this Town, dare not attend at Salem, unless escorted there, and back again by a large Force. . . . We hear of Nothing but Extravagancies in some Part or other, and of military Preparations from this place to the Province of New York, in which the whole seems to be united. . . . Your Lordship will know from various Accounts, the Extremities to which Affairs are brought, and how this Province is supported and abetted by others beyond the Conception of most People, and foreseen by none. The Disease was believed to have been confined to the Town of Boston, from whence it might have been eradicated no doubt without a great deal of Trouble, and it might have been the Case some Time ago; but now it's so universal there is no knowing where to apply a Remedy."

That was what Dartmouth understood in December of the tumultuous conditions in and beyond New England; those were the texts from autumn on the basis of which government in London was to fashion its winter remedies. But December 10, when the texts were under scrutiny, was only days from the Christmas holidays, so that in the event, policy was to be formulated no sooner than January. The king's cabinet would meet at last in mid-January and put together the plan that Lord North had been promising Parliament since before Christmas, a plan based on stale news of September and October, destined to reach Boston not before April of the new year—fall to winter to leafy spring required to encompass decisions so momentous.

The plan thus arrived at was at last forwarded to General Gage in the form of a secret, lengthy dispatch from the colonial secretary dated January 27. The dispatch finally made clear exactly what was to be done—issued the governor orders, in effect, that left him few options. Written, fatally written, dated January 27, 1775, sealed, transmitted into those broad tense silences sometime in February: and then it was London's turn to wait.

The strain told. Between the writing and the transmittal, Mr. Hutchinson on one occasion in Downing Street spent nearly an hour in conversation with the prime minister. North "seemed overborne with the weight of affairs," the governor noted, "and tho' he evidently wished for something to take hold of to bring forward an accommodation, professed to be resolved never to concede to the present claimes." As with the overwhelmed North, so with that other public servant Dartmouth. Hutchinson on February 15 was at Lord Dartmouth's levee: "I never saw him more dispirited. He asked me whether I thought no proposals could be made to satisfy the Americans?"

During this time, the governor would have known nothing specifically of the cabinet's plan, devised in secret last month, as he knew nothing of Dartmouth's January dispatch to Gage, which remained at the foreign office through much of February and was still there on the 21st, when favorable word from Boston arrived at Whitehall at last: "At Lord Dartmouth's, who I found in high spirits upon a letter from Gage, of 18 Jan. which he afterwards sent me to read."

No wonder Lord Dartmouth's spirits had soared with the good news that Gage was reporting, of order returned to Massachusetts. The directive to the governor-general could now be dispatched to a province where patriot fury had finally spent itself, where loyalty was prevailing, where events seemed splendidly to have confirmed the wisdom of the cabinet's earlier determinations: Hold fast, concede nothing.

What the cabinet had decided, what Dartmouth had written to Gage in secret January 27, what was being transmitted at last in late February aboard the *Falcon* was precise and detailed—and appeared very little interested in placating Americans. The lengthy letter begins by acknowledging the unfavorable light in which the general's reports of the fall had portrayed the province, as well as the "dangerous & alarming" behavior of colonials in resisting the execution of the law. Yet—and here at the very start unfurls the remainder of a stern, extended sentence of 168 words that the governor-general could hardly read otherwise than frowningly, given the gravity of the tone: Yet as Gage's reports "did not refer to any Facts tending to shew that the Outrages which had been committed were other than merely the Acts of a tumultuous Rabble, without any Appearance of general Concert, or without any Head to advise, or Leader to conduct that could render them formidable to a regular Force led forth in support of Law and Government, it was hoped that by a vigorous Exertion of that Force, conformable to the Spirit & Tenor of the King's Commands signified to you in my several Letters, any further Insults of the like nature would have been prevented, & the People convinced that Government wanted neither the Power nor the Resolution to support it's just Authority, & to punish such atrocious Offences."

A vigorous earlier exertion of force by the forbearing general might already have imposed peace: Gage was famously too timid, too tame, an old woman, as many thought. That unflattering judgment had been much in the air on both sides of the ocean lately; and if this official dispatch avoided saying so explicitly, the implication hovered over every page. For however brought on (implicitly, through Gage's failure to act?), conditions in New England, as reported in the general's autumn correspondence and as gleaned from other sources from America, amounted to "actual Revolt," Dartmouth wrote now, "and shew a Determination in the People to commit themselves at all Events to open Rebellion."

That was what Gage must deal with, then, and deal with decisively. Nothing less than rebellion. Moreover, "the King's Dignity, & the Honor and Safety of the Empire, require, that, in such a Situation, Force should be repelled by Force." There it was, plain enough; and that the stated policy might be implemented, Lord Dartmouth had the satisfaction of acquainting the general that orders had been issued this very day, January 27, for the immediate embarkation for Boston of seven hundred marines and three regiments of infantry, with one of light dragoons, from Ireland. The general was, moreover, reminded of other forces having been sent earlier and was encouraged to augment his present troops with "every Corps that could be spared from necessary Duty in every other part of America."

About crushing rebellion, government was in earnest. "It appears," wrote Dartmouth pointedly, "that your Object has hitherto been to act upon the Defensive, & to avoid the hazard of weakening your Force by sending out Detachments of your Troops upon any Occasion whatsoever; and," his lordship thought to add, "I should do Injustice to Your Conduct, and to my own Sentiments of your Prudence & Discretion, if I could suppose that such Precaution was not necessary."

That last seems added more from tact than conviction. In any case, henceforth perhaps somewhat less of discretion and prudence. With substantial reinforcements on the way, General Gage will be able "to take a more active & determined part." He will have sufficient strength "not only to keep Possession of Boston, but to give Protection to Salem, & the friends of Government at that Place." It may be assumed, indeed, that the governor will soon leave Boston and return to the designated capital, "without Hazard of Insult," and there exercise his administrative functions in accordance with his majesty's earlier instructions.

As for that, Governor Gage should not even be in Boston. He should be in Salem, capital of the province according to the terms of the Port Act. And from Salem the governor-general should implement the following policy. To repeat: "I have already said, in more Letters than one," wrote Dartmouth with a touch of impatience, "that the Authority of this Kingdom must be supported, & the Execution of its Laws inforced, & you will have seen in His Maty's Speech to both Houses of Parliament, & in the Addresses which they have presented to His Majesty, the firm Resolution of His Majesty and Parliament to act upon those Principles."

More specifically, it appears that large numbers in three of the provinces of New England—Massachusetts, Rhode Island, and Connecticut—have determined to cast off their dependence on the mother country. The only question remaining is how Gage's forces should be exerted to restore those provinces to obedience.

"It seems to be your Idea," the colonial secretary noted dryly, "that Matters are come to such a State that this is no otherwise attainable than by an absolute Conquest of the People of the three

Governments . . . & that such Conquest cannot be effected by a less Force than 20,000 Men."

But sir, you must be aware that such a force cannot be assembled without putting the empire on a war footing. If such were necessary, the stakes are high enough that it would be done; "yet I am unwilling to believe," wrote Dartmouth, "that matters are as yet come to that Issue."

No, what must occur, with a force rather less than the twenty thousand men requested, is the prompt arrest and imprisonment of the two or three leaders of the rebellion. And if provincial courts are not functioning, let the prisoners await their trials in jail until the courts do function. That will keep those firebrands out of mischief and add to their punishment. And if the people rise up in protest, what then? Let the seizure of their leaders be a test of the people's resolve.

Of course Governor Gage must have the final say; "in a Situation where every thing depends so much upon the Events of the Day, and upon local Circumstances, your Conduct must be governed very much by your own Judgement and Discretion." But here, in brief, is what his superiors expect of the general: "It is the Opinion of The King's Servants in which His Majesty concurs," wrote Dartmouth, "that the first & essential step to be taken towards re-establishing Government, would be to arrest and imprison the principal actors & abettors in the Provincial Congress (whose proceedings appear in every light to be acts of treason & rebellion)," as soon as the congress dares to meet again. Meanwhile, move from the defensive to the offensive; forcefully establish his majesty's authority over all of New England.

And what if large numbers resist—farmers, freeholders, mechanics, townspeople, country people? But they won't. If Gage moves after taking proper precautions and while using every means to keep his plan secret until ready to execute it, "it can hardly fail of Success," the colonial secretary adjudged from the safety of three thousand miles away, "and will perhaps be accomplished without bloodshed."

The people will not resist. And even if they do—and here Dartmouth displayed government's policy undraped: "I must again repeat that any efforts of the People, unprepared to encounter with a regular force, cannot be very formidable"—but how wrong! how utterly, crucially mistaken were his lordship and the king's other advisers on that point—"and though such a proceeding should be, according to your own idea of it, a Signal for Hostilities yet, for the reasons I have already given, it will surely be better that the Conflict should be brought on, upon such ground, than in a riper state of Rebellion."

There it was: Fight now rather than later. With those instructions in hand, the general could no longer doubt what was expected of him.

21

FATE OF THE PEACE PLANS

WHAT WERE LORD DARTMOUTH and his colleagues in London thinking of, devising such orders for Gage? But his majesty's army and navy together were the mightiest fighting instrument in the world, demonstrably so. Hardly a decade earlier those same forces had concluded the most astoundingly successful war in all of British history, against the most formidable of all foes on earth at that time, wresting from the powerful continental allies of France and Spain far-flung holdings in Canada, India, the West Indies, West Africa, Cuba, and the Philippines. One little island nation had accomplished that unprecedented feat. This was not jingoism, but fact. And England (not unlike America in the 1960s, a decade or so after its own great global triumph) was now to be defied by a mere province or two at the fringes of empire?

Hardly. Moreover, if colonials did foolishly resolve on armed defiance, an article of faith among loyalists presumed that the rebels would fight neither long nor well. Dr. Peter Oliver on the scene, in Boston in mid-February, at this very time, stated in writing to London no more than what was widely accepted as true. "Our country people," he reported, "are determin'd to oppose the measures of Parliament at the risk of their all, but it is doubted whether they will fight long."

And it was doubted whether they would fight well. In his orders to Gage, Dartmouth had made clear the low estimation in which government held such a foe: Any efforts of so ill-trained and ill-led a rabble "cannot be very formidable." Some few Englishmen were cautioning that that rabble was armed, unlike the Scottish rebels of thirty years earlier—armed, and numerous, and would be fighting for liberty on their home ground. But the prevailing opinion in London was to be expressed once more, notoriously, in Parliament in March, by the first lord of the admiralty, the same earl of Sandwich who had recently demanded the rejection of Chatham's peace plan as the scurvy clandestine handiwork of the American Franklin. "Suppose the Colonies do abound in men," Sandwich would rant from the security of the House of Lords; "What does that signify? They are raw, undisciplined, cowardly men. I wish instead of forty or fifty thousand of these *brave* fellows, they would produce in the field at least two hundred thousand, the more the better, the easier would be the conquest; if they did not run away, they would starve themselves into compliance with our measures."

Extraordinary. Imagine for one instant his derisive lordship, the good earl himself, exhausted and staggering in full retreat under fire from those same brave fellows through an April afternoon on the wretched way to safety in distant Charlestown—

Rubes and bumpkins, as he regarded them, Yankee Doodles likely to flee into the forests at the first explosion of gunfire. Such estimates of American skill and valor were based, the English thought, on experience with colonial troops in the French and Indian War, quite recent enough to be applicable. The late General Wolfe, conqueror of Quebec, had dismissed the Americans then as "in general the dirtiest, most contemptible cowardly dogs that you can conceive. There is no depending on them in action. They fall down dead in their own dirt and desert by battalions, officers and all. Such rascals as those are rather an encumbrance than any real strength to an army." Motley herd of street leavings and hayseeds, poorly armed, badly clothed, and worse disciplined; and although there were reasons that English regulars in those wars against the French might not always have seen the best of America's fighting spirit, opinions such as Wolfe's (and Lord Loudoun's, and Gage's, and many others at the time) were so decided, appeared so informed, and had been so often volunteered as to have taken on the force of dogma.

Those earlier opinions were being echoed from Boston at present, in letters home from officers who regularly dismissed as poltroons any potential opposition in view: raw militia drilling in their makeshift way on provincial greens, local farmers sullenly gathered on hillsides to watch his majesty's forces conduct their own smart maneuvers along country roads below. The disparity between brightly clad British regulars and drab colonials appeared obvious enough; and yet Lord Dartmouth in distant London, aware of all this, remained unhappy. His friend Hutchinson observed in mid-February, after the cabinet had determined its overseas policy and before the minister had dispatched that policy off to Gage, that his lordship had never looked more dispirited. "He asked me," we recall the governor noting, "whether I thought no proposals could be made to satisfy the Americans?"

Indeed, throughout the winter the gentle Dartmouth (with his stepbrother North the least belligerent of the king's ministers, despite those recent firm orders for Gage) had been secretly seeking just such proposals that would satisfy Americans. All this while, since early December, through intermediaries, he had been soliciting terms of Dr. Franklin, though avoiding for the purpose a face-to-face encounter with the agent of the Massachusetts Assembly. Of course the colonial secretary knew and on occasion had met with Franklin. Why now, in pursuing conciliation, his lordship chose not to confer directly with the American may be guessed at. For a peer of the realm to haggle over conditions and run a risk of rebuff would have been unseemly; and the doctor himself had opined in December that negotiations might enjoy more likelihood of success if his own role in them were kept secret, given the ministerial rage that Franklin's involvement in the affair of Hutchinson's letters had called forth a year earlier. But it was with that same Franklin that Dartmouth's emissaries had been dealing through recent weeks; and it was Franklin to whom Lord Howe, one of the colonial secretary's would-be peacemakers, had given assurances in late December "of a Certainty that there was a sincere Disposition in Lord North and Lord Dartmouth to accommodate the Differences with America."

Both the prime minister and the colonial secretary honestly wanted reconciliation; Franklin had heard Howe's authoritative confirmation on that point December 28 with joyous tears in his eyes. Lately, the American had about made up his mind, partly on the basis of the king's speech opening Parliament in November, that government had determined on war. Yet with North and Dartmouth's goodwill, there might yet be a way to save the empire while according the colonies the liberties to which they were justly aspiring. Lord Howe was asking the doctor what he thought of the idea of sending a commissioner overseas "to enquire into the Grievances of America upon the Spot, converse with the leading People, and endeavour with them to agree upon some Means of composing our Differences." Somebody well disposed, of sufficient rank and dignity, well respected in America, and as eager to see the colonial side as government's: Yes, such a person employed in that capacity could be "of great Use," Franklin thought—just such a man (the admiral's sister interjected at this conference among the three in late December) as Lord Howe himself. To be sure. And yes, the American would try to draw up the promised paper that his recent busy activities had prevented his putting together before now, a paper containing conditions that the colonials might agree to as a basis for peace.

Already, early in the month (as noted), Dr. Franklin had prepared one such paper, listing some fifteen "hints" toward a durable union, and had given it to Mr. Barclay and Dr. Fothergill, the latter Lord Dartmouth's personal physician. But Howe feared that those hints, which he had since seen, were too unyielding. At the admiral's request, Franklin would try again. Within a day or two, before year's end, he did present Lord Howe with a new set of terms that adhered closely to what his fellow countrymen, in congress assembled, had drawn up in petitioning the king. Franklin after all had no official authorization to negotiate (although the English persisted in thinking he did); all that the American could do was set down conditions that, should England consent to them, he assumed would be acceptable overseas—in this case, conditions that the congress in Philadelphia had already publicly agreed upon.

In his paper conveying the terms, Franklin reminded Admiral Lord Howe that the American congress had explicitly promised a restoration of harmony between colonies and mother country as soon as the various oppressive acts passed in Parliament's last session were repealed. Accordingly, government should do just that: Repeal the coercive acts. But here in London it was said that America must first commit itself to a course of loyal conduct in the future before any such step could be contemplated. Well, the colonies had already offered such a commitment, stating in their petition, as Franklin quoted it, "that when the Causes of their Appre-

hensions are removed, their future Conduct will prove them not unworthy of the Regard they have been accustomed in their happier
Days to enjoy."

Britain should trust the good faith of the congressional declaration. By doing so, it stood to lose nothing. Repeal the acts; and if
the colonies break faith, "she has it in her power at any time to resume her present Measures." But surely commitments such as the
congress's, freely given, might be more confidently relied upon
than any extorted by force.

What government should do, then: Trust the colonists; believe in
their declarations. Repeal the coercive acts. And withdraw the fleet
and the troops from Boston. Do that much as gestures of goodwill,
to indicate a change of disposition toward America and to show
the sincerity of England's desire for reconciliation. But do more.
Magnanimously remove some other grievance that the petitioners,
counting upon Parliament and the king's sense of justice, had left
unspecified. Franklin offered examples of such grievances, among
them "those relating to the Payment of Governors' and Judges'
Salaries." Address one such unasked. And, finally, acknowledge
the legality of the Continental Congress, set to meet again this
coming May. Even authorize the congress to meet—and send a
commissioner, "a Person of Weight and Dignity of Character," to
attend it. Once there, the commissioner could requisition the congress "of such Points as Government wishes to obtain, for its future
Security, for Aids"—that is, for funds in aid of the empire—"for the
Advantage of general Commerce, for Reparation to the India
Company, &c. &c."

The agent ended his paper with the assurance that government's
placing such confidence so generously in the colonies would lend
support to England's many friends there, helping them in their efforts to obtain from America "every reasonable Concession . . . that
can fairly be desired."

Here, then, were Franklin's recommendations for resolving the
present crisis, as of the first of the year 1775. Doubtfully, Lord
Howe looked over the paper, troubled that a recipe so rich with
governmental concessions would be coolly received, though he
did agree to "forward the propositions as intended."

This was on January 2. Weeks went by before Franklin heard
anything more of the matter. Meanwhile, about his "hints" for a

durable union, given earlier to his two Quaker friends, the agent had "wonder'd I heard nothing of them from Dr. Fothergill. At length however, but I cannot recollect about what time, the Dr. called on me, and told me, he had communicated them, and with them had verbally given my Arguments in support of them, to Lord Dartmouth, who after Consideration, had told him, some of them appear'd reasonable, but other[s] were inadmissible or impracticable." Britain would never submit to such humiliation as an acceptance of all the terms in Franklin's hints constituted. Dr. Fothergill, blunt spoken and on intimate footing with the colonial secretary, had thereupon answered Dartmouth, as he reported to Franklin, that England's conduct toward the colonies had been unjust; that she must bear the consequences and change her behavior; "that the Pill might be bitter; but it would be salutary, and must be swallow'd." In short, some such measures as these that the agent had proposed must sooner or later be followed "or the Empire," said the prescient Fothergill, "would be divided and ruined."

There matters rested through a busy interval early in the year. Dartmouth was in possession of two separate though related proposals, one from Dr. Fothergill, one from Lord Howe, both ultimately from Franklin, while Parliament reconvened after the holidays, the cabinet met, Lord North and his followers developed their own plan for addressing the situation in New England, and Lord Chatham rose at last with proposals in opposition for solving the all-consuming crisis.

February 1 had found Dr. Franklin in attendance as the great Chatham presented his far-ranging recommendations to the House of Lords. The debate that followed removed any remnant of whatever illusions the American might have clung to concerning government's good sense and reasonableness. In the course of expressing feelings that the occasion had outraged, Franklin was soon moved to pour forth one mighty rumble of a glorious sentence, laden with scorn and disgust:

To hear [he wrote] so many of these *Hereditary* Legislators declaiming so vehemently against, not the Adopting merely, but even the *Consideration* of a Proposal so important in its Nature, offered by a Person of so weighty a Character, one of the first Statesmen of the Age, who had taken up this Country when in the lowest Despondency, and conducted it to Victory and Glory thro' a War with two of the mightiest Kingdoms in Europe; to hear them censuring his Plan not only for their own Misunderstandings of what was in it, but for their Imaginations of what was not in it, which they would not give themselves an Opportunity of rectifying by a second Reading; to perceive the total Ignorance of the Subject in some, the Prejudice and Passion of others, and the wilful Perversion of Plain Truth in several of the Ministers; and upon the whole to see it so ignominiously rejected by so great a Majority, and so hastily too, in Breach of all Decency and prudent Regard to the Character and Dignity of their Body as a third Part [with king and Commons] of the National Legislature, gave me an exceeding mean Opinion of their Abilities, and made their Claim of Sovereignty over three Millions of virtuous sensible People in America, seem the greatest of Absurdities, since they appear'd to have scarce Discretion enough to govern a Herd of Swine.

After that disabusing exhibition by the House of Lords, the agent from Massachusetts had expected to hear no more about any negotiations toward amicably settling differences between colonies and mother country. But within a day or two, he received a note requesting yet another interview with Mr. Barclay and Dr. Fothergill. The three gentlemen met February 4.

Having come from the colonial secretary, Barclay was optimistic. He surprised Franklin with assurances "that a very good Disposition appear'd in Administration; that the *Hints* had been considered, and several of them thought reasonable, and that others might be admitted with small Amendments." For his part Dr. Fothergill, "with his usual Philanthropy," fell to musing on the miseries of warfare, remarking that America was growing steadily stronger and its population steadily increasing, so that "whatever she might be oblig'd to submit to at present, she would in a few Years be in a Condition to make her own Terms." Barclay alluded to the moralist and scientist Franklin's unique position in promoting an agreement, esteemed on both sides of the water, and what an honor it would be to bring such an agreement about. Moreover, government was sure to give the person who managed that laudable feat anything he might thereafter wish: wealth, titles, power.

An appeal to self-interest, which Lord Howe, too, was not above utilizing, invariably failed with Franklin: "I need not tell you, who know me so well, how improper and disgusting this Language was to me." To Barclay, the American answered that the ministry, far from giving him even his old position back as postmaster, "would rather give me a Place in a Cart to Tyburn, than any other Place whatever." To Dr. Fothergill, he remarked that America did not desire war and wanted nothing but what was necessary and reasonable for the colonies' well-being. And to both, Franklin added "that I sincerely wish'd to be serviceable, that I needed no other Inducement than to be shown how I might be so; but saw they imagined more to be in my Power than really was."

Yet the Quakers would have the agent attend once more to his hints read aloud and hear the ministerial response to each separate condition. The paper was produced. Six of Franklin's articles had been accepted outright; six more were accepted with reservations; three were rejected.

"We had not at this Time," the agent reported of the meeting, "a great deal of Conversation upon these Points, for I shortned it by observing, that while the Parliament claim'd and exercis'd a Power of altering our Constitutions at pleasure, there could be no Agreement; for we were render'd unsafe in every Privilege we had a Right to, and were secure in nothing."

There lay the crux of the matter, as it had been from the start: a question of sovereignty. Who would be sovereign? On the one hand, was America, with its charters at the mercy of the British, to be governed by a collection of parliamentary mediocrities hardly fit to govern swine? Or, on the other hand, was Parliament in its dignity to negotiate with irregular assemblies of tradesmen and plowmen overseas as though they were equals? It was toward the broad rock of sovereignty that any agreement was bound, and on that rock it was doomed to founder.

But for now, his present hosts were irritating Franklin once more, this time by hinting how necessary such an agreement was for America, vulnerable as were the defenseless colonial seaports to the wrath of the British navy. At this, wrote the agent, "I grew warm, said that the chief Part of my little Property consisted of Houses in those Towns"—of Boston and Philadelphia—"that they might make Bonfires of them whenever they pleased; that the Fear of losing them would never alter my Resolution to resist to the last that Claim of Parliament; and that it behov'd this Country to take

Care what Mischief it did us, for that sooner or later it would certainly be obliged to make good all Damages with Interest.

"The Doctor"—Fothergill—"smil'd, as I thought," added Franklin, "with some Approbation of my Discourse, passionate as it was and said he would certainly repeat it to morrow to Lord Dartmouth."

But all the talking in the world would not bridge this gap, grown wide as the ocean itself. And even if the British by some miracle of farsighted statesmanship had seen fit to accede and subscribe to Franklin's program, would that have saved the empire? Or were too many American interests—of northern merchants, southern gentry, speculators, settlers coveting lands to the west—by this time, by early 1775, already persuaded of the profits that would come hand in hand with independence?

The talk continued for all that. Through February, Franklin met on occasion with his Quaker friends and separately with Lord Howe. The ministry, he was assured, only wanted an opening. Troops were about to be dispatched to America. Pay for the tea, and orders might be issued to detain those troops at home. With that, the philosopher, relying on Massachusetts to reimburse him later, boldly offered his own private fortune to pay the East India Company—but would make the payment only after the coercive acts had been repealed. Government, in turn, declined to consider repealing the acts until the tea had been paid for.

Again, each side held fast, awaiting a move by the other. Franklin, in "the present dangerous Situation of Affairs"—and having withdrawn his offer—now warmly embraced the idea of a commissioner to be sent to America, a nobleman of Lord Howe's stature, "as it might be a Means of suspending military Operations, and bring on a Treaty, whereby Mischief would be prevented, and an Agreement by degrees be form'd and established." Lord Howe was willing to serve in such a capacity and urged Franklin to accompany him as his trusted adviser. Dartmouth, too, favored the idea, but the king and the king's other servants balked.

Earlier, his majesty had opined in private that he was "not so fond of the sending Commissioners to examine into the disputes; this looks so like the Mother Country being more affraid of the continuance of the dispute than the Colonies and I cannot think it likely to make them resonable." In his prim wisdom the sovereign protested that he sought to drive the colonies not to despair, only to submission; but that nothing except their feeling the inconvenience of their present situation seemed likely to achieve that end.

In time, a commissioner would be dispatched, Admiral Howe himself, when it was too late—more than a year from now. For now, America must suffer; government must show no signs of lessening the pressure. Grant one concession, and more would be demanded, until nothing less than independence would satisfy. Thus, Franklin negotiated all this while in vain.

On the last day of February, at his own request, he met with Howe once more. The admiral "said that he had not seen me lately, as he expected daily to have something more material to say to me than had yet occurr'd." So far there had been nothing of substance to report. But the American could wait no longer. In the message to his lordship that had sought this present interview, Franklin had written vaguely of measures that he must take if the admiral did not foresee his prompt departure from England as commissioner. Not understanding, Lord Howe now asked what measures Dr. Franklin had in mind.

"I answer'd, that having since I had last seen his Lordship, heard of the Death of my Wife at Philadelphia"—but of Deborah, the death of Debby, that "good and faithful Helpmate," so long silent, far away, dead—"the Death of my Wife at Philadelphia, in whose Hands I had left the Care of my Affairs there, it was become necessary for me to return thither as soon as conveniently might be; that what his Lordship had propos'd of my accompanying him to America, might if likely to take place, postpone my Voyage to suit his Conveniency, otherwise I should proceed by the first Ship." Having for some time heard nothing from the admiral, or from the Quaker emissaries either, this widower, informed only yesterday of Deborah Franklin's death and burial, was presuming that thoughts of commissioners or answers to grievances or accommodations by government as had been discussed—"all Thoughts of that kind were laid aside."

And all this while, since last December, at home, his wife of forty-four years—who as a young woman long ago, standing one Sunday morning in a Philadelphia doorway, had watched amused as an impoverished Boston lad on his first day in town, still in his working clothes, dirty and fatigued from traveling, had passed down Market Street with pockets laden and a great puffy loaf of bread under each arm, first sight of her "Benny," her "Pappy," as the young stranger would become—this faithful wife whom Franklin's eyes had last gazed on a decade earlier, would have borne her final illness, and died, and been put forever beyond the gaze of eyes.

22

ILLNESS OF MR. QUINCY

SHE HAD DIED OF A PARALYTIC STROKE at age sixty-six, on the 19th of December 1774. Two letters from Philadelphia, both dated December 24, had reached Franklin by the same ship in February, one from his son, another from his son-in-law. Neither correspondent had mentioned Mrs. Franklin's decline earlier, although William, the son and royal governor, now chose to write his father what he had not so much as hinted at before, at least in any surviving letters: that his mother had told him, "when I took Leave of her, on my Removal to Amboy, that she never expected to see you unless you returned this Winter, for that she was sure she should not live till next Summer. I heartily wish you had happened to have come over in the Fall, as I think her Disappointment in that respect preyed a good deal on her Spirits."

What was the philosopher to do with such tardy, gratuitous information? The son-in-law Mr. Richard Bache's letter was more comforting. Sunday evening, December 18, five days after the stroke that had robbed Mrs. Franklin of her speech, the family (Bache wrote) had "discovered a considerable change in her for the worse; She continued without seeming to suffer much Pain 'till Monday Morning about 11 o'Clock, when without a Groan or even a Sigh, she was released from a troublesome World, and happily relieved from all future Pain and Anxiety."

Franklin's relations with his common-law wife, although always civil, had not been close for years. His letters to her had continued to be regular enough, if hardly confiding; often they did little more than convey assurances of his good health with hopes that she herself was well. And if he sometimes still thought to send his Debby gifts of cloth and other goods from England, he had been considerably more generous to his sister Jane in Boston, just as the letters of the brother are far more lively and informative throughout this period than are the dutiful ones of the aged and absent husband.

Even so, the new widower's loss, with its grim reminder of transience and change and of earlier, happy times, must have been felt forcefully enough, all the more because of the many sad signs of endings that loomed everywhere around him. The empire itself was patently threatened. The doctor's long, fulfilling London years were winding down—all those friends to part from. And throughout this month of February, along with the frustrations that accompanied his secret and finally fruitless negotiations, hovered a concern arising from his protégé Quincy's sudden grave illness.

On January 23, Josiah Quincy had been taken sick, no more than a day after the young patriot was writing confidently home to Braintree to assure his father of his continued well-being. "Honoured and dear Sir," he had written on the 22nd, "I intend to say nothing more in this letter than that I am in health and spirits, having never had an ill day since my arrival in this island." But in his brevity, Quincy had been unable to refrain from sharing one bit of blissful news: Last Friday he had experienced the "great happiness" of hearing Chatham speak for hours in the House of Lords "on the concerns of my country." And then an ingratiatingly impertinent paragraph to conclude: "This letter is intended to contain nothing but what the spies of the ministry may be willing to let pass; and having gratified their own curiosity, I wish they may be candid and generous enough to let my friends gratify theirs also."

That on January 22, from a young man apparently in flourishing health, busy, engaged in doing his duty. But the frantic pace that Josiah Quincy had maintained ever since reaching England would appear to have been driven by the manic energy of the consumptive. The following night, "for the first time since my arrival, I was taken very ill with a fever and spasms."

He was no better in the morning. Dr. Fothergill, Franklin's friend and longtime physician, came to prescribe for him. The patient was to have dined at Mr. Towgood's that afternoon, with Drs. Franklin and Priestley, Dr. Price and Dr. Joseph Jeffries, "but my illness prevented that pleasure." And the next day the illness persisted gravely enough to warrant another visit from the physician, who peremptorily refused to take any fee for his treatment. "I consider this as a public cause, to which we must all contribute," Fothergill would explain when the patient spoke of fees.

Confined to his quarters near the Haymarket, only once venturing forth to dine, with Lord Shelburne and others, Quincy was soon judged to be too feeble to be left alone. Toward the end of January, he departed town for the northern suburbs, for Islington, to reside at Mr. Thomas Bromfield's, brother of his mother-in-law back home. "Received by this amiable family, and treated with the greatest hospitality and kindness," he noted gratefully in his journal. "It is now the third of February."

Only the briefest entries followed, days apart. Dr. Fothergill calls at Islington and prescribes new medicines. Again the esteemed physician absolutely refuses a fee. Unnamed friends visit the patient, "and great numbers send daily to inquire after my health, whom I never saw." Then it is February 26, a whole month passed in the vagueness of fifteen summary lines or so. On that day: "Rode out for the fourth time on horseback about twelve or fourteen miles. Evidently better when I am in the open air, and the motion of the horse not fatiguing. My friends redouble in the number and frequency of their visits." Among those who had called during the week just ended was Dr. Franklin.

But Quincy must leave the insalubrious environs of London. While in health, he had spoken of sailing for home in time to reach Philadelphia by May, in order to attend at the reconvening of the Continental Congress if the coercive acts were not repealed before then. But now he must set forth even sooner. He would depart as early as possible, for Massachusetts, even though neither he nor his physician favored such a plan.

"It is a good deal against my own private opinion and inclination," the patient noted privately, "that I now sail for America. I have had no letter from there since they knew of my arrival"—not a word yet from Boston in response to his own letters written from November onward. "I know not what my next letters may contain" from family. "Besides the fine season is now coming on here, and Dr Fothergill thinks Bristol air and water would give me perfect health."

And the return to Bristol would be so much more manageable. Why, in his condition, undertake the fatigues of an ocean voyage?

Invalided on the outskirts of the metropolis, Quincy brooded. His physician had given as his opinion that the patient should venture no farther than western England. "On the other hand, my most intimate friends (except Mr Bromfield) insist upon my going directly to Boston. They say, no letters can go with safety, and that I can deliver more information and advice *vivâ voce*, than could or ought to be written. They say, my going now must be (if I arrive safe) of great advantage to the American cause."

Ill as he was, Quincy was nevertheless being kept abreast of the many political developments of February, so that from friends of America he was possessed of confidences too sensitive to risk writing down. Those confidences he must take personally overseas to patriot leaders, share insights and advice "of great advantage to the American cause" with Adams, Warren, and others face to face. Or was the concern of his friends here principally for the alarming turn in the young man's health? Was that concern, cloaked in a mission that his patriotism would find irresistible, responsible for their urging him even against a distinguished physician's advice to make with all expedition for home?

To be sure, the February through which young Quincy had lain ill in the suburbs had been particularly rife with governmental activity concerning the colonies. The public knew nothing of Dartmouth's private dispatch to General Gage of January 27, which would be sealed aboard the *Falcon* bound for Boston, with a copy in a second vessel at sea. But on land, in Westminster, Lord North had this month at last publicly revealed and seen through Parliament the new proposals that constituted government's plan promised last December, a plan devised in cabinet sessions of mid-January. What the ministers had settled upon then, and Parliament had approved during February, during Quincy's retirement to Islington, was a three-part program designed less to appease than to overwhelm.

Near the start of the month, government had determined formally that the provincial congress of Massachusetts, by appropriating public moneys and organizing local militias, had engaged in acts of rebellion. Parliament therefore, February 2, addressed his majesty, humbly entreating that the rebellion be recognized for what it was. As the month advanced, steps were taken to reinforce Governor-General Gage with additional seamen to the number of 2,000, additional soldiers to the number of 4,000. The intention was to provide the general, if not with the 20,000 troops he had requested last fall, at least with no fewer than 10,000—a force ample enough, it was presumed, to overwhelm a mob of straggling, leaderless colonials.

Reinforcement was the first of the three responses that government had settled upon to deal anew with its rebellious possessions. The British fleet, augmented, would see that the second of the responses was implemented. That second took the form of a new coercive bill that Lord North introduced in Parliament on February 10. The bill sharply restricted where Massachusetts would be allowed to trade. And because Connecticut and Rhode Island had been supporting Massachusetts in its recent unruliness and because citizens of New Hampshire had last December seized the king's powder in Fort William and Mary, the bill included those three provinces as well, included, in other words, all of New England as then constituted in the restriction.

All four of the provinces were for the time being required to trade only with England and the British West Indies. The logic behind the restriction was simple. The congress at Philadelphia had declared that America would neither import from England, nor export to England, nor consume English goods until the coercive acts were repealed. Well then, England would deny at least the most recalcitrant of the colonies the right to trade anywhere else. If they refuse to trade with us, then let them trade with no one. And in weeks ahead, the ban would be extended to include colonies farther south that had persisted in supporting the Yankees: New Jersey, Pennsylvania, Virginia, Maryland, South Carolina.

Government's hope was in part to divide the colonies. Those that behaved themselves (New York and North Carolina were cited) would be exempt from the restriction and could trade where they chose. Perhaps other provinces would learn the wisdom of following such loyal examples. But there was a third part of the plan, which might also help to break down this new, awkward, and unforeseen colonial unity and lure the more reasonable provinces back to a proper obedience.

The third part offered conciliation as an accompaniment to reinforcement and coercion.

Lord North introduced his conciliatory measure February 16. It hardly amounted to a substantive concession, though what it did propose had doubtless arisen in part from Franklin's negotiations with Lord Howe and his Quaker friends and their subsequent representations to government. But even in its mildness, the measure provoked outcries of protest from members in Parliament supporting administration, convinced as they were that any concessions whatever would betray weakness and lead straight to colonial demands for independence. The king himself had grown alarmed at what North was doing, until the prime minister privately assured his majesty that the gesture "gives up no right, & that it contains precisely the plan which ought to be adopted by Great Britain; even if all America were subdued."

What North's proposal offered was to suspend any future taxation of colonies that on their own made an appropriate provision for the defense of the empire. Only "such Duties as it may be expedient . . . to impose for the regulation of commerce" in that mercantile age would be maintained, and income collected from those duties would be applied to the use of the provinces themselves. According to Chatham and others, taxation without representation had loomed as the great stumbling block; from now on, there would be no further taxing of colonies that on their own made adequate requisitions for the common defense.

This, then, was, as Franklin dryly labeled it, Lord North's "pacific Motion in the House for healing all Differences between Britain and America."

But who would determine what "adequate" was, as in "adequate requisitions"? Parliament would. Accordingly, when an English acquaintance inquired of Franklin soon after what objection could possibly be raised to the prime minister's recent generous proposal, the American's answer was prompt. "I replied," wrote the doctor, "the Terms of it were that we should grant Money till Parliament had agreed we had given enough, without having the least share in judging of the Propriety of the Measures for which it was to be granted, or of our own Abilities to grant; that these Grants were also to be made under a Threat of exercising a claimed Right of Taxing us at Pleasure, and compelling such Taxes by an armed Force, if we did not give till it should be thought we had given enough; that the Proposition was similar to no mode of obtaining Aids that ever existed, except that of a Highway-man who presents his Pistol and Hat at a Coach-Window, demanding no specific Sum, but if you will give all your Money or what he is pleas'd to think sufficient, he will civilly omit putting his own Hand into your Pockets. If not, there is his Pistol."

No, North's conciliatory gesture would hardly suffice to settle the differences, now so vast, between the contending parties in the empire. For, as Franklin went on to insist, referring to the various permanent coercive measures enacted last spring—the Government Act and the others: "a new Dispute had now been rais'd, by the Parliament's pretending to a Power of altering our Charters and establish'd Laws, which was of still more importance to us than their Claim of Taxation, as it set us all adrift, and left us without a Privilege we could depend upon but at their Pleasure; this was a Situation we could not possibly be in; and as Lord North's Proposition had no Relation to this Matter, if the other" about taxes "had been such as we could have agreed to, we should still be far from a Reconciliation."

Those were the agent's feelings as expressed March 1. By then, Franklin was convinced that any hope of harmonizing objectives with the present ministry had passed. He hardly regretted it. To a Philadelphia friend who had proposed a plan that would permanently establish the union between England and its colonies, the doctor had written a few days earlier, on February 25, stating his own lately formed conviction of why any such closer union was undesirable:

> When I consider the extream Corruption prevalent among all Orders of Men in this old rotten State, and the glorious publick Virtue so predominant in our rising Country, I cannot but apprehend more Mischief than Benefit from a closer Union. I fear They will drag us after them in all the plundering Wars their desperate Circumstances, Injustice and Rapacity, may prompt them to undertake; and their wide-wasting Prodigality and Profusion [open] a Gulph that will swallow up every Aid we may distress ourselves to afford them. Here Numberless and needless Places, enormous Salaries, Pensions, Perquisites, Bribes, groundless Quarrels, foolish Expeditions, false Accompts or no Accompts, Contracts and Jobbs devour all Revenue, and produce continual Necessity in the Midst of natural Plenty. I apprehend therefore that To unite us intimately, will only be to corrupt and poison us also.

The agent had begun clearing his desk as February ended, writing to friends and family overseas in preparation for setting off at last for home. He wrote not only to Joseph Galloway in

Philadelphia about the plan for union; he wrote to Boston to his sister Jane, and to Mr. Bowdoin, answering a letter from last fall by means of which young Quincy had been introduced to London. February 25: "I received your kind Letter of Sept. 6 by Mr. Quincy," Franklin began, then went on to assure that Bostonian of the justice of his censure back then of governmental measures; yet now, six months later, those measures "are still persisted in and will I trust continue to produce Effects directly contrary to those intended; will *unite* instead of *dividing* us, *strengthen* and make us more *resolute* instead of *intimidating* us, and work our *Honour* and *Advantage* instead of the *Disgrace* and *Ruin* designed for us."

Before concluding, the doctor alluded briefly to the new young friend that Bowdoin's introduction had furnished him. "I am much pleased with Mr. Quincy. 'Tis a thousand Pities his Strength of Body is not equal to his Strength of Mind. His Zeal for the Public (like that of David for God's House) will I fear eat him up."

And next day, on the same distressing subject, at more length, Franklin wrote another interested party near Boston, in Braintree, an old friend of twenty years, Josiah Quincy Sr.

London, February 26, 1775

Dear Sir,

I received, and perused with great pleasure, the letter you honoured me with, by your amiable and valuable son. I thank you for introducing me to the acquaintance of a person so deserving of esteem for his public and private virtues. I hope for your sake, and that of his friends and country, that his present indisposition may wear off, and his health be established. His coming over has been of great service to our cause, and would have been much greater, if his constitution would have borne the fatigues of being more frequently in company. He can acquaint you so fully with the state of things here, that my enlarging upon them will be unnecessary. I most sincerely wish him a prosperous voyage, and a happy meeting with his friends and family; and to you, my old dear friend, and the rest of those you love, every kind of felicity; being, with the truest esteem and affection, Yours,

BENJAMIN FRANKLIN

P.S. Besides that the air of this city is found extremely prejudicial to his health, all our friends here are of opinion that your son's return at this time, when writing is so inconvenient, may be of singular service.

The day after Franklin wrote that letter, the ailing young Quincy moved back from Islington to London. This was February 27. The journal that the patriot had begun when leaving Salem on his mission to England last September was to run only a few days longer. On the 28th, the invalid with Mr. Bromfield took a post chaise to Fulham to dine with Bromfield's partner, "a very amiable, sensible friend of liberty"; and on that day Quincy wrote his will. On March 1, he talked privately for an hour and a half with Dr. Franklin about "what course America, and especially New England, ought now and during the spring and summer to hold. I wish I might with propriety enter his discourse" into the pages of the journal. More talk about America on the 2d, with Sheriff Lee; and on March 3, "This day being the day before my departure, I dined with Dr Franklin and had three hour's private conversation with him." The agent remained confident that English manufacturers would not long tolerate the loss of American trade. "Let your adherence be to the non-importation and non-exportation agreement a year from next September, or to the next session of Parliament," Franklin predicted, "and the day is won." America's friends here— the Chathams and Shelburnes, the Camdens and Burkes—would, he felt certain, have come to power by then.

That same evening a last glimpse, happily of a young man feeling "great satisfaction"—Quincy sitting reading aloud to friends his reports of the debates in the House of Lords, those glorious outpourings by Chatham and others in support of redressing colonial grievances. His listeners judged the transcriptions that the American had taken down "exceedingly correct, and were amazed at the blunders, omissions, and misrepresentations of the printed accounts."

And at that point, abruptly, Quincy's English journal ends.

23

DEPARTURES

ACCORDING TO HIS JOURNAL, the ailing Quincy was to leave London on March 4, the day after a final conference with his patron Franklin. Perhaps he did; with the journal abandoned, the record becomes obscure. Perhaps he ventured by land to one of the port cities on England's southern coast. Or maybe illness delayed his departure. Or he may have boarded ship, but contrary winds prevented the vessel from casting off. Quincy's son and biographer has him departing for America no earlier than the 16th (though Thomas Hutchinson at the time recorded Quincy gone from London well before then). In any case, on March 16 the traveler, aboard ship for sure, dated a sheet of paper on which to write a letter postponed in the event a couple of days. It was redated March 18, and addressed to his host and caretaker Thomas Bromfield in Islington—

But here occurs one of those coincidences too unlikely for fiction. On that very day, March 18, Quincy's adversary Thomas Hutchinson records in his journal, uniquely, without further comment: "After dinner went with E[lisha] H[utchinson] and Mr Clarke, to make a visit to Mr Bromfield at Islington." During the visit, would there not inevitably have been mention among those Massachusetts merchants of the host's recent houseguest from Boston, Mr. Quincy?

That same Saturday, aboard ship entering Plymouth Harbor, Josiah Quincy was writing to his friend Bromfield back in Islington, the last letter he would ever write: "Dear Bromfield, Paper being scarce, I am obliged to take the remains of a letter I was beginning to you two days since, when the boat [that would have carried it ashore] put off and left the ship. The sea runs high and I can scarcely write legibly."

Those words being fashioned with an effort would not be read by the addressee. The letter was to remain among Quincy's papers, and the water-stained sheet now reposes in the Massachusetts Historical Society, as evocative as if written a week ago, its penmanship forever wrenched by the vessel's long-ago tossing: "The sea runs high . . . A word as to my health. My cough is far from better, though in the day time I am troubled a very trifle with it."

Other matters about the voyage seemed more troubling than the cough. "I wrote you I had been ill-used and deceived. I discover every day more instances of it." To what was the passenger referring: to disappointed hopes concerning support from English Whig acquaintances or to something more mundane, such as wretched accommodations aboard ship? "If we reach into Plymouth tonight," he went on, "I shall have a thousand minds to go to Bristol"—where Dr. Fothergill had suggested that the patient convalesce in any case, for a complete restoration of his health. Bristol, which Quincy had visited happily over the recent Christmas holiday: the temptation must have been very strong. "I am perplexed much what I ought to do."

Yet the vessel did not after all proceed into Plymouth Docks (at the start of his stay in England last November, a sightseeing Quincy, exulting in health that his voyage from America appeared to have restored, had stood awed before the specimens of England's martial might as revealed among armament and ships of the line at Plymouth Docks). The vessel instead made for the open sea, so that this his last letter remained on board, as the long voyage across the Atlantic got under way.

Quincy was gone—with hopes that the passage would restore his health, as had the passage eastward in the fall—and Franklin was going. In London a week before, on March 13, Thomas Hutchinson at Lincoln's Inn Hall had encountered the solicitor general, who reported having lately heard that Dr. Franklin would be setting out next week for America. Mr. Wedderburn was of the opinion the agent ought to be stopped. Governor Hutchinson had no difficulty understanding why—indeed, Lord Suffolk would say the same thing a week later: that Franklin should be prevented from leaving the country. But how? The governor and the solicitor general (those two whom Philadelphia had burned in effigy months before) "talked of the impossibility of conviction in America: the difficulty of punishing without." Once Franklin got back home he would be safe from prosecution, and yet there seemed to be no grounds for detaining him here. Mr. Hutchinson inquired of the jurist whether a bill might not be framed in Parliament to deal with the situation. Very likely—Wedderburn "advised me by a letter to put Lord North in mind of it." Accordingly, Hutchinson sat down that evening and wrote the prime minister, letting him know precisely that Quincy was gone and Franklin was going, "and the mischief I apprehended they designed, &c."

That mischief would take the form of giving comfort to the enemies of the empire. As the governor phrased it elsewhere, he was concerned "lest F——'s return to America should excite to still greater acts of revolt." Hold firm, the new arrivals from London were sure to urge colonials in Boston and Philadelphia; and, seeming to speak knowledgeably, they would be listened to. Continue to resist Parliament's laws. Decline to buy English goods. Friends of patriots in England—English merchants and manufacturers and politicians—would soon be uniting (they would say) to advance the resisters' cause. Such mischief as that those two would spread abroad, to keep up the spirit of opposition; and, in Hutchinson's view, it would all be lies, pernicious lies to threaten the peace and delay the resolution of a quarrel that England meant neither to leave nor to lose. There was no such support in England for the colonies as Franklin imagined; yet the doctor and young Quincy in the provinces would set about "advising measures to distress or ruin the Kingdom," such advice as already had "irritated the Ministry to that degree, that they don't now feel for the distresses of the Americans as they otherwise would do."

An example of ministerial irritation was much on Mr. Hutchinson's mind these March days. Not only had government proposed a bill to restrict New England's trade drastically; it was even now putting before Parliament a measure that would deny New England the time-honored use of fisheries off the Canadian and American coasts, those fishing grounds on the Georges Bank that stretch a hundred and fifty miles northeast from Nantucket

and that had provided provincials a hardy livelihood for generations.

The New England bill, including the restriction on the fisheries,
was debated in Parliament in late February and early March. As
with the deliberation of all such measures, this took many days—
to present the bill, allow speeches from supporters and opponents,
have various readings of it and vote on it in the Commons, then repeat the process in the House of Lords. Hutchinson watched apprehensively as the measure progressed through its various stages.
By March 8, it had passed the Commons on a third reading.

That same morning the governor had called on Lord Dartmouth,
who in the course of their conversation relayed the contents of a
dispatch from General Gage recently received, "of the 27th Jany,
advising that he had sent 100 men to Marshfield and Scituate,
many of the inhabitants having petitioned for them, and that he
was sending two Regiments to New Hampshire."

Gage's report, gratifying to the colonial secretary as evidence
that loyal Americans were starting to trust administration for aid
and to speak out at last against incendiaries, only added to the
governor's concern. Hutchinson was moved to urge his lordship to
support an amendment to the fisheries bill that was currently in
Parliament, lest "such as were now beginning to exert themselves"
in Marshfield, as Gage reported, "should be discouraged and fall
back." When Dartmouth asked his friend for alternatives to the
present measure, the governor suggested exempting from the
fisheries-restriction any Americans who demonstrated their loyalty by declining to abide by the Continental Congress's embargo
against English goods. The colonial secretary agreed to put the
suggestion before Lord North.

Later that day the governor, still troubled, addressed Dartmouth
in writing "and represented afresh the necessity of an alteration in
the Bill, as Marshf[iel]d and Scituate had much of their
depend[enc]e on the Mackerel fishery, which began in July, or
about that time, and ended in October or Novemb."

Thus loyal, innocent Marshfield fishermen would find themselves among the first to suffer from Parliament's latest measure.
Yet the very day that Governor Hutchinson wrote his letter urging
leniency, the fisheries bill passed the House of Commons, as he
was to learn to his dismay on the morrow. "I had rather no Bill had

passed than such an one as this," he complained promptly to a correspondent in America, "and as soon as I knew of it, gave my opinion that it would distress more of the friends, than of the enemies to Govt." To add to his dismay, the governor was told that during the debates before the passage yesterday, colony agents had been admitted to the galleries, where they would have heard such an indiscretion as this that one of the supporters of the bill had blathered forth: "We must pinch them," Lord Clare had cried of the colonials; "they must be compelled to submit without delay. If they are able to hold out, we know that we are not. What's done must be done at once, or they will finally conquer"—with, Hutchinson noted in his journal, "Franklin all the while in the Gallery, staring with his spectacles; and no doubt before this time, the relation of this speech is on its way to America."

Where it would give further encouragement to the foes of empire.

During these recent busy days, the bespectacled Franklin had indeed found time to attend debates in Parliament. The agent's date of departure from England was very close now; and with affairs to settle after a decade in residence, his hours were full. It was mid-March already. To a correspondent in Pennsylvania, Franklin was writing on March 13, much in the vein that Mr. Hutchinson supposed: "All the Hopes and Dependance of the Ministry, are in Dividing us, by working upon our Fears and Hopes. If we are faithful to each other, our Adversaries are ruin'd." And to another Pennsylvania correspondent the same day, to Charles Thomson, secretary of the Continental Congress, the agent made time to report on the congress's ill-fated petition to his majesty, delivered to Dartmouth in December and put before Parliament in January, which "has lain upon the Table of both Houses ever since it was sent down to them among the Papers that accompany'd it from above, and has had no particular Notice taken of it." Franklin and the other agents had sought to be heard in support of the petition, but their request had been "rejected with Scorn in the Commons; which must satisfy the future Congress," scheduled to meet in Philadelphia in May, "that nothing is to be expected here from that Mode of Application"— from humbly petitioning the king for redress.

The philosopher had other correspondents to deal with here at the last. March 14: "Purposing to embark for America in a few Days, I cannot depart without taking Leave of my dear Lord

Kaims, to whose Civilities and Friendship I have been so much oblig'd." March 16: "Dr. Franklin presents his respectful Compliments to Lord Bessborough, with Thanks for the obliging Invitation, which he should embrace with Pleasure, but that he expects to be at Sea on that Day in his Way to America." March 19, to his successor as agent, Arthur Lee: "I leave Directions with Mrs. Stevenson to deliver you all the Massachusetts Papers, when you please to call for them. I am sorry that the Hurry of Preparing for my Voyage and the many Hindrances I have met with, prevented my meeting you." A note as well to Mrs. Stevenson herself, his landlady, containing last-minute requests and instructions. And charges from friends to take on, such as that from the good Quaker Dr. Fothergill, at half past ten on the 19th: "Be kind enough to take the charge of the inclosed and convey them at thy leisure."

But even with all those claims on his time, Franklin had been at the House of Lords March 16, during the debate on the New England bill. He went specifically to attend as the eloquent Lord Camden, friend of America, spoke. (Hutchinson heard Camden's speech as well; and though the matter was not to the governor's liking, he had to admire the manner: His lordship "rose and spoke an hour and an half without the least hesitation. I never heard a greater flow of words, but my knowledge of facts in this controversy caused his misrepresentations and glosses to appear in a very strong light.") Franklin for his part was bothered by no such misrepresentations—thought Camden's speech admirable—but he did hear much in the Lords on that occasion to infuriate him. It was during this same debate that the earl of Sandwich uttered his notorious slander about the cowardice of Americans—how he wished there were a couple of hundred thousand of such poor, raw, dastardly fellows to take the field, instead of the forty or fifty thousand that were estimated. The more the better. Why, a thousand British regulars, his lordship boasted, would be able to drive a hundred thousand such poltroons into the sea.

Others supporting government spoke to the same purpose, if somewhat less immoderately, so that Franklin in the course of the debate felt himself "much disgusted . . . by many base Reflections on American Courage, Religion, Understanding, &c. in which we were treated with the utmost Contempt, as the lowest of Mankind, and almost of a different Species from the English of Britain; but particularly the American Honesty was abused by some of the Lords, who asserted that we were all Knaves, and wanted only by this Dispute to avoid paying our Debts; that if we had any Sense of Equity or Justice, we should offer Payment of the Tea &c."

Having attended two or three such outpourings, even the loyal Hutchinson was feeling "the high opinion" that he had earlier formed of the dignity of the Lords to be, as he put it gingerly, "lessened." As for Franklin, that gentleman left Parliament House now in cold fury and, in his indignation, went home to Craven Street and straightway drafted a scathing and most irregular memorandum to the colonial secretary.

A memorial it was, from Benjamin Franklin, agent of the province of Massachusetts Bay, to the right honorable the earl of Dartmouth, one of his majesty's principal secretaries of state. Given in London this 16th day of March 1775.

> Whereas an Injury done, can only give the Party injured a Right to full Reparation; or, in case that be refused, a Right to return an equal Injury. And whereas the Blockade of Boston, now continued nine Months, hath every Week of its Continuance done Damage to that Town equal to what was suffered there by the India Company; it follows that such *exceeding* Damage is an *Injury* done by this Government, for which Reparation ought to be made. And whereas Reparation of Injuries ought always (agreeable to the Custom of all Nations, savage as well as civilized) to be first required, before Satisfaction is taken by a Return of Damage to the Aggressors; which was not done by Great Britain in the Instance above mentioned. I the underwritten, do therefore, as their Agent in the Behalf of my Country and the said Town of Boston, protest against the Continuance of the said Blockade: And I do hereby solemnly demand Satisfaction for the accumulated Injury done them beyond the Value of the India Company's Tea destroyed.
>
> And whereas the Conquest of the Gulph of St. Lawrence, the Coasts of Labrador and Nova Scotia, and the Fisheries possess'd by the French there and on the Banks of Newfoundland, so far as they were more extended than at present, was made by the *joint Forces* of Britain and the Colonies, the latter having nearly an equal Number of Men in that Service with the former; it follows that the Colonies have an equitable and just Right to participate in the Advantage of those Fisheries. I do therefore in the Behalf of the Colony of the Massachusetts Bay, protest against the Act now under Consideration in Parliament, for de-

priving that Province, with others, of that Fishery (on pretence of their refusing to purchase British Commodities) as an Act highly unjust and injurious: And I give Notice, that Satisfaction will probably one day be demanded for all the Injury that may be done and suffered in the Execution of such Act: And that the Injustice of the Proceeding is likely to give such Umbrage to *all the Colonies*, that in no future War, wherein other Conquests may be meditated, either a Man or a Shilling will be obtained from any of them to aid such Conquests, till full Satisfaction be made as aforesaid.

B FRANKLIN

This was neither the language of diplomacy nor the terms in which one addressed a peer of the realm. "I do . . . solemnly demand Satisfaction"; "I . . . protest . . . an Act highly unjust and injurious: And I give Notice, that Satisfaction will . . . be demanded for all the Injury that may be done and suffered in the Execution of such Act." Franklin, that able diplomat, of course knew as much. Accordingly, having poured out his feelings, the politic agent cooled enough to show his handiwork to an English friend, who "lookt at it and at me several Times alternately, as if he apprehended me a little out of my Senses." Perhaps so; the philosopher was harried and hurried in these late days. Would his friend be so good as to show the memorial to Lord Camden for his opinion?

The friend did so, at once, and in a note of that same date returned Franklin's memorial, "which it is thought," he wrote pointedly, "might be attended with dangerous consequences to your person, and contribute to exasperate the Nation."

Leave the memorial unpublished—and to make sure, lest the written message should miscarry, Franklin's friend hunted him up and delivered Camden's negative concurrence in person.

Thus, the document joined those other articulate specimens of the philosopher's temper—his famous letter to William Strahan after war had begun ("You are now my Enemy, and I am, Yours."), his withering and well-deserved reproach to the incorrigible Arthur Lee from Passy in April 1778—that were composed to ease a nature overstrained, then never sent.

In the present case, it hardly mattered one way or the other. Government's policy was already irretrievably committed, in the form of Dartmouth's dispatch to Gage, the original and a copy, aboard ships somewhere off the English coast and bound for

America. Nothing that Franklin or anyone else might say would alter that fact. Meanwhile, in the two or three days remaining to him in England, the agent continued preparing for his departure, giving out to his many acquaintances that he would be leaving London on Monday morning, March 20.

Actually, he left on the 21st. His final evening he chose to spend, without molestation of additional farewells, with an old and dear friend, one of the Club of Honest Whigs, Dr. Joseph Priestley, discoverer of oxygen. Years afterward, Priestley recalled having passed that last day in London with Dr. Franklin, "without any other company; and much of the time was employed in reading American newspapers, especially accounts of the reception which the 'Boston Port Bill,' met with in America; and as he read the addresses to the inhabitants of Boston, from the places in the neighbourhood"—supporting the port in its ordeal—"the tears trickled down his cheeks."

Even before the agent was gone, Mr. Hutchinson was hearing gossip of his having set out. This same Monday, as Franklin in seclusion perused his newspapers with Priestley, the governor was already learning from friends that "a crony of F——n's," calling at Craven Street on the 19th, had been informed that the philosopher had left for Portsmouth the day before.

That gossip Hutchinson was apprised of March 21, the actual day of departure. And on Tuesday the 22nd, at the colonial office in Whitehall, the governor learned at last of Dartmouth's momentous letter to Gage written in late January. "Knox read to me the Instructions to Gage, to apprehend the Leaders of the Congress, if they refuse, upon his Proclamation, to separate. This is the Provincial Congress; and he is directed to do it though a conflict with his troops should be like to be the consequence."

The instructions, the governor noted, were "intended by the *Falcon*, who was under sailing orders about the 20th of December." But the *Falcon* as late as March 12 was known to be no farther along on its voyage than Torbay, in western England. "Duplicate went by the *Nautilus*, who on the same 12th of March, was at Portsmouth: so that it's most likely both original and duplicate are yet within Scilly"—nearly three months later, for whatever reason, not even as far along on the crossing as the Scilly Isles off England's southwest coast.

But the two vessels would be westward bound in any case, however haltingly, bearing the fate of the empire with them, making
moot all those recent, windy, heartfelt debates in the House of
Lords—of Viscount Dudley and the earl of Sandwich and the duke
of Grafton and the rest—about trade and fisheries and American
cowardice.

24

MR. QUINCY'S
VOYAGE HOME

DR. FRANKLIN LEFT LONDON for Portsmouth and his passage to America on March 21, 1775. Three days earlier, on the 18th, from Plymouth in the west of England, the Boston packet on which Franklin's young friend Josiah Quincy had earlier embarked had at last set course for the open sea.

The tubercular's voyage proved long and dreadful, week following miserable wave-tossed week. Through the length of the crossing, the weather was damp and cold, forcing the patient from more wholesome air topside down into the noxious confines of his cabin. And the days and nights dragged on, seaborne, unreal, plunging toward catastrophe.

During those same days, back on solid ground in London, Mr. Thomas Hutchinson continued to take his airings about the city, tirelessly made his social calls, wrote his numerous letters as March yielded to April. The governor was growing increasingly concerned, fully aware of the significance of what Mr. Knox had shared with him at the colonial office on March 22: that Lord Dartmouth had dispatched orders to Gage to apprehend the leaders of the provincial congress in Massachusetts, even if "a conflict with his troops should be like to be the consequence." Never for a moment did Hutchinson doubt that such instructions bound westward on the high seas must, upon reaching their destination, one way or another precipitate the resolution of the long crisis of these late months and years.

Not that Dartmouth's instructions, as the governor judged them, appeared anything less than necessary. They would, in fact, in the end serve to deliver America from its enemies. "I hope," he wrote a friend overseas after learning what his lordship had ordered, "your deliverance draws near." Then added: "Dr F—— is gone out to deceive the Colonies, and some say to gather them together in battell: but the more general opinion is, that he intends no more than to keep them from complying with any conciliatory proposals by an assurance that if they can hold out another year, the Kingdom will be so distressed that it must concede to every demand of the Colonies. Never was there a more distracted scheme."

For if that was Dr. Franklin's expectation, it was the merest madness. England stood united behind government's policies as never before. "Perhaps at this distance," Mr. Hutchinson wrote another of his numerous American correspondents at the time, "I have observed more distinctly than you who are upon the spot, that your affairs, step by step, have been constantly growing worse and worse ever since I left you." By now every report from Boston, from New York, from up and down the seaboard told of confusion approaching anarchy. Accordingly, the hour for leniency had passed. Troop reinforcements had been dispatched to restore order, and a firm course of conduct, with appropriate conciliation, had been legislated. Faced with such resoluteness, the colonies must give in, must cease their lawlessness and resume a posture of respectful obedience to Parliament and the Crown.

But perhaps provincials in their delusion meant to defy the will of virtually the entire English nation. Lord Dartmouth feared they might. His lordship "seems very apprehensive," Hutchinson had noted in his journal March 29, "that the New England people will resist the King's troops, and does not know but some action between them will be best." As well, perhaps, to have it out now as later. Yet for his part, the governor dreaded the thought of blood being spilled. "I hope," he wrote Thomas Oliver on April 8, "your opinion, that the people will not resist the King's troops is well founded for I do not wish for the loss of a drop of blood." Any such resistance, he insisted, would be irrational, as "nothing can be gained" by it "and everything may be lost." Indeed, there were those here in England who were saying (Hutchinson took care to relay the opinion to his New England correspondents) that the greatest misfortune that could befall the Americans would be to defy and triumph over the British army now in the colonies; for such a pyrrhic victory "would bring upon them the boundless rage and fury of the whole British nation, which I hope in mercy to them they will never feel."

But surely matters had not proceeded so far. "I cannot yet believe," he wrote his son on April 10, "Mr Adams will be able to persuade our people to so irrational a step as to form themselves into a body to oppose the King's troops." Not that Americans were cowards—of course they were not. Hutchinson knew them. But neither were they madmen: "They are not," as he put it, "so distracted." So would they fight or submit? "Before this reaches you," the governor added prophetically, "it will be determined."

And maybe the Hutchinsons would be back at their Milton home, order restored, by summer's end. Elisha longed to be there even sooner. The governor's son was feeling like a prisoner here in London, "with my heart and affections in New England." The young man's wife was over there, his family, a child born to him since he had left Boston. To Polly, Elisha confided on April 9: "I have all along been pleasing myself with the thoughts of returning to you in the spring"—in this very season—"and had determined in my own mind, to take passage in *Daverson*, but when I came to mention it, a few days ago, so far from finding any of my friends consenting to it, they all advised against it, and my letters by Robson discourage it, and tell me that I may think myself fortunate in being here at this time."

So here the exile must stay, he and his father and his sister and Billy, in London while spring advanced. The weather, at any rate, was remarkably pleasant, the season far forward of New England springtimes. The afternoon of April 12, Wednesday, Governor Hutchinson, anticipating a debate on the bill restraining the trade of the southern colonies—of Maryland, Virginia, South Carolina—attended at the House of Lords. But to his surprise, the bill passed "without a word of debate," so determined was Parliament on the intimidating course it had chosen to pursue. And on the following day, Hutchinson's son Elisha was at the upper chamber as well, "where," he wrote Polly, "I saw the King give his assent to one of the American Bills, and a number of others. I wish you could have gone with me. The King is such a figure of a man, that, seated on his throne in his Royal Robes, there is nothing here that affords such a feast to my eyes."

So the Restraining Bill—that declaration of economic war, extended now to colonies north and south—would pass effortlessly through Parliament and receive his majesty's approval. For his part, Josiah Quincy, resting his own eyes some weeks earlier on the spectacle that provided a feast for Elisha's—sovereignty bedecked in threads of gold—had been affected differently. Quincy had written disrespectfully of George III's "gigling and phiz," of his face and his foolish manner. But that was sometime back, at the opening of Parliament in November. Now, through March and these same days of April, as the Hutchinsons in London loyally awaited American news, as Parliament and his majesty adhered to their fateful policies, the Boston packet bearing young Quincy, by this time grievously ill, was all the while beating slowly westward, through rough seas and weather, toward New England.

On board, the time of arrival in America had been predicted for midmonth, but April 15 came and went with no land in sight. Confined to his cabin, the patient grew ever weaker. He was dying, and by now knew it. No longer did he have strength even to lift a pen. The hope of his heart was to survive long enough to make his way to Boston, there to speak with Samuel Adams and Dr. Warren. But more days were passing with only the sea in sight; and finally, as late as April 21 (momentous interlude ashore where the vessel was headed), Quincy was forced to summon a member of the ship's crew to his berth, to take down what the patient would have written if he could.

"Mr. Quincy is so low, that he probably will not be able to read a word of the foregoing but it is to be hoped it will be intelligible with a little pains," explained the ill-lettered seaman at the end of the pages on which had been inscribed final thoughts of a dying man. "Ever since I have been out," that feeble voice lamented of the voyage, "almost every thing has been different from what I expected, instead of pleasant weather"—which might have restored him—"the most inclement and damp which removes me entirely from the deck,—and although I was flattered with the hope of getting into port six days ago, I am here as distant from it as I was when the encouragement was given me. Had Providence been pleased that I should have reached America six days ago, I should have been able to converse with my friends. I am persuaded that this voyage and passage are instruments to put an end to my being. His Holy will be done!"

Yet in his anguish, this mortal felt bound to explain his recent conduct. Quincy had not wanted to sail for America, nor had his physician, the good Dr. Fothergill, wanted him to. But the voyage had seemed preferable to remaining in unwholesome London, and there had been no friend to accompany the patient to Bristol, no lodger in England able to give him the round-the-clock care that his malady required. However, "the most weighty motive of all that determined my conduct," he struggled to explain as the seaman wrote, "was the extreme urgency of about fifteen or twenty most stanch friends to America, many of them the most learned and respectable characters in the kingdom for my immediately proceeding to Boston." The patriot had perfectly known what those friends thought about the contest between Britain and America, indispensably valuable considerations that he would have been able to share orally with colonial leaders at home. During such tense times as these, sentiments and strategies from England could not prudently have been set down in writing. But to Quincy they might safely be entrusted, "and I was immediately on my arrival to assemble certain persons to whom I was to communicate my trust, and had God spared my life, it seems it would have been of great service to my country."

Here at the very last then, the patriot's regret lay most in being denied the opportunity one final time to serve his country. A few words must be added about the disposal of his remains. He would have his father build a tomb in Braintree, "a large durable stone tomb," near that of his ancestors. Erect a monument on it—"But all this is on the supposition that my most dear and beloved wife will consent to her being laid by my side . . . at her death. To this purpose I am willing to be interred any where, and pray that my request may not be derided, because some people may think it whimsical."

Thus, on the 21st, Quincy's late thoughts found utterance, during another dismal Friday at sea. What patriot wisdom would perish with him? The 22nd came and went, and the 23rd, and the 24th; and his feeble frame still clung to life. At last, on April 25, 1775, the vessel entered Gloucester Harbor, some twenty-five miles north of

Boston. At once a boat put ashore to summon physicians. Those gentlemen hurried aboard, with "other respectable persons" of the town (according to the local *Essex Gazette*), but could only stand in the close cabin helplessly by Quincy's berth and watch the patient expire, his native province so close, just there, beyond his dying view, his dying mind unaware of the astounding events that had occurred a few miles south only a week before.

They tried to locate Mrs. Quincy with their sad news. But she had left Boston—the burdens that humanity must bear!—her infant daughter having died only two weeks earlier, April 13, and her only other child, a boy of three, ill with a sickness that appeared to be mortal. The mother and her one surviving child had withdrawn to Norwich, Connecticut, to be with family there. And there, just turned thirty, Abigail Phillips Quincy must grieve the separate devastations of losing a daughter and a husband, yet in her grief would somehow manage to nurse back to health her only son.

That surviving son was to grow up to lead a long and most distinguished life, another Josiah Quincy, the third, dying himself as a grand old man not before he had lived past ninety, having served as renowned mayor of Boston in the 1820s (Quincy Market was inspired by and is named for him) and president of Harvard College, public speaker, prolific author, father in turn of another mayor of Boston, yet another Josiah Quincy, in the 1840s, and grandfather of still another Boston mayor, one more Josiah Quincy, the fifth, in the 1890s. The family that at the nation's birth had seemed on the verge of extinction would thus recover and flourish through an abundance of often impressive descendants, down even into the present.

But all that future brightness lay hidden behind the clouds of the mournful afternoon of April 25, 1775, as the patriot Quincy breathed his last aboard ship in Gloucester Harbor, his destination in sight, unattainable, his messages to colonial leaders undelivered, their purport forever unknown.

And ashore at the time, all was in turmoil. Seven days earlier, at no great distance from Gloucester, Governor Gage in Boston had finally taken the step that brought on the Revolution.

The governor had had little choice in the matter. Despite the care his excellency had exercised throughout the fall and the winter to avoid just such an outcome, events had conspired to make it irresistible. Far back, at the beginning of September, Gage had ordered a strike on a powder house in Charlestown across the river from Boston, sending some 250 regulars out in the predawn hours to confiscate what was stored there. The mission had been executed successfully, the numerous half barrels of powder secured. Such a venture was thus shown to be practicable. Now, when the governor learned that colonials were assembling military supplies in the village of Concord eighteen miles inland to use against his majesty, he had good reason to think that an expedition properly managed, planned in secret, and taking advantage of surprise in the darkness of early morning would succeed as well in Concord here in April as it had in Charlestown last September.

Governor Gage knew very well what the colonials were up to. A network of spies kept him admirably well informed of all their moves—spies even within the provincial congress itself, where one of the trusted patriot leaders, Dr. Benjamin Church, regularly attended at the secret meetings and promptly informed the governor of everything that had gone on. Spies were in Concord, too, to report to Gage precisely where the magazines of powder and cartridges were, and in which houses, even in which rooms of those houses were stored the cannon and coehorns, the flour, the fish and salt and rice that provincials had lately been gathering against the king's peace.

Moreover, during stagnant winter months the general had taken to exercising his town-bound troops by having them march forth from Boston into the countryside, one battalion one day, another the next, and along different routes; so that provincials had become glumly accustomed to seeing ranks and files of redcoats leaving the town toward various unspecified destinations and returning. One more foray westward might not be remarked upon. In addition, Gage had taken care secretly to have the roads to Concord sketched and mapped, in order that his forces would know where along the way to be wary, where to meet the enemy advantageously if an encounter should prove unavoidable.

To such a point had matters come by mid-April: colonial arms and supplies being assembled and stored nearby, Gage informed of it and inclined to believe that a surprise strike over mapped roads in predawn hours might successfully destroy those stores. That was the local situation on the evening of April 14, when HMS *Nautilus* put in to Boston from England, bearing copies of dispatches from the secretary of state for the American Department, including one dated January 27.

As we have seen, Dartmouth's dispatch of that date all but insisted on action. The general, it was hoped, would henceforth "take a more active & determined part" and would no longer allow himself to be bottled up in Boston, cowed by rebel farmers in the countryside. Against such an impromptu enemy, "Force should be repelled by Force." A relatively small contingent of British regulars, such as were in Massachusetts even now, should be able (in his lordship's opinion from distant Westminster) to deal with a disorganized, undisciplined multitude—rather more successfully, in fact, than a larger army, reinforced from home, might do later, after the people had had time to form themselves into a well-armed, confident fighting unit. Moreover, in confronting such a ragtag, poorly supported force of provincials as this at present appeared to be, "every thing must be put to the issue of a single Action." Strike at once, Dartmouth seemed to be urging, and the incipient rebellion might be doomed in a day.

Those orders at last in hand, the cautious Gage (who liked Americans, had lived in America nineteen years, was married to an American) knew what he must do. His numerous spies had laid the obvious opportunity before the general. If he should take proper precautions and use every means to keep his plan secret until ready to execute it, "it can hardly fail of Success," the colonial secretary had written encouragingly in his dispatch, "and will perhaps be accomplished without bloodshed."

Keep the plan secret. But considerable numbers of people must finally be involved in such an operation; and the provincials had their spies as well, had developed their own network over the winter, as they scowled down upon British regulars on their marches out of Boston into the countryside. Farmers and townspeople had learned to scrutinize the troops closely and to spread word of their movements fast and far. Thus in mid-April, patriots in the town, already aware through ships bringing news from England that reinforcements to Gage's army were on the way, guessed at once what certain irregular movements in and about the British camp just now must mean.

Boats of the royal fleet in the harbor were being brought ashore and repaired. Elite companies—grenadiers, light infantry—of the troops about town were being relieved of regular duties to prepare for special exercises. The true nature of those exercises patriots anticipated, and they divined to what use the boats would be put. So confident of Gage's intentions were the colonials that villagers in Concord had already been alerted to hide their military supplies; already they were burying cannon balls in local ponds and wheeling other materiel by oxcart into the surrounding woods.

On the chilly night of April 18, twenty-one companies of light infantry and grenadiers—some seven hundred of his majesty's troops—gathered as quietly as twenty-one companies were able, in moonlit darkness at the foot of Boston Common, along the water's edge. It was about ten o'clock. Lieutenant Colonel Smith bore orders to proceed with the troops by boat across to Charlestown, then march them overland the eighteen miles through Menotomy and Lexington and on to Concord, where they should arrive just before sunup, around 5 A.M., and there secure the bridges of the village and destroy any military stores, before returning to Boston by noon.

That was the plan: a neat, swift, secret and silent strike. But as it turned out, the foray was none of those things. Lights in a Boston church steeple signaled patriots over the water in Charlestown precisely what the troops were up to before they were well into their boats to be ferried across the bay. Patriot horsemen, one of them Paul Revere, sped ahead down the roads toward Concord to warn country folk of the British approach. Meanwhile, that approach was delayed by not untypical military bungling: an insufficient number of boats, more rations needed and sent back for, an uncomfortable wait in the frigid swamps at the river's edge on the Charlestown side until confusions could be cleared up.

At last the troops were mustering on dry ground opposite Boston, ready to march. But already it was two in the morning, so that by five, when they should have been in Concord, they were no farther along than Lexington, seven or eight miles shy of their goal. And at Lexington the nervous British encountered a ragged force of sixty or seventy colonials, armed, gathered at dawn on the village green.

Major Pitcairn of the marines quite properly commanded his troops to surround and disarm the locals; he could hardly have passed by and left them with their weapons at his back. But in the confusion that followed, someone—British or American—fired, and all at once others were firing, horrific loud explosions and the acrid smell and the thick puffs of smoke rising. Before order could be restored, eight colonials lay dead on the green, ten more wounded.

Even then, could peace have been salvaged? No English life had yet been lost. Perhaps if the king's forces had turned and marched back to Boston? But they could not turn back; they were under orders to proceed to Concord. And even if they had disobeyed those orders, the word of provincial deaths on the village green would have spread rapidly through the surrounding neighborhood, as it did spread, and the way home to Boston would have been turned into the nightmare journey that it did in fact become.

The troops marched on to Concord as ordered, arriving about eight in the morning, in full daylight three hours behind schedule. As they had been ordered to do, they secured the two bridges, north and south, that gave entrance to the village from the west. Then they began searching the houses that the information of spies had guided them to, piled in the middle of town whatever combustible stores they discovered—gun carriages, wagon wheels, barrels—and set the pile on fire.

At the bridge beyond the northern edge of the village, soldiers were meanwhile watching uneasily as an alarming number of locals gathered above them on nearby Punkatasset Hill to the west. Not just Concord farmers; farmers from Lincoln and other settlements nearby, maybe four hundred up there in all, each one appearing to be armed with his musket, frowning down from the ridge at the British contingent of ninety or so soldiers—four light-infantry companies—moving to secure the little wooden bridge below.

Smoke could be seen beyond the trees, rising from the village. At the village center the British were torching colonial stores, but there was no way to see that from here. Only the smoke rising: The sight stirred those indignant farmers on the crest of the hill to action. "Will you let them burn the town down?" one of their number demanded of Colonel Barrett; and with that challenge ringing in the April air, the farmers began to descend the ridge to the water's edge.

On opposite ends of the bridge over the narrow river, two groups of men—the one to the west in homespun and linsey-woolsey, the other to the east in brick-red uniforms—stood glaring at each other.

What followed lasted no longer than three minutes. The British fired first, and the Americans returned the fire: into the vaunted, fearsome strength that represented England's military might. Suddenly blood was blooming red on English flesh and uniforms, as one, two, three English soldiers staggered and fell. His majesty's forces had been fired upon, and three of their number lay dead on the ground, eight were wounded, and—astounding sight in the noise and smoke and shouting—the other redcoats were all at once fleeing in disarray, in panic, back toward Concord, would flee from there with all haste through a long, long afternoon of weariness and torment and death toward the distant safety of Charlestown, which the exhausted survivors reached finally at sunset.

The Revolution—pivotal event of modern times—had begun.

25

FINAL YEARS OF
MR. HUTCHINSON

BEFORE THE AMERICAN REVOLUTION, the plant of liberty had been deemed the rarest and frailest, if most beautiful, of sovereign flowers, capable of blooming only in sheltered valleys of Switzerland, behind dikes of the Low Countries, briefly and gloriously in ancient Greece and Rome. The Revolution and its aftermath demonstrated that liberty could be nurtured into a tree of such abiding robustness as to offer shade that would span a continent and beyond.

From the American seed grew at once the French Revolution, then the various revolutions in South and Central America, still later the American Civil War—undertaken to preserve the Union that the Founding Fathers had established—and more recently still, those many movements in our own times that have represented themselves as seeking to secure the blessings of freedom for all the world's peoples, to shelter them all under liberty's ample branches.

That centuries-long convulsion commenced irrevocably in the incidents of an April morning in 1775, in a village in Massachusetts Bay. There, British troops—they of the earlier awesome, unanswerable volleys, of the famous, devastating bayonet charges that filled their enemies with dread—had been fired upon. British lives had been lost. And soldiers in red disarray were fleeing into Concord village, to regroup and commence their long march back toward Boston, under withering shot of colonials following closely through the surrounding woods. The episode proved a disaster for his majesty's forces: infantry wearily on the move from eight one evening through to the following sundown, assaulted at the last by an enemy formidable in its wrath, murderous in its skill, maddening in its elusiveness. When the long day finally ended, British casualties numbered over 270 dead, wounded, or missing. American casualties amounted to one-third of that.

The action initiated the only modern war that England has lost. Of the opening rout, Dr. Franklin would give voice to the universal amazement felt about what had happened when General Gage had drawn the sword and begun hostilities. Meeting opposition at Concord, "His Troops made a most vigorous Retreat," Franklin wrote ironically, having learned the facts on his arrival in Philadelphia, "20 Miles in 3 Hours, scarce to be parallell'd in History: the feeble Americans, who pelted them all the Way, could scarce keep up with them." In truth, the retreat had extended over a longer span of horror than three hours, ample time for provincials to vindicate themselves from those charges of pusillanimity leveled in noblemen's speeches to which the agent for the Massachusetts Assembly had been obliged to listen in the House of Lords shortly before leaving England.

News of the violence that had erupted in and around the peacefully named Concord in mid-April reached London not before late May. The patriot version of events arrived first, in the form of an account from Salem aboard a schooner hired by the provincial congress; Captain Derby brought the *Quero* into Southampton on May 27 and was in London with his astounding news the following evening.

Governor Hutchinson took note in a diary entry of the 29th. "Capn Darby came to town last evening. He is sent by the Prov. Congress in a vessel in ballast"—not even waiting to gather a cargo—"to publish here their account of an action between the troops and the inhabit[an]ts on the 19th of April. A vessel which sailed four days before with dispatches from Gage, is not arrived." Derby brought also, as the governor noted, "advice of Quincy's death the night after he landed." But whatever of events in Concord was being bruited about—events far overshadowing young Quincy's demise—however inauspicious or exaggerated this of Gage's expedition into the countryside sounded, the reports just arrived appeared "very unfavourable," Hutchinson did admit, "if not being known that they all came from one side." The congress "hurry away a vessel that their partial accounts may make the first impression. I think Gage's will be different."

Ten days would pass before the general's version of the exchange reached Whitehall. When it arrived, it brought little comfort. Writing April 22, three days after the battle, Gage had done as much as he could to regularize what was extraordinary, first routinely acknowledging receipt of letters from England before commencing matter-of-factly: "I am to acquaint your Lordship that having received Intelligence of a large Quantity of Military Stores being collected at Concord, for the avowed Purpose of Supplying a Body of Troops to act in opposition to His Majesty's Government, I got the Grenadiers and Light Infantry out of Town under the Command of Lieut Colo Smith of the 10th Regt and Major Pitcairne of the Marines with as much Secrecy as possible, on the 18th at Night and with Orders to destroy the said Military Stores." The general went on briefly to recapitulate events of that fateful night and morning, and to allude to the horrible afternoon that followed: "Notwithstanding a continual Skirmish for the Space of Fifteen Miles, receiving Fire from every Hill, Fence, House, Barn, &ca," the troops had returned successfully to Charlestown and been ferried over to Boston. Casualties on both sides had been heavy. Too much praise could not be given the leaders of the expedition: Colonel Smith, Major Pitcairn, Lord Percy reinforcing.

What had to be told was reported succinctly, but Gage's dispatch provided no reassurance. "The whole Country," he ended, "was assembled in Arms with Surprizing Expedition, and Several Thousand are now Assembled about this Town threatning an Attack, and getting up Artillery. And we are very busy in making Preparations to oppose them."

Little in that business could friends of government find to crow about, in London or in Boston either. Nor would much happen to hearten them in days immediately ahead. In Boston, for instance, as of June 1, the situation had deteriorated so that it was "beyond description almost," according to the loyalist Dr. Peter Oliver's vigorously descriptive pen, employed from that place at that time. "You seem in England to be entirely ignorant of the temper of our people. They are as much determined from Florida to Hallifax to oppose you at home, do what you will, as I hear the Ministry are determined to pursue their plan. I am in no doubt but you will be able to conquer America at last, but a horrid bloody scene will be opened here, as never was in New England before. . . . By the time this reaches you havvock will begin, and whether we shall ever see one another in this world, I am not clear in."

Havoc had begun already. Lord Dartmouth and the other ministers could infer as much as soon as Gage's dispatch describing the Concord action reached them June 10: "Though relieved from suspense," wrote Hutchinson then, "yet received but little comfort, from the accounts themselves being much the same with what Darby brought." Indeed, in the time stretching before him, precious little comfort would arrive from his native land to relieve the former governor in exile, destined to feel anguish even up to the bleak June day, five years in the future, when he would die here on foreign soil an exile still.

What Thomas Hutchinson was required to endure in those five final years was appalling. The war itself, the Revolution, at once made him irrelevant. No longer were the issues facing government theoretical ones of taxation and sovereignty, nor was this Bostonian's unique expertise in the intricate politics of Massachusetts Bay to be of much use during a tumultuous period calling for the pursuit of military strategy and tactics and logistics on a continental scale. "I say nothing about public affairs," the governor would be reduced to explaining within a year or two, in a comment that measured how far his life had changed, "nor do I ever concern myself with them: nor am I ever inquired of or consulted about them; and I am glad I am not."

Perhaps he was glad. Perhaps this inveterate politician had come to feel well out of a role filled so many years so thanklessly. Now with the war arrived, Hutchinson would hear himself excoriated by both sides in the struggle. Patriots had long been accusing him of single-handedly creating hostilities between colonies and mother country through his malicious and self-serving misrepresentations to the ministry. Had he not, as proof, been demonstrably intimate, ever since arriving in England, with ministers at the highest levels of government? But now the English had taken to accusing this same gentleman of informing them about American attitudes before the war inaccurately—of, as he wrote, "neglecting to give advice of their intentions to revolt, and representing the body of the people as disposed to live quietly under the authority of Parliament, and to take no exception to any other acts than those of taxation." Lord North in a conciliatory gesture at the last had even gone as far as to agree, on the basis of such advice, to cease altogether taxing provinces that voluntarily contributed to the common defense. And still the colonies had risen in revolt. In the violent sequel, Mr. Hutchinson—he of the scrupulous rectitude, of the exquisite sense of duty—was charged by both sides, English and American, with betrayal.

The assignment of all that blame he must endure, and endure much more. Word reached him not long after war had begun that rebels had seized his beloved home in Milton. They were using it as a barracks—the well-known, most loved spot, those cherished rooms on the hilltop overlooking Boston Harbor. And then, to his dismay, the exile was led forcibly to recall having taken to Milton, at the time of the Tea Party disturbances six months before his own departure for England, a trunk from Garden Court full of personal letters, of having left the trunk in an attic space, and in the crush of events having forgotten about it.

Rebels had found the letters, of course, and began promptly and widely publishing whatever among the pages seemed most incriminating, wrenching passages from contexts, providing commentary to furnish tendentious interpretations, casually altering to suit patriot purposes what the governor had actually written for the private consideration of his friends. On June 26, Hutchinson would note in his diary: "Mr Quincy came in at breakfast time"— Josiah's older brother Samuel, the loyalist Boston attorney and Hutchinson's friend and correspondent, just arrived in town as a refugee. "Mr. Quincy came in at breakfast time, a passenger in Callahan, with letters from my son, &c., and an account of their distress; which has made this the most distressing day to me I have had since I have been in England. My house at Milton in possession of the rabble: all my letters, books, papers, &c. taken and carried away, and the publication of some of them already begun."

He must worry over the loss of belongings (silver epergne, Turkey carpet, "2 Bronzes, Shakespear and Milton," family portraits, all those loved irreplaceable possessions), while abiding the serial appearance of his letters in American newspapers, as week followed week through the summer—then must absorb besides, with the rest of London, alarming news arriving in late July concerning a costly engagement between troops and rebels on Bunker Hill ("a few such victories would ruin us"). Indeed, there was no relief from the relentless press of his anguish. August 1, he confided to an American correspondent: "I am under continued distress for the state of my children and friends, and cannot enlarge or write anything upon such a subject without pain."

Even in his anxiety, the governor persisted in his social rounds, attending at levees and dinners, restlessly gleaning what scraps of news he could; but the town's so-called pleasures only exasperated him. He had never been one for such distractions; and now his diary is spotted with his annoyance at the lord mayor's show, at the concert hall, at a magician's deceptions—"too low an amusement ever to attend again"—at rare visits to the theater. He saw Garrick in *The Beaux's Stratagem* without satisfaction, judging the actor miscast. And only "to avoid being singular," he dragged himself one afternoon at six to the regatta, where he "tarried till eight, and had patience no longer. The people were innumerable."

And insufferable. News, confirmed or unconfirmed, was all he sought, over the endless dinners and teas. What he heard he recorded. "Mr Strahan, stationer, and Member of Parlt an old friend of Franklin's, told me at Court he [Franklin] went away in a most rancorous state of mind, declared he had rather have his health drank by the Congress than be Lord High Treasurer of England." Hutchinson noted that Franklin was in Philadelphia, had been named to the congress; that congress's views were grown so radical as to have outdistanced even those of the philosopher. Again, August 23: "Mr Strahan showed me a short letter from Franklin of 7 July from Philadelphia . . . puts Strahan in mind of what passed between them in England, and that he (F.) had not proved a false prophet: they had now got to cutting throats—horrid war: the people of England might burn and destroy their towns, but that would not make the Americans to be better customers, nor better to pay their debts. He concludes with saying he was in good health, and never busier in his life."

Thus, Franklin, returned home, appeared vindicated and was thriving, as summer yielded to a fall that brought no relief in London. "Called upon Col. James at his lodgings, Charing Cross," the exile Hutchinson, hardly busy at all, would note in September.

"The more I hear of the state of Boston the more I am distressed: the prospect of ruin is so great." Then to add to his worries, in October the entire family in the London quarters—father, daughter, and both sons—came down with influenza. In mid-November the governor was writing his son Tommy, prematurely as it happened: "We have all been sick for three weeks past with a most malignant disorder, called the Influenza, which has been very epidemical, not one in ten escaping. I have not had so much of a fever for 35 years past, but through the goodness of God, we are upon the borders of health"—after many visits from the doctors, intense pain at night, quantities of blood taken from Billy and Peggy, great doses of medicines: oil of almonds, syrup of balsam, alexiterian simple.

Before the family could be restored to health, General Gage had returned to London, relieved of his New England command, and Lord Dartmouth had been replaced as colonial secretary. Such relocations moved the former governor even farther from the centers of power. November 11 brought news on a smaller scale, but personally vexing: "Washington, it is said, rides in my coach at Cambridge"—the rebel commander in Hutchinson's familiar carriage that had brought his excellency, that last day in America, to the wharf before Castle Island, on his way to England and the beginning of this long unnatural displacement.

Through the winter and spring approaching, more and more American loyalists, old friends of Hutchinson's, would arrive in London: Mr. Thomas Flucker, Mr. William Vassall, Mr. Charles Paxton, Treasurer Harrison Gray, finally whole droves of them, fleeing the deprivations of rebel-invested Boston. By mid-February 1776, the governor must acknowledge bleakly: "We Americans are plenty here and very cheap. Some of us at first coming, are apt to think ourselves of importance, but other people do not think so, and few, if any of us are much consulted, or inquired after." The new arrivals were reduced to coping as best they could, often partaking of the governor's generous hospitality—this little society of expatriates, sometimes impoverished, invariably superfluous, obliged to wheedle and plead their cases at court or to whoever would listen, soon becoming embarrassments among the British, becoming annoyances, bores.

Winter crept on, fearsomely cold, the enfeebled governor continuing to suffer from the months-long aftermath of his influenza.

Government meanwhile was known to be preparing reinforcements—"a prodigeous armament." New commanders were in place in America. A spring offensive promised news from overseas more inspiriting. But what spring brought instead to London, in early May, was word of the fall of Boston, that calamity coupled at last with what must be seen as good news personally. May 2: "About four o'clock I came in, and to my surprise found Colo Browne arrived from Boston, having left it the 26 March in the *Lord Hyde* packet, and arrived at Falmouth the 31st April. But I was more surprized when he told me he left my son and daughter and their children, and Miss Sanford aboard the packet, and that the troops had quitted Boston, and were embarked, and many of them sailed with the packet to Halifax, and the rest to sail the next day."

Boston had been evacuated, was in the hands of the rebels; but at any rate Tommy and his family were safe on these shores, and Hutchinson's other daughter, Sarah, and her husband Dr. Peter Oliver, and eventually Elisha's wife Polly with their three children, would arrive in England—so that the governor's inadequate London quarters must at one time accommodate some twenty-five people, and his hardly ample purse provide for them all.

Even so, the family was safe, and together. Hutchinson sought help from the ministry. He made application in writing, reminding those officials that his administration in Massachusetts had been generally successful, "and if it had not been for the plot laid by Franklin and others here in England, and the sending over my private letters, and the false representation made of them, I doubt whether there would have been a rebellion to this day." Voluntarily, this servant of the Crown had surrendered the governorship, trusting to assurances at the time "that I should be no sufferer by the discontinuance of the King's commission, and that some distinguishing mark should be shown of His Majesty's approbation of my conduct. The former part I gratefully acknowledge has been complied with"—his salary had been continued after his arrival in England—"the latter remains."

The approbation he now sought was in the form of government's redeeming an oft-made promise of a place for his son Billy, perhaps in Canada, and then employment for his older sons, who had suffered for no reason other than their having remained loyal to the king. But no such rewards were forthcoming, now or ever.

What did come forth in the summer—no balm at all to his purse, though it brought the governor's spirits enormous satisfaction—was the conferral upon him, at Oxford University, of the distinction of an honorary degree.

No other award in his long life meant more to him. Never mind that the self-educated Dr. Franklin had preceded Hutchinson on the dais at Oxford by fourteen years. The exile was thrilled to find himself clothed in the scarlet gown, the cap and band of the honoree, introduced by the beadles into the noble theater, there to attend to the orchestral and vocal music, the Latin speeches, the encomiums, before a distinguished and respectful audience numbering some two thousand. The date on which Thomas Hutchinson received the degree of D.C.L. Oxon. was July 4, 1776.

When in mid-August he learned what had happened in America on that very date, learned of the colonies' "declaring for Independency," the governor in his exasperation set about composing strictures in the form of a "Letter to a Noble Lord," wherein he assiduously sought to reveal the fraudulence of the Declaration's claims and grievances. He would, for example, "wish to ask the delegates of Maryland, Virginia, and the Carolinas how their constituents justify the depriving more than an hundred thousand Africans of their rights to liberty and the pursuit of happiness, and in some degree to their lives, if these rights," as claimed, "are so absolutely unalienable." The letter Hutchinson proceeded to publish as a pamphlet—his final intrusion into public affairs—but no one in the hurry of events paid it much attention.

Thereafter, he occupied himself with bringing his earlier *History of Massachusetts Bay* to the present, in a third volume that was finished at last, though not printed until long after his death. And he kept abreast of the news, and fretted, and brooded. His beloved daughter Peggy fell ill during this fall of 1776, and the illness wore on and grew worse, grew alarming the following summer, as through late summer days of 1777 the young invalid visibly, heartbreakingly sank toward death. "In this kind of life," the father wrote, "the days and nights pass incredibly swift, and I am six months older and nearer to my own death, than when my daughter's illness began; and it appears like the dream of a night." Those six months had been fixed exclusively on Peggy's recovery, but she became "more feeble and more emaciated from week to week"—

great soreness at her breast, her eyesight failing, no relief except from laudanum, unable to take a step without help, "the last stage threatening." She died, twenty-three years old, September 21, 1777—namesake of Hutchinson's adored wife, herself adored and now gone.

The exile never recovered from this loss. His own health suffered, and word from overseas provided no palliative. Rebels were mounting obstinate resistance through the fall of this year—the "boundless rage and fury of the whole British nation" that Hutchinson had warned against was proving not so formidable; and on the first of December 1777 came incredible news—news that brought "universal dejection"—of the loss of General Burgoyne's entire army to the rebel Gates at Saratoga. "Everybody in a gloom," the governor wrote at midmonth; "most of us expect to lay our bones here."

At last he realized that he would never see Boston, never see Milton again, nor would he lie again beside his wife, "of all earthly objects ever known, deservedly the dearest." Through eternity, an ocean must separate them. The new year brought worse war news yet, in March, of the treaty that the relentless Franklin had negotiated with the French, introducing that power into the conflict. On the 17th, on a line of its own, a single stupefied exclamation in the governor's diary: "Everybody is struck dumb!" and the following day, his glum concession: "America seems to be lost."

But peace would not come in this man's lifetime. The war dragged on, through bloody campaigns of 1778, 1779. And in July 1779, Hutchinson learned of his official banishment from the fledgling United States.

"I wish it may be in my power," he had written two years earlier, "to convince my countrymen of one truth (which I feel the force of to my own great comfort every day) that I never, in my public character, took any one step in which I did not mean to serve their true interest, and to preserve to them every liberty consistent with it, or with their connection with the kingdom. Whether they, or I, mistook their true interest, time will discover."

Time was no longer his friend. Two months after word of the banishment came, Hutchinson's son Billy spat blood, and that young man too must dwindle into infirmity as the governor watched forlorn, watched him slowly die. February 19, 1780: "I sat by my son after his brothers [Tommy and Elisha] and sister [Sally] left him this evening, until between 11 and 12, all this time struggling for life, and longing for his dissolution." He expired the following day, "without a groan . . . I could not help taking a look at his dead countenance, which I wished I had not. . . . This my youngest son, was 27 years of age last August."

So many gone, and his daughter Sally desperately ill; she would die in late June, and her infant soon after. But Governor Hutchinson, spared little of anguish, would at least be spared that. From Billy's death onward, he had been only half alive himself, existing morose, dazed, and despairing through the weeks of spring. The morning of June 3, as London recoiled under the most destructive riots it had ever witnessed, the anti-Catholic Gordon riots that would spread through a succession of terrifying, anarchical days— in that antithetical atmosphere, with a mob soon to destroy Lord Mansfield's home here in the city even as Hutchinson's own home had been destroyed in Boston years before—in that boding atmosphere, with all that the governor had feared come to pass, with all he had valued lost, Thomas Hutchinson, in his sixty-ninth year, started weakly, wearily, dutifully toward his carriage for yet another morning's airing, when he suddenly uttered a cry—"Help me!"—fell into his servant's arms, and within minutes lay dead on the floor at his entrance hall.

26

Dr. Franklin, American

THREE LIVES, THREE DEATHS.

Josiah Quincy, cut down in his prime, and he on the side of history, so that, had he lived ("God preserve you in health and longevity," his brother had written, to become "at length the father of your country"), his career might have provided yet another, glorious example of a founder of the republic—selfless, idealistic, utterly committed to the cause that dominated the thoughts and acts of his brief adulthood. If his life could have been extended into old age, into the nineteenth century, Americans might now know and revere Josiah Quincy as they know Jefferson, or John Adams, or Washington.

A second life and death: Thomas Hutchinson's, he a man of the utmost probity and honor, permitted to live through the length of such years as were denied Quincy, living out his allotted time consistently loyal to the values of his youth and heritage. Through four decades, Hutchinson devoted himself to public service, demonstrating wisdom and courage and incorruptibility and a generous forbearance toward his enemies. Yet his final years were poisoned; as his nineteenth-century biographer has written, "It would scarcely be possible for a human life to close among circumstances of deeper gloom." At the end, everything for which the man had lived appeared consumed in catastrophe. His loved ones were adrift or bereft or dead themselves, his friends defeated, his deepest wishes denied, discord in the ascendant, and the cause he cherished doomed.

And last, Benjamin Franklin's life and death. Franklin's life—
which had begun like that of the other two in Boston, and in his
case most modestly, and which had led him in youth to play the
part of a runaway, arriving at seventeen in Philadelphia virtually
penniless—had encompassed a rise from such humble beginnings
to astonishing heights as printer, publisher, businessman, soldier,
author, inventor, scientist, moralist, postmaster, philanthropist,
founder of useful and long-lived societies, and finally politician,
diplomat, and statesman. Franklin's time in Philadelphia from
1723 to 1757—thirty-four years—amounted to a complete life in itself, rich and full and varied.

He was over fifty and world renowned when he began a new
life, in London as a provincial agent, first for interests in
Pennsylvania, then for wider colonial interests. That new life, cen-
tered for the most part agreeably in Craven Street, extended from
1757 to 1775, nearly twenty years as a Londoner. When it was
ended, the cosmopolitan Franklin, aboard ship bound for America,
was about the age of Hutchinson at his death, was sixty-nine.

At such an age, with such full and varied accomplishments in
two geographical worlds and in many more worlds of the mind
and spirit behind him, the voyager was presuming that his
evening had come, and the time had come for repose. But fresh
challenges awaited this remarkable human being when he de-
barked. Soon after his arrival home in May, Franklin wrote to his
sister in Boston "just to let you know I am return'd well from
England; that I found my Family well; but have not found the
Repose I wish'd for, being the next Morning after my Arrival dele-
gated to the Cong[ress] by our Assembly."

He was to join those representing Pennsylvania at the Second
Continental Congress, which had opened its sessions on May 10
with the regathering in Philadelphia of delegates from the various
American colonies.

Franklin's was by no means an honorary appointment to that
historic body. Despite his age, he attended sessions faithfully and
served on numerous important committees, including a vital one
to procure gunpowder and another to conduct the foreign affairs
of the evolving nation. Congress elected him postmaster general,
and he was charged with preparing and submitting a draft of
Articles of Confederation for the united provinces. In the autumn,

he was chosen as one of three delegates to journey to Cambridge, across the river from Boston, to confer with Washington on needs and regulations of the new Continental army that the general was there forging into shape. And the following spring, from late March to the end of May 1776, Franklin with three much younger delegates undertook an arduous journey overland to Montreal, in a vain effort to persuade Canadians to make common cause with their neighbors to the south against the English.

Although that last took a toll on his health, the old man persevered in serving this new collection of independent colonies moving toward nationhood. Back in Philadelphia, congress chose him in June to serve on the committee to prepare the Declaration of Independence. That done, with John Adams (and sharing a bed along the way) he journeyed in late summer to Staten Island, to meet with his old acquaintance Lord Howe, recently put in command of the British fleet in North America, now come too late as peace commissioner. Civilly, but with a proud decisiveness, the American emissaries rejected Howe's pacific overtures.

In early autumn, on September 26, 1776, Franklin found himself appointed commissioner to France—an absolutely crucial assignment, inasmuch as gaining the support of the French might well mean the difference between the success and failure of the Revolution. He sailed from Philadelphia in late November.

People marveled at the daring of it. Lord Rockingham, who had led the administration that had repealed the Stamp Act a decade before and now was in opposition in Parliament, on learning of Franklin's arrival in France rose in the House of Lords to recall that gentleman's humiliating treatment by the solicitor general in the Cockpit there in Westminster three years earlier. "The horrid scene at a Privy Council is in my memory, though perhaps not in his. It may not excite his conduct. It certainly deters him not. He boldly ventures to cross the Atlantic in an American little frigate"— England's enemy, through seas that English ships patrol—"and risks the dangers of being taken and being once more brought before an implacable tribunal. The sight of Banquo's ghost could not more offend the eyes of Macbeth than the knowledge of this old man being at Versailles should affect the minds of those who were principals in that horrid scene. Depend upon it, he will plead forcibly."

No one, no one in all of America could have pleaded with the French government to such good effect as did Benjamin Franklin. In France he was to remain eight years—yet another distinct and most remarkable life for this phenomenon who at the start of it was seventy-one. Very soon the visitor would learn to love these new surroundings, in "the civilest nation upon Earth," as he described it. "'Tis a delightful People to live with." And ever afterward his most enjoyable dreams, he said, were set there.

But if Franklin soon came to love the French, the French adored Franklin, and from the first. He reached Paris at the end of 1776 and was before long established in the village of Passy, two miles out of the city. Within a month he found himself lionized; and the enthusiasm felt for the sage old republican, plain-clothed, unaffected, immensely knowledgeable, he who with his invention of the lightning rod had wrenched thunderbolts from the sky as he was now wrenching the scepter from the tyrant's hand—the wild enthusiasm of the French for such a one scarcely diminished in all the time that he lived among them. They hung engravings of his image over their mantels, displayed busts of him, portraits, prints; reproduced his familiar features on medallions for their rings and snuffboxes. Amazed by the fashion that persisted, the object of it felt moved two years after his arrival to write his daughter back home about the number of such reproductions, an incredible number, "copies upon copies . . . spread everywhere," with the result of having made "your father's face as well known as that of the moon, so that he durst not do any thing that would oblige him to run away, as his phiz would discover him wherever he should venture to show it."

Noblewomen of Louis XVI's court vied for his time and attention, carried on flirtations to which he responded with charming bagatelles printed on his own press at Passy. But his new life involved much more than celebrity and fashion and the writing of bagatelles. From the start he busied himself persuading the French to support the American cause by providing the new nation overseas with loans and supplies for its ragged army. He worked hard to negotiate commercial treaties with the French, to commission privateers, to secure aid for American vessels in French waters. And triumphantly, he was able, scarcely before the first year of his stay was done—and with the success of American arms at Saratoga supporting his efforts—to pave the way for signing, on the evening of February 6, 1778, at the office of the ministry for foreign affairs in the Hôtel de Lautrec in Paris, treaties of alliance and amity between France and the United States of America.

That diplomatic coup was as decisive a victory as any on the battlefield. To the signing ceremony, this good republican chose to wear an old blue coat of Manchester velvet. His fellow commissioner from America, Silas Deane, wondered whether that might be overdoing republicanism; why was he dressing so plainly on such an occasion? The philosopher explained that he wore the coat "to give it a little revenge," having last had it on four years earlier, the day Wedderburn had abused him at Whitehall.

The news of France's entry into the war appalled the English, dumbfounded them, left them desperate. At once a peace proposal went off from Whitehall to Philadelphia, what amounted virtually to a capitulation. All American grievances were to be redressed. Commissioners would be dispatched with full authority to treat with the American congress, with authority to negotiate a truce, grant pardons, repeal all the acts of Parliament since 1763, provide for home rule within the empire—precisely what Franklin had urged three years earlier. Whatever Americans wanted, short of outright independence, was to be granted. The English vessel bearing such gladsome tidings all but raced across the Atlantic against the French ship bringing news of Franklin's diplomatic triumph. Word of the triumph arrived first. Congress approved the new alliance with France in early May 1778, and the war went on.

Franklin remained in Passy through war's end and beyond. The blunt John Adams in Paris in the spring of 1779 remarked in wonder on the old gentleman's popularity there, pronouncing his fellow Bostonian's reputation among the French to be "more universal than that of Leibnitz or Newton, Frederick [the Great] or Voltaire; and his character more beloved and esteemed than any or all of them." Throughout the kingdom, "there was scarcely a peasant or a citizen, a *valet de chambre*, coachman or footman, a lady's chambermaid or a scullion in a kitchen who was not familiar with it and who did not consider him a friend of mankind." When the people spoke of Franklin, "they seemed," as Adams noted in amazement, "to think he was to restore the golden age."

Deliberately, ever efficient of voice and movement, the old man labored on, beseeching funds from the French treasury to support the American war effort, bargaining for more supplies, conducting himself through the labyrinths of diplomacy with unvarying tact and skill. But the long effort drained him, and in March 1781, now seventy-five years old, he sought to be relieved of further duties. "I have been engaged in public affairs," he wrote the congress in Philadelphia, "and enjoyed public confidence, in some Shape or other, during the long term of fifty years, an honour sufficient to satisfy any reasonable ambition." He pleaded that someone else represent American interests at Versailles. For answer came word in August that the minister was to remain where he was, in order to act as one of the commissioners to negotiate a peace with England. And within three months the time for peace was brought nearer, as joyous news reached Paris of a decisive French-American victory over General Cornwallis at Yorktown.

Despite victory, making peace proved a long and delicate process. Finally, preliminary articles were agreed upon toward the end of 1782; and in January 1783, Franklin and John Adams attended at the signing that led to an armistice. David Hartley, Franklin's English friend and correspondent (and author some years earlier of an "intended speech" for the king to use in opening his new Parliament), signed the definitive treaty for Great Britain that September. "We are now Friends with England and with all Mankind," the successful American diplomat exulted in writing to Josiah Quincy Sr., within days of the signing—and added: "May we never see another War! for in my opinion *there never was a good War, or a bad Peace.*"

Even after the peace, it was not until the summer of 1785 that Franklin, now nearly eighty, at last left Passy, laden with honor, and proceeded to Le Havre to board ship for home. His long residence in France was finally ended. A brief stop at Southampton, a final passage across the Atlantic, and on September 14 the statesman arrived in Philadelphia, at Market Street wharf, where as a youth from Boston he had first set foot in the town on an autumn day like this, sixty-two years before.

This later landing was yet another triumph, a speedier ship having informed townspeople of their beloved Franklin's progress westward, thus allowing them time to prepare a reception. "The affectionate Welcome I met with from my Fellow Citizens," he wrote soon after, "was far beyond my Expectation." Cannon had boomed as he stepped ashore; bells had rung in all the churches as he made his slow, crowded way the four blocks to Franklin Court, to his waiting daughter and to grandchildren he had never seen. For days after the return, visitors flocked to the great man's door to pay homage and show their regard.

In what time lay ahead, Franklin busied himself enlarging his home in Market Street, building a dining room that would seat twenty-four people, a library that would house his four thousand books. And still the octogenarian was called upon to serve the public, as president of the Supreme Executive Council of Pennsylvania, as president of the Society for Political Enquiries, as president of the Society for Promoting the Abolition of Slavery. Most notably, through the summer of 1787 he sat as a member of the Constitutional Convention. "I attended the Business of it 5 Hours in every Day from the Beginning," he reported. "You may judge from thence, that my Health continues." And it was Franklin who gave the closing speech of the convention, urging each delegate to "doubt a little of his own infallibility" in order that the new Constitution, with all its controversial clauses, might be approved unanimously.

Having seen so much and participated in so much, still the old man lived on, to witness the election of the first president of the United States and to sign a final public document as late as February 1790, petitioning congress against slavery and the slave trade. Two months later, on April 8, he answered a written inquiry from Jefferson, who had succeeded him as minister to France and was now secretary of state; this was his last public service.

Nine more days remained to him. On the evening of April 17, 1790, about eleven at night, Benjamin Franklin, in his eighty-fifth year, died quietly at his home in Philadelphia, his daughter and son-in-law nearby, his friend Polly Hewson with his two grandsons taking their turn at his bedside.

But so glorious a life, so filled with honor and achievement and friendship and the grateful esteem of his contemporaries, had not passed without its share of suffering. What life does? Seven months before his death, Franklin had written to congratulate President Washington "on the growing Strength of our New Government under your Administration. For my own personal Ease," he had confided on that occasion, "I should have died two

Years ago, but, tho' those Years have been spent in excruciating Pain, I am pleas'd that I have liv'd them, since they have brought me to see our present Situation."

Anguish of another sort the old man had borne for a long time. Not just the bladder stone that had made movement a trial ever since his late days in France. There was a wound within, and the will that he wrote shortly before his death disclosed that wound still festering. To his daughter's family and to his sister in Boston and to various public institutions he would leave generous bequests. Moreover, on a much admired compatriot he took care to bestow his fine crab-tree walking stick with the gold liberty-cap handle—that treasured possession to go to his friend, "and the friend of mankind, *General Washington*. If it were a Sceptre, he has merited it, and would become it."

But to the loyalist son William, imprisoned in Connecticut during a part of the Revolution and now living in England, were left only the worthless claims to land held in Nova Scotia, books already in his possession, and a forgiveness of whatever debts were owed his father. It was about as much forgiveness as the old man could manage. "The part he acted against me in the late war, which is of public notoriety," the will explained in words that disclose a lasting bitterness, "will account for my leaving him no more of an estate he endeavoured to deprive me of."

There had been a time, after the war, when William had tried to mend the rift with his father. "I . . . am glad," wrote the elder Franklin from Passy in response, August 16, 1784, "to find that you desire to revive the affectionate Intercourse, that formerly existed between us. It will be very agreeable to me; indeed nothing has ever hurt me so much and affected me with such keen Sensations, as to find myself deserted in my old Age by my only Son; and not only deserted, but to find him taking up Arms against me, in a Cause, wherein my good Fame, Fortune, and Life were all at Stake."

Putting in at Southampton on his voyage home from France, Franklin had been greeted by his son, come down from London the night before for the purpose. It was their first sight of each other in a decade, but the meeting was brief and formal, soon ended and never repeated. Why could not the royal governor of New Jersey have remained neutral in the crisis of their lives? William had felt that his duty to his king required that he act as he had, a vigorously belligerent Tory in wartime. "I ought not to blame you," the father had written after the patriot cause was won, "for differing in Sentiment with me in Public Affairs. We are Men, all subject to Errors. Our Opinions are not in our Power; they are form'd and govern'd much by Circumstances, that are often as inexplicable as they are irresistible." Still: "Your Situation was such that few would have censured your remaining Neuter, *tho' there are natural Duties which precede political ones, and cannot be extinguish'd by them.* This is a disagreable Subject. I drop it."

But the subject was not easily dropped, could never really be dropped—this source of the greatest pain that one man ever knew.

To be sure, perhaps late in life Franklin felt on occasion yet another regret. In the year before he was briefly, coldly meeting with his loyalist son a final time, from France on May 12, 1784, the philosopher, then nearing eighty, had written his old Boston friend and contemporary Samuel Mather—Cotton Mather's son, born in the year of Franklin's birth, in 1706, now an old man, too. "I long much," one Bostonian had told the other, "to see again my native place, and to lay my bones there."

Thomas Hutchinson (brother-in-law of that same Samuel Mather) had longed likewise, from the dreamlike exile of England, to lay his bones in the soil of his native place. And Josiah Quincy, feverish and dying aboard ship in Gloucester Harbor, had at the last felt a similar sharp longing and anguish to be in Boston once more.

As with those others, Franklin retained his love for the Yankee town of his birth. Very late in life he wrote, to a friend and neighbor of his homebound sister, of the pleasure he took in the company and conversation of Bostonians, "when any of them are so good as to visit me; for, besides their general good sense, which I value, the Boston manner, turn of phrase, and even tone of voice, and accent in pronounciation, all please, and seem to refresh and revive me."

Not that much time remained by then for revival. He had become an ancient gentleman, this philosopher, teeth gone, body emaciated by the loss of appetite from laudanum that his pains demanded. His bones, soon to be buried, were all too evident: "Little remains of me but a skeleton covered with a skin." Yet even so,

even in these very last months, Franklin was busy bestowing bene-
factions, designating among beneficiaries of his will not only loved
ones and societies, but whole cities as well, two cities specifically:
Philadelphia, with which his name is forever linked, and Boston,
where he had been born and reared. To each, the philanthropist left
one thousand pounds to aid young apprentices, ingeniously set up
in a way that has allowed the funds to go on multiplying, so that
two hundred years later the bequests were continuing to bestow
their ample benefits, the endowments in each case having grown
to a value of over four million dollars.

In such tangible ways the past flows into the present, a past including among so much three lives here described, and one year
when those lives intermingled. One life was arrested in its prime,
its potential unfulfilled. A second was protracted into the gloom
and despair of a pathetic old age. The third, however, the longest—
broadest in scope, highest in the honor it achieved, alert and curi-
ous to the end—the third, shapely life of perhaps the most affec-
tionately regarded of all Americans would be allowed after far
voyages to cease at last at home, quietly, surrounded by loved
ones, its multifarious tasks completed and the great cause that had
called forth its finest labors triumphant.

NOTES

The events of 1774–1775 recounted herein have been told in the words of the participants whose actions the text follows. Thus, numerous citations come from three sources: Hutchinson's *Diary and Letters* (abbreviated HDL in the notes), *The Papers of Benjamin Franklin* (PBF), and the *Memoir of the Life of Josiah Quincy Jun.*, by his son (QMQ). To reduce the number of notes, I have omitted identifying a relevant page where a date in the text seems adequately to locate a passage from a source frequently cited.

Various of Hutchinson's and Quincy's manuscripts are in the Massachusetts Historical Society. Hutchinson's letterbooks are in the Massachusetts Archives. Among other primary sources consulted, repeatedly and gratefully, were Gage's *Correspondence, American Archives,* Wroth's *Province in Rebellion,* and *Documents of the American Revolution.* Of the many valuable secondary texts that have guided me, I owe particular debts to Lawrence H. Gipson's *The British Empire Before the American Revolution,* to Carl Van Doren's *Benjamin Franklin,* and to Bernard Bailyn's indispensable, superlative *The Ordeal of Thomas Hutchinson.*

Full titles of sources appear on pp. 271–276.

CHAPTER 1: MR. HUTCHINSON

1 "We, Merchants and Traders." "Address" 43–44. *Am. Arch.* 1:346, 358, 363, 364. Stark 128–129.

2 "13 months' absence." HDL 1:52.

3 The Port Act. Gipson 12:113–116. Text in *Am. Arch.* 1:61–66.

4 Hutchinson's response to the petition. *Am. Arch.* 1:362.

4 "Early mark of his favor." Lord Dartmouth to Hutchinson, privately, 4-9-74. Bailyn 271.

4 "Foresee the Consequences." Gage to Dartmouth, Boston, 5-30-74. Gage 1:356.

5 Hutchinson's career. In addition to Bailyn and Hosmer, Shipton's is a good brief account. Freiberg's is thorough on both the public and the private lives. Pencak's study attempts to establish Hutchinson as the formulator of a consistent conservative philosophy, "a far more original and powerful thinker than Bailyn gives him credit for" (vi).

5 "Best man in America." Frothingham 107. Adams, *Diary* 1:306 (3-17-66).

6 "Indefateguable Patrioat." Jane Mecom to Franklin, 12-30-65. *Letters Mecom* 87.

6 "'Very good Gentleman.'" James Otis's remark, quoted Bailyn 15.

6 "Pretty Ladies." *Boston Gazette*, 1-31-63; quoted Miller 25–26.

6 "More than human." HDL 1:54.

6 "Best of husbands." HDL 1:55.

7 Vile serpent: Adams, *Diary* 2:81 (4-24-73). Viper: Schlesinger 152. "Damn'd *arch-traitor*": Andrews 328.

CHAPTER 2:
DR. FRANKLIN AND THE LETTERS

8 One of the best actions. Smythe 10:270.

8 Franklin's life. Books, dozens and dozens of them, have been written on every phase of it, and on each of the many roles enacted in its long course. An excellent general biography is Wright's, in which the crucial impact of Boston in forming Franklin's character is discussed at 23–28. (As late as 1750, in his midforties, this Boston native was still referring to himself as a "Stranger" in Pennsylvania; p. 74.) Van Doren's remains an immensely readable biography, and Lopez and Herbert's is a fascinating account of Franklin's relationships with intimate friends and with his wife and children—an account not always favorable to the head of the family. Middlekauff's study explores Franklin's dealings with foes (William Smith, Thomas Penn, Hillsborough, Hutchinson, Arthur Lee, Ralph Izard, and others), all but inevitably acquired over a long and active lifetime.

10 The Stamp Act. Gipson 10:246–281. Morgan, esp. 53–113.

11 "Whom I am not . . . permitted to name." PBF 21:419. Speculation on Franklin's informant is in Bailyn 224–236 and PBF 19:403–407.

13 "An abridgment of . . . English liberties." Hosmer 436–437. Hutchinson's six letters are reprinted as Appendix C in Hosmer 429–438. All nineteen are in PBF 20:541–580. Though Hutchinson himself, like many others, blamed the letters for his downfall, Schlesinger has argued that the Whigs had been determined to drive the governor from office as early as January 1773, when he condemned their committees of correspondence. Even so, he retained authority for nearly a year after the furor over the letters had died down. According to this source, not until his mishandling of the tea crisis as late as December 1773 was the governor's usefulness to the crown compromised. Schlesinger 150, 152.

15 Franklin's letter about the duel. PBF 20:515–516.

16 "False and Erroneous allegations." PBF 21:70. The complete "Report of the Privy Council Committee" is at 68–70.

16 "As sacred . . . as their family plate." PBF 21:51. Wedderburn's diatribe is given entire at 43–67.

18 "The Happiness once more of seeing you." 4-28-74. PBF 21:205.

CHAPTER 3:
A THIRD BOSTON GENTLEMAN

19 "United all Parties here against our Province." 3-22-74. PBF 21:152.

19 "That Shadow of a Man." Upton 293.

20 The Tea Party. Labaree, esp. 104–193. The names of participants, as "generally supposed," are in Drake xcii–iv.

20 Quincy's life. The rather meager published sources are his son's *Memoir*, Nash, "Radicalism," and Sibley 15:479–491. Unpublished letters are in the Massachusetts Historical Society.

21 "Manuscripts & other papers." To Richard Jackson, 8-30-65. Freiberg 111.

21 "Big with the greatest anxiety." "Extracts" 48–49.

22 The Boston Massacre. Zobel, esp. 184–205 (a comprehensive and thoroughly readable work on the subject).

23 "Good God! Is it possible?" 3-22-70. QMQ 34–35. For Quincy's conduct of the case, Beach 208–212, Zobel 241–294.

23 "This whole people will . . . REJOICE." 3-26-70. QMQ 37. Captain Preston was acquitted, as were four of the six British soldiers. The other two were convicted of manslaughter. Upon pleading benefit of clergy, those two were branded on the hand and, with their companions, returned to their regiment. Zobel 265, 294.

24 Quincy's voice. Sibley 15:486. On the formation of the Boston committee of correspondence and its early work involving Quincy, Richard Brown 58–80.

24 "Let us weigh and consider." 12-16-73. "Tea-Party" 197.

25 *Insatiable* enemy of my country." *Boston Gazette*, 2-7-74; quoted Bailyn 249.

25 "Pettyfogging Attorney." Sibley 15:489.

26 "YOUR WELLWISHER." QMQ 153, 156.

26 "Alone, or in company." QMQ 157, 158.

CHAPTER 4:
BOSTON IN MAY 1774

29 Boston in 1774. Bridenbaugh's detailed study considers aspects of Boston along with four other American seaports. See esp. Part 2 (1760–1776), 215–425. For descriptive evocations, Scudder; Nash's

Crucible, esp. 185–189, 224–233; Warden, esp. 291–317. Andrews and Rowe kept vivid contemporary journals that convey a sense of lives as actually lived in Boston throughout the period.

29 Tories and Whigs. The Court and the Country, or Popular, Parties, out of which grew Tories and Whigs, are contrasted in Patterson 44–45. See also 70–90, and Knollenberg 199–203.

30 "What used to be common civility." To John Pownall, 3-26-70. Hosmer 189.

32 Gage's arrival in Boston. Alden 206–211. Rowe 269–271. Wroth 58–63. A good brief sketch of Gage's career is in Shy, "Empire" 75–107. See also Richmond 59–70.

33 Quincy's *Observations.* The text is in QMQ 361–469. Citations at 377, 368, 379, 380.

36 "The father of your country." QMQ 160–162.

CHAPTER 5:
CROSSING THE ATLANTIC

37 "A Negro man." Elisha Hutchinson's diary. HDL 1:152.

38 Cheerful farewells. Hosmer 315–316. HDL 1:152.

38 "Not be of long duration." Hutchinson, *History* 3:458.

39 "The Governor . . . very sick." HDL 1:154.

39 "Neither . . . have dared to appear." 3-9-74. HDL 1:131.

40 Elisha's visit to Plymouth. [Hulton] 70.

40 "Running from a mob." To Polly Hutchinson (Elisha's wife), 1-25-74. HDL 1:108.

40 "The grandeur of the ocean." To his wife, 6-27-74. HDL 1:155.

41 Miss Hulton to Mrs. Lightbody. [Hulton] 72.

42 Mr. Oliver's funeral. HDL 1:133. Oliver 112. Hosmer 313–314.

43 "Died in great distress." HDL 1:154.

44 "I am longing to hear." To Mr. Montagu, 4-30-74. HDL 1:141.

44 "See him . . . next day at noon." HDL 1:155.

CHAPTER 6:
A FLATTERING RECEPTION

45 Lord Dartmouth. Valentine 528–529, under William Legge. Bargar 1–56. Trevelyan 158–166.

46 "The Daniel of the age." George Whitefield's judgment. Bargar 13.

46 "Introducing me . . . to the King." HDL 1:157. The entire interview is given at 157–175.

47 "A handsome drawing-room." HDL 1:194.

47 George III's mastery of detail. Guttmacher 129. For the life, Brooke; Mumby, esp. 281–405; Guttmacher, esp. 120–139.

47 "Much reduced . . . by seasickness." HDL 1:158.

48 "Not one bonfire kindled." Marshall 6.

52 "Put it in his power." HDL 1:175–176.

52 "Relief for the T. of B[oston]." To Thomas Flucker, 7-7-74. HDL 1:178.

CHAPTER 7:
EARLY WEEKS IN ENGLAND

53 "Bringing them to a speedy submission." Fortescue 3:116. On the different understandings of what was said at the interview, Norton 47.

53 "Friendly . . . beyond conception." 7-20-74. HDL 1:190.

54 "My advices to the 9th of June." 7-14-74. HDL 1:188.

54 "Never met with greater civility." 7-16-74. HDL 1:192.

55 "I do not believe it." HDL 1:217.

56 "An answer to this letter." HDL 1:190.

56 Peggy's letter. HDL 1:200–201.

58 Gage dissolves the Assembly. Gipson 13:151–152.

60 "No step can be taken." 8-8-74. HDL 1:215.

60 "Forget that I am an American." HDL 1:215.

62 "Make them very ridiculous." 8-25-74. HDL 1:229.

62 "The prospect . . . was very favorable." 8-29-74. HDL 1:231.

CHAPTER 8:
DR. FRANKLIN LINGERS

63 "So dangerous a conspiracy." 7-8-74. HDL 1:185.

64 "Nothing would more alarm our Ministers." To Thomas Cushing, 7-7-73. PBF 20:273.

64 "A very trimmer—a very courtier." 5-3-73. "Journal" 473–474.

65 "Cause your accounts to be made up." 1-31-74. PBF 21:74.

66 "I am very angry." To Thomas Cushing, 2-15-74. PBF 21:93.

66 "The consequences are plain!" PBF 21:82.

66 "Harmony between the two Countries." To Samuel Cooper, 2-25-74. PBF 21:124.

67 "No Conception of the Rage." To Samuel Cooper, 2-25-74. PBF 21:124.

67 "Wonderfully supports a Man." "Extract of a Letter from London," 2-19-74. PBF 21:114.

67 "Lime-Stone and Marble." To Condorcet, 3-20-74. PBF 21:151. "Your Brother Chymists." To Benjamin Rush, 7-22-74. 21:248. "Subjects of Natural History." To Rush, 7-25-74. 21:258.

69 Coercive acts. Gipson 12:116–132.

71 Franklin compared to Jesus. 11-3-74. PBF 21:346–347 ("I think it is not Profanity to compare you to our Blesed Saviour who Emploued much of His time while hear on Earth in doing Good to the bodys as well as souls of men and I am shure I think the compareson Just").

71 "An infamous Falshood." 7-28-74. *Letters Mecom* 145.

71 Franklin's sister and son. On Jane Mecom, *Letters Mecom*, intro., 3–33, and, more extensively, Van Doren, *Mecom*. On William Franklin, Randall (which provides a much less sympathetic portrait of the father than does the present work).

CHAPTER 9:
CHATHAM

73 "What a fellow is this Pitt!" Williams 2:195. See also on the life, Ayling, esp. 338–418, Sherrard, esp. 336–359. In Plumb's brief, splendid account, see esp. 143–153.

73 "Amazing powers and influence." Rockingham's judgment. Williams 2:196.

74 "Our bells are worn threadbare." To George Montague 10-21-59. Walpole 9:250–251.

74 England in the early 1760s. Lecky 3:1–138, Gipson 10:3–52, 200–245.

74 "Americans are the sons . . . of England." 1-4-66. Williams 2:190.

75 "When were the colonies emancipated?" Williams 2:193.

75 Chatham's letters to the king. Pitt, *Correspondence* 3:228 (3-3-67). The letter perseveres: "He entreats most humbly to renew the tender of his devoted services (grieving to think how feeble they are); every hour more and more animated by the truly royal magnanimity of his Majesty." Other representative specimens at 76–77 (9-25-66) and 343–344 (10-14-68).

76 "Pitt's love letters, alas! survive." Rosebery 355. They have been published in Ethel Ashton Edwards, ed., *The Love-Letters of William Pitt First Lord Chatham* (London, 1926).

78 "We . . . waited on Lord Stanhope." PBF 21:547.

79 Hayes. Ayling 325.

79 Franklin's interview with Chatham. PBF 21:547–549.

81 "Sentiments . . . such as you could wish." 9-27-74. PBF 21:319.

81 "The Tone of publick Conversation." To Thomas Cushing, 9-3-74. PBF 21:280.

CHAPTER 10:
A SECRET MISSION

82 "In a most critical Situation." PBF 21:276.

84 Texts of the coercive acts. *Am. Arch.* 1:104–112 (*"An Act for the Better Regulating the Government of the Province of the* Massachusetts Bay . . . *"*); 129–132 ("An Act for the Impartial Administration of Justice in the cases of Persons questioned for any acts done . . . for the Suppression of Riots and Tumults, in . . . Massachusetts Bay . . . "); and 170 ("An Act for the better providing suitable Quarters for Officers and Soldiers in his Majesty's service in North America"). For the document that the acts would in effect abrogate, see "Charter."

84 Gage notifies the councillors. Salem, 8-25-74. Gage 1:364. The oath administered (8-8-74) is in Wroth 522.

84 Loyalist ladies "pelted." Outrages are enumerated in *Am. Arch.* 1:1260–1263 ("An address to the Provincial congress of Massachusetts," 2-23-75).

85 Donations. Letters from Boston gratefully acknowledging specific aid from other towns and provinces are in "Correspondence."

86 Solemn League and Covenant. Knollenberg 250–251. Matthews, "League" (containing text, related letters, and discussion). Wroth 458–459.

86 The "better Sort of People." 7-5-74. Gage 1:358.

87 "Allways impetuous and vehement." To Abigail Adams, from Arundel, 7-4-74. *Adams Family Corresp.* 1:122.

87 "Taken a Bed together." 7-5-74. *Adams Family Corresp.* 1:123.

87 "An harrangue, upon Air and cold." New Brunswick, 9-9-76. "Autobiography." Adams, *Diary* 3:418.

87 John Adams. In Page Smith's two-volume biography, see esp. 1:144–195, from the Tea Party to the Concord skirmish. Ellis's fine brief work is less a life than an analysis of character, but no less interesting for that. Also Shaw, esp. 76–88.

87 "Unequal to this Business." 6-20-74. Adams, *Diary* 2:96.

88 "The *better Sort,* the *Wiser Few.*" To Abigail Adams, *Adams Family Corresp.* 1:130.

88 "Opposition to her designs." 1-1-1819. Adams, *Novanglus* vi ("Preface").

89 "Servants well mounted and arm'd." Andrews 339.

89 "Kind wishes and fervent prayers." Adams, *Diary* 2:97.

89 Samuel Adams. The best brief account is in Maier 3–50, which manages to humanize the remote and austere figure. See also Knollenberg 242–245, Beach, esp. 249–285, and Miller (a far better study than its title might suggest).

89 "Embark for London." To John Dickinson, QMQ 173.
90 "No Design has appeared of Opposing." Boston, 5-30-74. Gage 1:356.
92 "The Arrival of the late Acts." 9-12-74. Gage 1:374.

Chapter 11:
Mr. Hutchinson's Autumn

93 "All our advices . . . discouraging." HDL 1:231.
94 "Strolling about the country." HDL 1:231.
95 "My thoughts day and night." 10-10-74. HDL 1:261.
96 Mr. Oliver's letter. *Documents* 8:182–184. HDL 1:265.
97 "Any prospect of relief." HDL 1:274.
99 The Suffolk Resolves. HDL 1:272. Gipson 12:157–159, 244–246. Knollenberg 249. Text in *Am. Arch.* 1:776–779, Wroth 914.
100 Dartmouth "thunderstruck." HDL 1:273.
100 "Without this reflection." To Sarah Oliver (daughter), 11-1-74. HDL 1:281.
101 "I have not known more tranquility." HDL 1:283.

Chapter 12:
Journey Overland

103 Hutchinson's waning influence. As late as 9-29-74, he was writing his son Tommy, "The Ministry are always inquisitive after my Intelligence." By 3-10-75, "There never has been a question asked me about America for a long time past." Norton 46, 48.
104 "I determined it must be Quincy." 11-18-74. HDL 1:296.
104 "A nine days' wonder." From Nathaniel Appleton, 11-15-74. QMQ 201.
104 "Sameness of a sea life." At sea, 11-5-74. QMQ 218, 219.
105 "Indignation against public conspirators." 11-8-74. QMQ 221.
106 "The country and cultivation surpass description." To Mrs. Quincy, 11-8-74. QMQ 222.
106 *"The brave Bostonians."* QMQ 222–223.
107 Quincy's English journal. An annotated transcription slightly less genteel is in Howe. Wet sheets in which Quincy imprudently slept, for instance, and which are omitted from the discreet QMQ, are noted there, as is the "ruddy bloom" of English women. Howe 435 (11-9-74).
108 London. Rudé, esp. 40–48, 64–81. Besant, esp. 31–33, 236–245, 399–432, 446–450. Barker and Jackson, 176–234.
109 "Your enemies are to be gratified." 1-3-75. QMQ 213.
110 "I received many civilities." QMQ 227–228.
111 "Hardly in the nature of things." 6-10-71. Lee 1:218, 217.

CHAPTER 13:
FIRST DAYS IN THE CAPITAL

113 "I am very glad of it." QMQ 229.

114 "Now nine long Months." PBF 21:303.

115 "They ought first to do Justice." 7-3-74. PBF 21:238.

116 "I am in perpetual Anxiety." To Thomas Cushing, 10-6-74. PBF 21:328.

116 "My situation here is . . . hazardous." To Joseph Galloway, 10-12-74. PBF 21:334.

117 "A Tumult in the street." Boston, 11-3-74. *Letters Mecom* 150.

118 "Dangerous to my Health." To Joseph Galloway, 10-12-74. PBF 21:334.

119 "A cheerful affability." QMQ 233.

121 "Wondered how 'I dared to come.'" QMQ 237.

122 "You know the author of it." QMQ 240–241.

122 "The man . . . to curse of all others." Governor Pownall was the observer. 11-27-74. QMQ 249.

122 There is a certain *influence.* QMQ 245.

123 "I am in a delicate situation." To Mrs. Quincy, 11-24-74. QMQ 243–244, 249.

CHAPTER 14:
THE KING BEFORE PARLIAMENT

125 "A bad, insidious man." HDL 1:301.

126 "What passed between him and Quincy." 11-25-74. HDL 1:304–305.

127 "The ugly state of North America." To Horace Mann, 10-6-74. Walpole 24:44–45.

128 "The K. Speech will be very general." Lord Beauchamp's opinion. 11-23-74. HDL 1:301.

128 "The intended speech." Smyth 6:299–301. About the attribution, PBF 21:359–360.

129 "Without *grace* in the heart." Howe 445.

130 Elisha, writing his wife. HDL 1:310 n.

131 "The world is in amaze here." To Horace Mann, 11-24-74. Walpole 24:61.

131 "Blows must decide." 11-18-74. Fortescue 3:153.

131 "A most daring Spirit of Resistance." *Am. Arch.* 1:1465. Gipson 12:272–273.

132 "The King's Speech . . . is strong." 12-10-74. HDL 1:316.

CHAPTER 15:
A STRANGE SILENCE

133 "In Newgate, or at Tyburn." QMQ 258.

135 "Will you believe me." QMQ 256–257.

136 "Except such persons as should be named." 12-9-74. HDL 1:319.

136 "BOSTON WAS NOW IN ASHES." 12-7-74. QMQ 255.

136 Gossip in London. HDL 1:322, 318, 332. Quincy's insistence that Lord North requested specifically to see him is at QMQ 243.

137 "The long-expected sloop is arrived." To Henry Seymour Conway, 12-15-74. Walpole 39:226. Showing more penetration than his bellicose countrymen, he goes on: "Our conduct has been that of pert children: we have thrown a pebble at a mastiff, and are surprised it was not frightened."

137 Petitions to be sent. Gipson 12:255–257. Texts in *Am. Arch.* 1:934–938, 917–921.

137 A "piece of Insolence." Gage to Barrington, 2-10-75. Gage 2:191.

137 "What could be done?" 12-14-74. HDL 1:324.

138 "It is a matter of speculation." HDL 1:328.

139 "I only throw it out." 10-17-74. Gage 2:175.

140 Gage recommends suspending the coercive acts. Gage to Hutchinson, 9-17-74. Alden 220. Donoughue 210. Fortescue 3:154.

140 "By artful & designing Men." Dartmouth to Gage, 12-10-74. Gage 2:178.

141 "There's a strange silence." HDL 1:329.

CHAPTER 16:
PEACE PLANS

143 "The congress . . . shine unrivalled." QMQ 323.

144 The petition to the king. 10-26-74. *Am. Arch.* 1:934–938.

147 "Decent, manly, and properly express'd." 12-26-74. PBF 21:569.

147 Franklin's chess match. PBF 21:550 ff. The account is in Franklin's "Journal of Negotiations in London," written aboard the Philadelphia-bound packet in late March 1775 as a self-justifying letter to his son. PBF 21:540–599. On the peace plans, Trevelyan 299–304. Donoughue 214–215, 221–222, 244–247. Weldon Brown 35–57.

148 Admiral Richard, Lord Howe. Gruber, esp. 44–55. Barrow 85–89.

151 "The Tears of Joy." 7-20-76. *Writings* 993.

151 "HINTS for *Conversation*." PBF 21:366–368.

152 "He saw some *light*." 12-11-74. PBF 21:377.

152 "Receive it very graciously." PBF 21:399. On the role of Franklin and other colonial agents in the political maneuvering, Kammen, esp. 282–308.

CHAPTER 17:
TWO VISITS TO BATH

153 "Laying down some line of conduct." QMQ 253.
155 "Commercial leeks and onions." QMQ 302.
156 North "spoke exceeding well." HDL 1:327.
159 "The most elegant city in England." To Mr. Green, 1-10-75. HDL 1:354.
161 "A dream, rather than a reality." 1-15-75. HDL 1:351.

CHAPTER 18:
IN THE HOUSE OF LORDS

163 "Dr Franklin's birthday." QMQ 317.
165 "Saying aloud, this is Dr. Franklin." PBF 21:576.
166 The Boston Cicero. To William Wirt, 1-5-1818. Adams, *Works* 10:271.
166 "He seemed like an old Roman senator." QMQ 318–319. The transcription of Chatham's speech is at 319–328. Citations from 319–320, 320–321, 321, 322–323, 326–327, 320, 327, 328. A somewhat different version appears in *Am. Arch.* 1:1493–1498.
169 "I had great Satisfaction in hearing his Motion." PBF 21:576. Text in *Am. Arch.* 1:1504–1507.
170 "The Bayonet was at their Breasts." PBF 21:570.
170 "Whistling of the Winds." PBF 21:577.
170 "Dr. F. is fill'd with Admiration." PBF 21:456.
171 "Daily Business and Company." PBF 21:578.
171 "Such a Visit . . . flattered . . . my Vanity." PBF 21:579.

CHAPTER 19:
MR. HUTCHINSON'S WINTER

174 "I have despaired." HDL 1:357.
174 "Franklin will still write." 1-27-75. HDL 1:359.
175 "A mob of several hundred people." HDL 1:365–366, *Am. Arch.* 1:1042–1043, Scott 508–509.
176 "The just rights of the people." *Am. Arch.* 1:1505. Donoughue 235–236.
176 "A most excellent Speech." PBF 21:581.

176 Lord Sandwich. Valentine 614–615, under John Montagu, 1718–1792.

177 "He is not easily interrupted." PBF 21:580.

178 "What has that man to answer for!" HDL 1:356.

179 "Never shewn his head." 1-10-75. HDL 1:356.

180 "The People's Minds are greatly cooled." Gage 1:390.

181 "The uncertainty of human affairs." 11-22-74. HDL 1:301.

181 "The appearance of a dream." 1-15-75. HDL 1:351.

182 "I am . . . drove here by the mob." HDL 1:371.

Chapter 20:
The Ministry Commits Itself

183 "Exceedingly inconvenient for me." 8-30-74. Matthews, "Documents" 480. Letters of others declining the honor are in Wroth 525–534.

184 "Cut the throats of honest people." *Am. Arch.* 1:1168.

185 "Combine together for their Mutual Defence." Gage 1:391.

186 "A Damp upon the Faction." Gage 1:392.

187 "Sedition flows . . . from the Pulpits." Gage 1:374.

188 "Overborne with the weight of affairs." 2-9-75. HDL 1:375.

188 Dartmouth's dispatch of January 27. Gage 2:179–183. Alden 233–241.

Chapter 21:
Fate of the Peace Plans

193 "It is doubted . . . they will fight long." To Elisha Hutchinson, 2-18-75. HDL 1:371.

194 "Raw, undisciplined, cowardly men." 3-16-75. *Am. Arch.* 1:1681.

194 "Such rascals as those." From Louisburg, 8-7-58. Mumby 94. Gage in the same war voiced similar sentiments (New Englanders were the "greatest Boasters & werst Soldiers on the Continent . . . infamously bad." To Washington, 5-10-56. Hamilton 1:254). So did Amherst, of provincial soldiers, who "if left to themselves would eat fryed Pork and lay in their tents all day long." Shy, *Lexington* 93. See further Leach, Boorstin 365, Ammerman 127.

194 Earlier opinions echoed. For example: "Upon paper they are the bravest fellows in the world, yet in reality I believe there does not exist so great a set of rascals and poltroons." 7-6-74. Evelyn 27. Lord Percy was of the same opinion ("a set of sly, artful, hypocritical rascalls, cruel, & cowards." 8-8-74. Percy 31), until he encountered the rebels in action.

195 "Proposals . . . to satisfy the Americans?" 2-15-75. HDL 1:377.

196 "Enquire into the Grievances of America." PBF 21:571.

197 "Not unworthy of the Regard." PBF 21:410.

198 "Other[s] were inadmissible." PBF 21:575.

199 "Govern a Herd of Swine." PBF 21:582–583.

199 "I need not tell you." PBF 21:584. The "you" is Franklin's son, to whom the account of these negotiations is directed. Franklin's various efforts toward peace are summarized in Knollenberg 254–257.

201 "The present dangerous Situation of Affairs." PBF 21:587.

201 "Not so fond of the sending Commissioners." To North, 12-15-74. Fortescue 3:156.

202 "Good and faithful Helpmate." *Autobiography* 129. On the marriage and Deborah Franklin's death, Lopez and Herbert 164–173.

CHAPTER 22:
ILLNESS OF MR. QUINCY

204 Two letters from Philadelphia. PBF 21:401, 402.

205 "My illness prevented that pleasure." QMQ 337.

206 "The fine season is now coming on." 1-24-75. QMQ 340.

209 "Gives up no right." Lord North to the king, 2-19-75. Fortescue 3:177. Text of North's motion quoted in Weldon Brown 43–44.

209 "For the regulation of commerce." *Am. Arch.* 1:1598.

209 North's "pacific Motion in the House." PBF 21:591.

209 "A Highway-man . . . presents his Pistol." PBF 21:594–595. The acquaintance was Lord Hyde.

CHAPTER 23:
DEPARTURES

214 "I can scarcely write legibly." QMQ 343–344.

215 "F——'s return to America." 3-24-75. HDL 1:410.

215 "Measures to distress . . . the Kingdom." 3-10-75. HDL 1:401.

216 "100 men to Marshfield." HDL 1:403. Gage 1:391.

217 "I had rather no Bill had passed." 3-10-75. HDL 1:401.

217 "We must pinch them." HDL 1:404.

217 "No particular Notice taken of it." PBF 21:521.

218 "Lord Kaims . . . Lord Bessborough." For Kames, scholar and writer (1696–1782), Valentine 461, under Henry Home. For the Second Earl of Bessborough (1704–1793), 711–712, under William Ponsonby.

218 Franklin "much disgusted." PBF 21:598. Trevelyan 295.

219 "The high opinion . . . lessened." HDL 1:410.

220 "A little out of my Senses." PBF 21:598. The friend was Thomas Walpole.

220 "You are now my Enemy." 7-5-75. *Writings* 904. And to Lee, 4-3-78. *Writings* 999–1000.

221 "Tears trickled down his cheeks." PBF 21:526 n.

CHAPTER 24:
MR. QUINCY'S VOYAGE HOME

224 "Your deliverance draws near." 4-11-75. HDL 1:434.

224 "Affairs . . . have been . . . growing worse." 4-6-75. HDL 1:431.

225 "Boundless rage and fury." 4-10-75. HDL 1:431.

225 "Returning to you in the spring." HDL 1:427.

226 "A feast to my eyes." HDL 1:427–428.

226 "Gigling and phiz." Howe 445.

226 "Mr. Quincy is so low." Howe 471.

228 "Other respectable persons." 5-2-74. Sibley 15:491.

229 The Charlestown foray. Richmond 1–7. Alden 213–214.

230 "Take a more active & determined part." Gage 2:180.

232 "Will you let them burn the town down?" Fischer 209. Three of the
many accounts of the Lexington-Concord skirmishes are French's still
reliable brief narrative, Tourtellot's more thorough study, and Fischer's
recent, comprehensive, and absorbing examination of the battles in their
larger contexts. A contemporary account is in Wroth 1804–1829 ("A
Narrative of the Excursion and Ravages of the King's Troops . . . on the
nineteenth of April, 1775"), which includes twenty-three depositions,
related affidavits, and a casualty list.

CHAPTER 25:
FINAL YEARS OF MR. HUTCHINSON

234 Significance of the Revolution. For a recent estimate (one among
many), Wood 3–8. For instance, "it was one of the greatest revolutions the
world has known, a momentous upheaval that not only fundamentally
altered the character of American society but decisively affected the
course of subsequent history" (p. 5). The introduction elaborates, elo-
quently and persuasively. Wood's study is filled with fascinating insights
on differences between the revolutionary age and our own.

235 "A most vigorous Retreat." To Edmund Burke, 5-15-75. PBF 22:41.

236 "I am to acquaint your Lordship." Gage 1:396.

236 A situation "beyond description almost." To Elisha Hutchinson.
HDL 1:458–459.

237 "I say nothing about public affairs." To James Murray, 3-3-77.
Hosmer 344.

237 "Neglecting to give advice." 3-3-77. Hosmer 343.

239 "A few such victories." To Hardwicke, 6-26-75. Bailyn 340.

239 "Too low an amusement." 7-11-76. HDL 2:78. And Garrick, 12-1-75.
1:574. And the regatta, 6-23-75. 1:475.

239 "Mr. Strahan . . . at Court." 6-22-75. HDL 1:475.

240 "The prospect of ruin is so great." 9-7-75. HDL 1:529.

240 "Upon the borders of health." 11-17-75. HDL 1:558–559.

240 "Plenty here, and very cheap." 2-16-76. HDL 2:40.

241 "A prodigeous armament." 2-16-76. HDL 2:40.

241 "Sending over my private letters." 7-76. HDL 2:79.

242 The colonies' "declaring for Independency." 8-14-76. HDL 2:89.

242 "An hundred thousand Africans." Hosmer 339.

242 "Like the dream of a night." 8-16-77. HDL 2:156. Bailyn 362–363.

243 "Everybody in a gloom." 12-12-77. HDL 2:171.

243 "Deservedly the dearest." 2-20-80. HDL 2:342.

243 "Time will discover." To Edward Hutchinson (cousin), 8-5-77. Bailyn 372.

244 "Help me!" HDL 1:451–452. Bailyn 373. Hosmer 347–349. On the Gordon riots, Rudé 221–227.

CHAPTER 26:
DR. FRANKLIN, AMERICAN

245 "God preserve you in health." QMQ 162.

245 "Circumstances of deeper gloom." Hosmer 348.

246 "I am return'd well from England." 5-26-75. *Letters Mecom* 156–157.

247 Franklin and Adams as peace commissioners. Weldon Brown 118–126.

247 "The sight of Banquo's ghost." Van Doren 572–573.

248 "The civilest nation upon Earth." To Elizabeth Partridge, 10-11-79. *Writings* 1012.

248 "His phiz would discover him." To Sarah Bache, 6-3-79. *Writings* 1008.

249 "Give it a little revenge." Van Doren 594.

249 "He was to restore the golden age." 5-15-1811. Adams, *Works* 1:660.

250 "The long term of fifty Years." 3-12-81. Smyth 8:221.

250 "Now Friends with England." 9-11-83. Smyth 9:96.

250 "Far beyond my Expectation." To John Jay, 9-14-85. Smyth 9:466.

251 "My Health continues." To Jane Mecom, 9-20-87. *Letters Mecom* 298.

251 "Doubt a little of his own infallibility." 9-17-87. *Writings* 1141.

252 "I should have died two Years ago." 9-16-89. Smyth 10:41.

252 "He has merited it." Smyth 10:508. Franklin's Last Will and Testament is at 493–510.

252 "Revive the affectionate Intercourse." 8-16-84. *Writings* 1096–1097. On William Franklin's vigorous Tory leadership during the war, Lopez and Herbert 241–242, 249–250, Randall 461–479.

253 "To see again my native place." *Writings* 1093.

253 "The Boston manner, turn of phrase." To Rev. John Lathrop, 5-31-88. Smyth 9:651.

253 "A skeleton covered with a skin." Van Doren 772.

SOURCES

The list comprises only those titles cited in the notes.

Adams Family Correspondence. Edited by L. H. Butterfield et al. 4 vols. to 1782. Cambridge, Mass., 1963–.

Adams, John. *Diary and Autobiography of John Adams.* Edited by L. H. Butterfield et al. 4 vols. to 1780. Cambridge, Mass., 1961–.

———. *Novanglus, and Massachusettensis . . . To Which Are Added a Number of Letters, Lately Written by President Adams, to the Honourable William Tudor . . .* New York, 1968; reproduced from the first edition of 1819.

———. *The Works of . . .* Edited by Charles Francis Adams. 10 vols. Boston, 1850–1856.

"Address 'To Governor Hutchinson,'" as printed in the *Massachusetts Gazette*, 6-2-74, Massachusetts Historical Society *Proceedings* 12 (1873):43–44.

Alden, John Richard. *General Gage in America, Being Principally a History of His Role in the American Revolution.* Baton Rouge, La., 1948.

American Archives: Fourth Series, containing a Documentary History of the English Colonies in North America, from the King's Message to Parliament, of March 7, 1774, to the Declaration of Independence by the United States. Edited by Peter Force. 6 vols. Washington, D.C., 1837–1846.

Ammerman, David. *In the Common Cause: American Response to the Coercive Acts of 1774.* Charlottesville, Va., 1974.

Andrews, John. "Letters of John Andrews, Esq., of Boston, 1772–1776." Massachusetts Historical Society *Proceedings* 8 (1864–1865):316–412.

The Autobiography of Benjamin Franklin. Edited by Leonard W. Labaree et al. New Haven, 1964.

Ayling, Stanley. *The Elder Pitt, Earl of Chatham.* London, 1976.

Bailyn, Bernard. *The Ordeal of Thomas Hutchinson.* Cambridge, Mass., 1974.

Bargar, B. D. *Lord Dartmouth and the American Revolution.* Columbia, S.C., 1965.

Barker, Felix, and Peter Jackson. *London: 2000 Years of a City and Its People.* London, 1974.

Barrow, Sir John. *The Life of Richard Earl Howe, K. G. . . . .* London, 1838.

Beach, Stewart. *Samuel Adams: The Fateful Years, 1764–1776*. New York, 1965.

Besant, Sir Walter. *London in the Eighteenth Century*. London, 1903.

Boorstin, Daniel J. *The Americans: The Colonial Experience*. New York, 1958.

The Boston Gazette, and Country Journal, Containing the freshest Advices, Foreign and Domestic. 1774–1775.

Bridenbaugh, Carl. *Cities in Revolt: Urban Life in America, 1743–1776*. New York, 1955.

Brooke, John. *King George III*. New York, 1972.

Brown, Richard D. *Revolutionary Politics in Massachusetts: The Boston Committee of Correspondence and the Towns, 1772–1774*. Cambridge, Mass., 1970.

Brown, Weldon A. *Empire or Independence: A Study in the Failure of Reconciliation 1774–83*. Baton Rouge, La., 1941; reissued Port Washington, N.Y., 1966.

"Charter of the Province of the Massachusetts Bay, 1691." Colonial Society of Massachusetts *Publications* 2 (1913):7–29.

"Correspondence, in 1774 and 1775, between a Committee of the Town of Boston and Contributors of Donations for the Relief of the Sufferers by the Boston Port Bill." Edited by Richard Frothingham. Massachusetts Historical Society *Collections*, 4th series, 4 (1858):1–278.

Documents of the American Revolution, 1770–1783: Colonial Office Series. Edited by K. G. Davies. 21 vols. Dublin, 1972–1981.

Donoughue, Bernard. *British Politics and the American Revolution: The Path to War, 1773–75*. London, 1964.

Drake, Francis S., ed. *Tea Leaves: Being a Collection of Letters and Documents relating to the Shipment of Tea to the American Colonies in the Year 1773, by the East India Tea Company*. Boston, 1884; reprinted Detroit, 1970.

Ellis, Joseph J. *Passionate Sage: The Character and Legacy of John Adams*. New York, 1993.

Evelyn, Captain William Glanville. *Memoir and Letters of Captain W. Glanville Evelyn of the Fourth Regiment*. Edited by G. D. Schull. Oxford, 1879.

"Extracts from the Diaries of Josiah Quincy, Jr." Massachusetts Historical Society *Proceedings* 4 (1858–1860):47–51.

Fischer, David Hackett. *Paul Revere's Ride*. New York, 1994.

Fortescue, John, ed. *Correspondence of King George the Third from 1760 to December 1783*. 6 vols. London, 1927–1928.

Freiberg, Malcolm. "Prelude to Purgatory: Thomas Hutchinson in Provincial Massachusetts Politics, 1760–1770." Ph.D. diss., Brown University, 1950. Copy in Massachusetts Historical Society.

French, Allen. *The Day of Concord and Lexington, the Nineteenth of April, 1775*. Boston, 1925.

Frothingham, Richard. *Life and Times of Joseph Warren*. Boston, 1865.

Gage, Thomas. *The Correspondence of General Thomas Gage with the Secretaries of State, and with the War Office and the Treasury 1763–1775.* Edited by Clarence E. Carter. 2 vols. New Haven, 1931–1933.

Gipson, Lawrence H. *The British Empire Before the American Revolution.* 15 vols. Caldwell, Idaho, 1936–1970.

Gruber, Ira D. *The Howe Brothers and the American Revolution.* New York, 1972.

Guttmacher, Manfred S. *America's Last King: An Interpretation of the Madness of George III.* New York, 1941.

Hamilton, Stanislaus Murray, ed. *Letters to Washington and Accompanying Papers.* 5 vols. Boston, 1898.

Hosmer, James K. *The Life of Thomas Hutchinson, Royal Governor of the Province of Massachusetts Bay . . .* Boston, 1896.

Howe, Mark A. DeWolfe, ed. "Journal of Josiah Quincy, Jun . . . September 28th, 1774, to March 3d, 1775." *Massachusetts Historical Society Proceedings* 50 (1916–1917):433–471.

[Hulton, Anne]. *Letters of a Loyalist Lady: Being the Letters of Anne Hulton, sister of Henry Hulton, Commissioner of Customs at Boston, 1767–1776.* Cambridge, Mass., 1927.

Hutchinson, Peter Orlando, ed. *The Diary and Letters of His Excellency Thomas Hutchinson, Esq . . .* 2 vols. Boston, 1884–1886. [HDL].

Hutchinson, Thomas. *The History of the Colony of Massachusets-Bay . . .* 3 vols., 1764, 1768, 1828. Reprint edition, New York, 1972.

Kammen, Michael G. *A Rope of Sand: The Colonial Agents, British Politics, and the American Revolution.* Ithaca, 1968.

Knollenberg, Bernhard. *Growth of the American Revolution, 1766–1775.* New York, 1975.

Labaree, Benjamin W. *The Boston Tea Party.* New York, 1964.

Leach, Douglas Edward. "Brothers in Arms?—Anglo-American Friction at Louisbourg, 1745–1746." *Massachusetts Historical Society Proceedings* 89 (1977):36–54.

Lecky, William Edward Hartpole. *A History of England in the Eighteenth Century.* 8 vols. New York, 1891.

Lee, Richard Henry. *Life of Arthur Lee, LL.D.* 2 vols. Boston, 1829.

The Letters of Benjamin Franklin & Jane Mecom. Edited by Carl Van Doren. Princeton, 1950.

Lopez, Claude-Anne, and Eugenia W. Herbert. *The Private Franklin: The Man and His Family.* New York, 1975.

Maier, Pauline. *The Old Revolutionaries: Political Lives in the Age of Samuel Adams.* New York, 1980.

Marshall, Christopher. *Extracts from the Diary of . . . kept in Philadelphia and Lancaster, during the American Revolution, 1774–1781.* Edited by William Duane. Albany, 1877.

Matthews, Albert. "Documents Relating to the Last Meetings of the Massachusetts Royal Council, 1774–1776." Colonial Society of Massachusetts *Publications* 32 (1933–1937):460–504.

———. "The Solemn League and Covenant, 1774." Colonial Society of Massachusetts *Publications* 18 (1915–1916):103–22.

Middlekauff, Robert. *Benjamin Franklin and His Enemies*. Berkeley, 1996.

Miller, John C. *Sam Adams, Pioneer in Propaganda*. Boston, 1936.

Morgan, Edmund S., and Helen M. Morgan. *The Stamp Act Crisis: Prologue to Revolution*. Chapel Hill, N.C., 1953.

Mumby, Frank Arthur. *George III. and the American Revolution: The Beginnings*. London, 1924.

Nash, Gary B. *The Urban Crucible: The Northern Seaports and the Origins of the American Revolution*. Cambridge, Mass., 1986.

Nash, George H. III. "From Radicalism to Revolution: The Political Career of Josiah Quincy, Jr." American Antiquarian Society *Proceedings* 79 (1969):253–290.

Norton, Mary Beth. *The British Americans: The Loyalist Exiles in England 1774–1789*. Boston, 1972.

Oliver, Peter. *Origin & Progress of the American Rebellion*. Edited by Douglass Adair and John A. Schutz. San Marino, 1961.

The Papers of Benjamin Franklin. Edited by Leonard W. Labaree and William B. Willcox. 28 vols. to February 1779. New Haven, 1959–. [PBF].

Patterson, Stephen E. *Political Parties in Revolutionary Massachusetts*. Madison, Wis., 1973.

Pencak, William. *America's Burke, The Mind of Thomas Hutchinson*. Washington, D.C., 1982.

Percy, Hugh Earl. *Letters . . . from Boston and New York, 1774–1776*. Edited by Charles Knowles Bolton. Boston, 1902.

Pitt, William, Earl of Chatham. *Correspondence . . .* Edited by William Stanhope Taylor and Captain John Henry Pringle. 4 vols. London, 1838–1840.

Plumb, J. H. *Chatham*. London, 1953.

Quincy, Josiah. *Memoir of the Life of Josiah Quincy Jun. . . .* Boston, 1825. [QMQ].

Randall, Willard Sterne. *A Little Revenge: Benjamin Franklin and His Son*. Boston, 1984.

Richmond, Robert P. *Powder Alarm 1774*. Princeton, 1971.

Rosebery, Lord (Archibald Philip Primrose, Fifth Earl of). *Chatham, His Early Life and Connections*. London, 1910.

Rowe, John. *Letters and Diary of John Rowe, Boston Merchant . . .* Edited by Anne Rowe Cunningham. Boston, 1903.

Rudé, George. *Hanoverian London, 1714–1808*. Berkeley, 1971.

Schlesinger, Arthur M. *Prelude to Independence: The Newspaper War on Britain, 1764–1776.* New York, 1958.

Scott, Kenneth. "Tory Associators of Portsmouth." *William and Mary Quarterly,* 3d series, 17 (1960):507–515.

Scudder, Horace E. "Life in Boston in the Revolutionary Period." In *The Memorial History of Boston . . . 1630–1880,* edited by Justin Winsor, vol. 3, pp. 149–188. Boston, 1881.

Shaw, Peter. *The Character of John Adams.* Chapel Hill, N.C., 1976.

Sherrard, O. A. *Lord Chatham and America.* London, 1958.

Shipton, Clifford K. *Thomas Hutchinson.* Vol. 8. Boston: Massachusetts Historical Society, pp. 149–217, of John Langdon Sibley and Clifford K. Shipton, *Biographical Sketches of Graduates of Harvard University.* Cambridge, Mass., 1873–1975.

Shy, John. "The Empire Militant: Thomas Gage and the Coming of War." In Shy, *A People Numerous and Armed,* pp. 73–107. Oxford, 1976.

_____. *Toward Lexington: The Role of the British Army in the Coming of the American Revolution.* Princeton, 1965.

Sibley, John Langdon, and Clifford K. Shipton. *Biographical Sketches of Graduates of Harvard University . . .* 17 vols. Cambridge, Mass., 1873–1975.

Smith, Page. *John Adams.* 2 vols. Garden City, N.Y., 1962.

Smyth, Albert Henry. *The Writings of Benjamin Franklin . . .* 10 vols. New York, 1905–1907.

Stark, James H. *The Loyalists of Massachusetts.* Boston, 1910.

"Tea-Party Anniversary, 1873." Massachusetts Historical Society *Proceedings* 13 (1873–1875):151–216.

Tourtellot, Arthur B. *William Diamond's Drum: The Beginning of the War of the American Revolution.* Garden City, N.Y., 1959.

Trevelyan, Sir George Otto. *The American Revolution, Part I, 1766–1776.* London, 1899.

Upton, L.F.S. "Proceedings of Ye Body Respecting the Tea." *William and Mary Quarterly,* 3d series, 22 (1965):287–300.

Valentine, Alan. *The British Establishment 1760–1784 . . .* 2 vols., consecutively paged. Norman, Okla., 1970.

Van Doren, Carl. *Benjamin Franklin.* New York, 1938.

_____. *Jane Mecom, the Favorite Sister of Benjamin Franklin . . .* New York, 1950.

Walpole, Horace. *Correspondence . . .* Edited by W. S. Lewis et al. 48 vols. New Haven, 1937–1983.

Warden, G. B. *Boston, 1689–1776.* Boston, 1970.

Williams, Basil. *The Life of William Pitt, Earl of Chatham.* 2 vols. London, 1913.

Wood, Gordon S. *The Radicalism of the American Revolution.* New York, 1992.

Wright, Esmond. *Franklin of Philadelphia*. Cambridge, Mass., 1986.
Writings of Benjamin Franklin. Edited by J. A. Leo Lemay. New York, 1987.
Wroth, L. Kinvin et al., eds. *Province in Rebellion: A Documentary History of the Founding of the Commonwealth of Massachusetts, 1774–1775*. Catalog volume and microfiche. Cambridge, Mass., and London, 1972.
Zobel, Hiller B. *The Boston Massacre*. New York, 1971.

INDEX